KT-522-581

365 Days

from Genesis Through Revelation

J. Ellsworth Kalas

Abingdon Press
Nashville

365 DAYS FROM GENESIS THROUGH REVELATION

Copyright © 1993 by Abingdon Press

All rights reserved.
No part of this work may be reproduced or transmitted in any form or by
any means, electronic or mechanical, including photocopying and recording, or by any information storage or retrieval system, except as may be
expressly permitted by the 1976 Copyright Act or in writing from the pub-
lisher. Requests for permission should be addressed to Abingdon Press, 201
Eighth Avenue South, P.O. Box 801, Nashville, TN 37202.

93 94 95 96 97 98 99 00 01 02   —   10 9 8 7 6 5 4 3 2 1

This book is printed on acid-free, recycled paper.

Library of Congress Cataloging-in-Publication Data

Kalas, J. Ellsworth, 1923-
 365 days from Genesis through Revelation / J. Ellsworth Kalas.
  p.   cm.
 Includes index.
 ISBN 0-687-46626-1 (alk. paper)
  1. Devotional calendars. I. Title. II. Title: Three hundred sixty-five
days from Genesis through Revelation.
 BV4811.K35   1993
 242'.2—dc20   93-3742
                                                                    CIP

Scripture quotations, unless otherwise indicated, are from the New Revised
Standard Version Bible, copyright 1989, by the Division of Christian Education of the National Council of the Churches of Christ in the U.S.A.

Scripture quotations noted NIV are taken from the *Holy Bible: New International Version*. Copyright © 1973, 1978, 1984 by the International Bible
Society. Used by permission of Zondervan Bible Publishers.

Scripture quotations noted KJV are from the King James Version.

MANUFACTURED IN THE UNITED STATES OF AMERICA

With profound gratitude to
Gene Palmer,
who started me in a lifelong
habit of daily Bible reading

Arden Bud Hoff,
who insisted that this book be written

Chad and Jennifer Bentz,
who affirmed Bud's insistence

Before You Begin

Soon after I was converted, I felt a call to the ministry. A few months later, a Presbyterian evangelist, Gene Palmer, came to our little Iowa Methodist church for special services, and to our home for Sunday dinner. My mother, with typical maternal pride, told him of my call. When the meal was finished, Mr. Palmer excused himself from adult conversation so he could talk with this eleven-year-old about the ministry.

I remember only one part of the conversation:

—*Have you read the Bible through yet?*
—*Uh-hunh, I read the Bible.*
—*No, I asked if you've read it through.*
—*All the way?*
—*All the way! How can you hope to be a preacher if you haven't read the Bible through?*

Then he gave me his formula, which was so simple yet so difficult. If I would read three chapters every weekday and five chapters every Sunday, I would finish the Bible in a year.

Young and earnest as I was, I believed him, and I did it. I've done it any number of times since then, and have recommended it to each of the congregations I've served in my thirty-eight years of pastoral ministry.

When I retired from the pastoral ministry a few years ago, I received a letter from one of those persons who had taken my urging seriously—a Lutheran layperson in Madison, Wisconsin, Arden "Bud" Hoff. "There's a book that hasn't been written yet," he said, and I was to write it. It would lead a person through the Bible in daily devotional fashion, with "each day's reading . . . in a parable suitable for children of any age."

I knew it was a quite impossible assignment, but also that it was one that deserved to be tried. This is the book.

I ruled out the three-chapters-daily-five-on-Sunday pattern, because Sundays shift from year to year. Instead, we have three chapters daily except for certain days, usually the third and sixth, when we have four chapters.

Psalms and Proverbs appear in consecutive readings scattered through the book. This is partly in recognition that these books don't lend themselves to the kind of summary we're seeking, and partly because by such an arrangement I'm able to balance out certain readings.

The aim of this book is simple, yet complicated. I am seeking to cover the entire Bible in a year, from Genesis through Revelation, so that as you read, you will have guidance in your reading. The guidance is not a study, as such, but neither is it meant to be simply a series of meditations. Particularly, it isn't meant to be a daily sermonette from a verse that stimulates the preacher in me. I hope to summarize without being tedious, and to inspire without being trivial. And I want you to get the grand sweep of the Book, something I feel isn't possible when you follow one of those schedules which give daily portions from several parts of the Bible.

Gene Palmer, thanks be to God, got me reading the Bible through when I was a pre-teenager, and for that I am indebted to him into eternity. I would like to repay my debt in some measure by helping others read the whole, wonderful Book. A layperson once told me, "Everyone wants to read the Bible through, but it's intimidating." I pray that this book will make it less so, and that its daily portions will make the project manageable. Yes, and exciting, too!

J. Ellsworth Kalas

Expand

When Genesis draws back the curtain on the Eternal Drama, there's only one Person on stage. *God* and *Beginning* are synonymous. Without God there is no beginning, and there is no beginning before him. So the drama begins, and God quickly establishes lighting (1:3) and time (1:5), then begins moving in scenery—waters, sky, dry land, vegetation.

+ 2 sources, Yahwhist & Priestly

Then there are creatures with a possibility of being more than scenery: birds, fish, animals, crawling things. At last, human beings (1:26-31), creatures who will play opposite God in this drama. They can fill this role because they are made in God's image and are therefore able to communicate with him.

It's an awesome picture, and all the more so because of the simplicity with which it is drawn. The writer sees no need to accumulate adjectives; it is enough that God will say, at intervals, *Good!* If God feels that way about it, what other word is needed? *or flesh, foreskins...?*

I am impressed that the creation is such an intimate process. The Creator might be portrayed as a Master Engineer or the Ultimate Computer. Instead, Genesis tells us that God has soul; he wants to talk with someone. So the creation develops step by step on the framework *"God said."*

Science speaks increasingly of a Big Bang at creation. Genesis tells of a big conversation. But of course science is talking about *how*, while Genesis is telling us about *who*.

PRAYER: Help me, O God, on this day of new beginnings, to have all my beginnings in you. Amen.

GENESIS 2; PSALMS 3, 4   *Week 1, Day 2*

*G*enesis 1 told us we are made in the image of God. That's exciting, but from practical experience it's also confusing. We don't feel that God-like all the time; some days, we don't feel God-like at all.

Genesis 2 helps by telling us more about ourselves. We are creatures of the dust, which is easy to believe. Our physical person will decay into dust, and our personality is earthy enough to suggest our origins. But into that dust, God breathes something of the divine. Here is both our dilemma and our glory—that we are a bit of sod and a breath from God.

Perhaps the best evidence of our God-likeness is that we desire, like God, to communicate. Genesis 1 pictured both male and female created at once (1:27), but this chapter uses a beautiful story to let us know that we human beings need one another. We are bone of each other's bone and flesh of each other's flesh. John Donne underlined the point centuries later by saying that when one person dies, every person is diminished.

The intimacy of which we human beings are capable is uniquely expressed in marriage, partly because in marriage there is the possibility of engaging with God in the creation process.

There is a kind of divine humility in this chapter. Though the man is able to commune with God, he isn't expected to find fulfillment in God alone. "It is not good that the man should be alone" (2:18). We need God, but we also need one another.

PRAYER: Help me, I pray, to see every human being as part of my very being. Amen.

GENESIS 3, 4; PSALMS 5, 6   *Week 1, Day 3*

When Genesis 2 ends, all is perfect; man and woman have each other, they are in communion with God, happily employed, and blessed with idyllic housing and food.

Then, enter the villain. He is known by a variety of names, but probably the most significant is *Adversary* or *Accuser*. He enters our story making accusations against God, but it is soon evident that the object of destruction is the human creature.

The sin, quite simply, is disobedience to God. What Adam and Eve wanted was itself admirable (as is often the case with sin); they wanted to "be like God." But they pursued their goal in the wrong way.

The results were catastrophic. They found themselves distanced from God, from each other, from nature, and from their own selves.

The pain continued into the next generation, and it con-

8

tinues to our own time. All our deeds, for good or ill, have consequences. In Adam and Eve's case, the tragedy grew monstrous when their older son murdered the younger.

But there's a note of grace from the very beginning. When Adam and Eve sinned, they received a message that traditional scholars over the centuries have seen as a promise of the Messiah (3:15); and when godly Abel was killed, there was a birth of new hope in Seth.

PRAYER: Save me, O God, from the day of temptation; and if I fall, teach me to repent. Amen.

GENESIS 5, 6; PSALM 7   *Week 1, Day 4*

There's much to be learned from reading an obituary column, chief of which is that we will all die. That, as Samuel Johnson would say, concentrates the attention. Genesis 5 is the first obituary column; its brief biographies are identical in their endings: *and he died.*

All but one. Enoch is a different sort of human being. In a setting of dying, he insisted on living, by means of his extraordinary communion with God.

Genesis 6 is an obituary column of another kind. It portrays a dead society. The smell of destruction is all about it, in proportions so ugly that "every inclination of the thoughts of their hearts was only evil continually," until at last "the LORD was sorry that he had made humankind."

But here, too, there was an element of wondrous life, in the man named Noah. He "found favor in the sight of the LORD," for with evil all around him, he was "blameless in his generation." Further, he managed to communicate his goodness to his family, so that his wife, his sons, and his daughters-in-law accepted his spiritual leadership.

No one else did, however. Though a New Testament writer calls Noah a "herald of righteousness" (2 Peter 2:5), his message was not heeded. Perhaps it was achievement enough to be good and godly in a thoroughly perverse time, even to the point of winning his own household.

PRAYER: Grant me, dear Savior, the grace to be a child of life, no matter how great the measure of death around me. Amen.

9

*I*f Hollywood were telling this story, a large share of the screen time would be invested in scenes of terrifying destruction. Genesis tells us the proportions of the rain (forty days and nights), the total involvement of nature ("the fountains of the great deep burst forth, and the windows of the heavens were opened" [7:11]) and the long wait for the waters to subside, but there is no description of human terror or of vast areas of desolation.

Instead, the emphasis is on restoration. We are told much about what was saved of both animal and human life, and of the patience and faith with which Noah waited for an end to his journey. Then, a moving interaction between Noah and God. Noah builds an altar and presents a sacrifice to God, and God, in turn, expresses divine pleasure at Noah's act. Never again, God vows, will there be such destruction; seedtime and harvest, cold and heat, summer and winter, day and night, shall not cease.

In this scene of judgment the overriding quality is mercy. Judgment has come so a worse fate can be avoided. God's judgments are never for pointless destruction or revenge, but for redemption. So, too, the flood is not an end, but a beginning. And what a beginning it is! A human being in trusting worship, and God responding with the assurance of continuing mercy.

PRAYER: When I face judgment, dear Lord, help me to see it as redemption at work; in Jesus' name. Amen.

*T*he Bible is a book of new beginnings. When sin seems to have destroyed an age or an individual, there is always a place of starting again.

It is as if the flood had washed the earth clean for this new start. The "first generation" was told to "be fruitful . . . and fill the earth" (1:28); now Noah and his family are given the same instructions (9:1). And as if in recalling the sins of Cain and Lamech, a warning is reiterated against the shedding of blood (9:6).

But things soon began to go wrong. Even as the rainbow of the covenant fades from view, Noah falls into drunkenness and one of his sons mocks his shame. Then, as the descendants of Noah multiply, a new spirit of rebellion appears: "Come, let us build ourselves a city, and a tower with its top in the heavens" (11:4). So the original sin repeats itself: a people would, by their own devices, become like God and perhaps even displace him.

Their effort ends in disarray. When we set ourselves against God, whether as a civilization or as individuals, we put ourselves out of joint with the very nature of things and we are captured by confusion. Not only is communication with others broken, but within our own souls we speak a multitude of tongues.

But now, a new ray of hope: "Terah was the father of Abram. . . . The name of Abram's wife was Sarai" (11:27, 29). God has a friend, and who can say what good lies ahead?

PRAYER: Deliver me, dear Savior, from the confusion that comes from my rebellions against your love. Amen.

GENESIS 12, 13; PSALM 10   *Week 1, Day 7*

*A*braham is known as the father of the faithful (Gal. 3:6, 7). These two chapters show why he deserves the title. They also show that faith almost always follows an uneven course, because it resides in human vessels.

Abraham's faith begins in a dramatic act: "Get up and go!" That could be said to be the essence of faith, because faith leads to action. So Abraham and Sarah, who were partners in the faith venture, left all that was familiar and dear to follow a promise.

But faith, as I said a moment ago, takes an uneven course. In Egypt, Abraham seems to retreat into doubt through his fear of the Egyptians. One would think that a person who was ready to go into the wilderness of the unknown would confront Pharaoh with confidence, but we human beings are rarely that consistent. That's why we need God's grace.

Abraham returns to his position of sublime strength, however, when there is conflict with Lot's herdsmen. He makes a decision based on character and trust, letting Lot have the far better portion, and only after the choice is made is Abraham revisited by God with a message of grand assurance. God said, "Raise your eyes now, and look from the place where you are. . . . All the land that you see I will give to you" (13:14, 15). And with that, Abraham moved on, and "built an altar to the LORD" (13:18).

PRAYER: When I fail, dear Savior, help me to trust in you and rise up to try again; in Jesus' name. Amen.

GENESIS 14, 15; PSALM 11   *Week 2, Day 1*

*I*n those ancient days, wars between city-states went on constantly. Abraham was himself a kind of traveling city, with his 318 trained men; and his little army turned the tide. I think the writer of Genesis sees the victory as an achievement of faith and of Abraham's skilled leadership.

Abraham refuses any reward for himself, but he gives a tithe to Melchizedek, king of Salem (which means *peace, shalom*). Melchizedek is a mysterious figure, open to our speculation. The New Testament pays him particular attention (Hebrews 5–7), portraying him as a forerunner of Christ.

But again Abraham struggles. When the Lord says, "Do not be afraid, Abram . . . ; your reward shall be very great" (15:1), Abraham reminds God that he still doesn't have an heir. Will his holdings simply pass to his steward, Eliezer of Damascus, "a slave born in my house" (15:3)? It is a plaintive cry.

What follows is at once inspiring, mysterious, and symbolic. After God has reassured Abraham of the divine plan, God asks him to make a sacrifice. Abraham has to drive scavenger birds away from the sacrifice; they seem like a malevolent force. Then Abraham has a terrifying dream, which reveals some of the peril that will one day threaten his descendants, even as the scavengers have invaded his place of worship.

PRAYER: When I am in a dark and uncertain place, O God, reassure me with your presence and promise; in Christ our Lord. Amen.

12

S arah, who is of course as fine an example of faith as Abraham, wavers as does Abraham. In frustration, she attributes her childlessness to God (16:2), and judges (as Abraham seems to have done in (chap. 15) that she will have to take matters into her own hands.

Her solution was probably a rather common one in that time and culture; she and Abraham use her maid as a surrogate mother. But when the maid, Hagar, finds that she has succeeded where her mistress could not, she feels scorn for Sarah. So Ishmael is born; and since the Arab world looks upon him as their ancestor and the Jews upon Isaac as theirs, the strife between Sarah and Hagar continues to our day.

Thirteen years pass, and when Abraham is ninety-nine (17:1) God promises again that he and Sarah will have a son. It has been a long wait! At this moment his name is changed from Abram (exalted ancestor) to Abraham (ancestor of a multitude), and Sarai is changed to Sarah. Still, Abraham wants to cling to what is present and visible: "O that Ishmael might live in your sight!" (17:18). No wonder, when he and Sarah had waited so long and to no avail.

But God assures Abraham that there will be an Isaac and commands that the covenant mark of circumcision be instituted. From this point on, the Hebrew scriptures divide the world, by this mark, into the circumcised and the uncircumcised.

PRAYER: Thank you, gracious Lord, for not giving up on me when I wonder and wander! Lead me on, I pray; in Jesus' name. Amen.

GENESIS 18, 19; PSALMS 13, 14   *Week 2, Day 3*

W hen the New Testament writer urges that we be hospitable to strangers because by doing so "some have entertained angels without knowing it" (Heb. 13:2), he may well have had Abraham and Sarah in mind.

These desert visitors brought good news and bad news. Abraham and Sarah are told again, this time with a specific detail, that they will have a son. Sarah laughs—half, I think, in doubt and half in incredulous joy—but the strangers say it will be so. But then they confide in Abraham that Sodom and Gomorrah, whose sins are "very grave," will soon be destroyed.

Abraham begins bargaining. He is half saint and half merchant in a Middle Eastern bazaar, and the marvel is this: that it is only when Abraham stops asking that God stops giving. The two cities will be saved if only there are ten righteous.

But the righteous element in Sodom and Gomorrah was almost nonexistent. Even Lot's attempt to get together a Noah-like family contingent falls short; his sons-in-law think he is jesting. This may say as much about Lot's quality of witness as about the young men's sensitivity. At last even Lot's wife shows how tied she has become to the life and culture of Sodom and Gomorrah.

It is a sad and instructive story, and the postscript about the Moabites and the Ammonites only accentuates the irony.

PRAYER: Give me, please, the faith of Abraham, to plead and work for the redemption of the times in which I live; to your glory. Amen.

GENESIS 20, 21; PSALM 15   Week 2, Day 4

The Bible is a wonderfully honest book. It portrays us as we are, even as it holds before us the ideal of what God wants us to be. Once again Abraham, the man of faith, conducts himself more like an artful manipulator. God respects the heart integrity of Abimelech (20:6) and—in what may seem almost irony—instructs the king to solicit prayer from Abraham. Because Abraham, whatever his occasional lapses, is a servant of God.

And now the promise is fulfilled and the child Isaac—Laughter—is born. Abraham is a hundred years old, and Sarah is ninety; are these ages according to our length years, some will ask? Whatever the case, Genesis wants to make one point clear: Abraham and Sarah are far past childbearing age, and Isaac is a miracle, a gift.

But now the tension between the child of logic and the child of faith grows to the point of disaster, and Hagar and

Ishmael are forced out. From the Bible's point of view, Isaac is the issue of the story, because the witnessing line and the redemptive line will come through him and his descendants. Nevertheless, God watches over Hagar and her son. When she reconciles herself to death, an angel chides her: "What troubles you, Hagar? Do not be afraid" (21:17). Perhaps this is what theologians call common grace; for while Ishmael is not the key figure in the eternal drama, his life is nevertheless preserved and blessed.

PRAYER: Help me, Lord of all, to have room in my heart to see you at work in those who are different from me; in Christ. Amen.

GENESIS 22, 23; PSALM 16   *Week 2, Day 5*

*W*hen Abraham lifted the knife to kill Isaac, it would be a triple murder. He would kill his son, his dream, and the product of his faith. The enormity of the act is shown in the command: "Take your *son*, your *only* son Isaac, *whom you love*" (22:2). Abraham had waited decades for God to fulfill the promise in this son; now he has been asked to destroy him. Even God's miracle is not allowed to compete with God.

Abraham is faithful, and Isaac, who is strong enough to resist his aged father, cooperates with him. It is an awesome father-son partnership of faith. At the last moment, God's angel intervenes. Generations later the writer of Hebrews will say that, "figuratively speaking," Isaac was raised from the dead (Heb. 11:19).

Abraham must have asked himself what kind of God it would be who would make such a monstrous request. He must also have wondered how God's plan could be fulfilled with Isaac gone. But he believed in the face of all his questions. However much this man of faith may have faltered on other occasions, there is no apparent faltering here.

The story stumbles us. We claim to be troubled by its primitive quality, but what bothers us most is its insistence on an ultimate commitment. Our era is not comfortable with ultimate commitments—not in marriage, patriotism, friendship, or faith. It is hard to follow Abraham up this mountain because it is hard to be an ultimate disciple.

15

PRAYER: Grant me, O Lord, the grace to trust you with all of my being, for all of your purposes; in Jesus' name. Amen.

GENESIS 24, 25; PSALMS 17, 18   *Week 2, Day 6*

W e have had two miracles in Isaac—first his birth, then his preservation. But there will not be a family line through Isaac unless he becomes a father, so there must be a marriage.

That seems simple enough, but Abraham felt otherwise. He was convinced that his son must not marry a daughter of the Canaanites, but he was equally sure that his son must not settle back in the land he and Sarah left so long ago. Both these convictions sprang from Abraham's understanding of the plan of God in his life and in that of his family.

So he sent his trusted servant (whose name, perhaps significantly, is never mentioned) on an expedition of trust, and the servant brings back a wife for Isaac, the beautiful and clever Rebekah.

The developing plot has its own pain. Rebekah conceives, but finds a war in her womb. The twins, born only a moment apart, are as different as if from alien cultures. As they grow up, Esau is his father's favorite and Jacob is his mother's. By convention, Esau should be the primary heir, as the older son, but Jacob is the one who is chosen by God. In many ways, he does not appeal to us; he is too crafty and too ready to dupe his brother. But Esau is interested only in the needs and excitements of the moment, and he gladly sacrifices his birthright to fulfill an evening's appetite. Whatever his other limitations, Jacob has a better grasp of life's ultimate values.

PRAYER: Lord of life, teach me to prize what truly matters most; in Jesus' name. Amen.

GENESIS 26, 27; PSALM 19   *Week 2, Day 7*

I saac seems to have inherited something of both his father's strength and his weakness. He follows the same pattern of deception regarding his wife; yet like Abraham, he enjoys God's blessing on all he does (26:12, 13), and in time God confirms for him the promise that was previously made to his father (26:24). And like his father, Isaac becomes a builder of altars.

Esau continues to be a person who seeks his fulfillments regardless of other commitments, and marries out of the will of his parents. And Jacob continues to be Jacob! This time he has the help of his mother. It is not a pretty story. They combine forces to deceive blind Isaac; and they succeed, so that Jacob receives the blessing that was intended for Esau. In the previous instance, Esau was equally at fault, but this time the sin is all Jacob's. And Esau, hating Jacob, vows that when his father has died, he will kill his younger brother. It appears that the Cain and Abel story is about to be re-enacted.

Yet even from this ugly scenario, some good will come. Rebekah, her own cleverness turning in upon her, knows that she must send her favorite son away. But she uses the crisis to be sure that Jacob marries, as both his father and his mother desire, from other than the Canaanite women. The hour of extremity will become an occasion of opportunity.

PRAYER: Heavenly Father, may I never be so anxious for a desirable end that I use an unworthy means; in Jesus' name. Amen.

GENESIS 28, 29, 30   Week 3, Day 1

Almost any circumstance of life can be endured if only occasionally there is a Bethel. As it happens, our Bethels often come when the circumstances are most bleak. Jacob is a fugitive now, alone in a trackless wilderness, but God visits him in a dream and promises him blessings for himself and his offspring.

The blessing begins soon thereafter in the household of his uncle Laban, as he falls in love with Laban's daughter, Rachel. But the blessings come with a price, because Jacob and Laban are cut from the same cloth. It's fascinating to watch these two clever dealers outwitting each other.

Jacob's cleverness is no match, however, for the problems he encounters in being married to the sisters Leah and Rachel. It is Rachel whom he loves, but it is Leah who is fruitful; and as the years go by he is caught between their jealousies and resentments.

But his family grows, and so does his wealth. Clever as Laban is, Jacob is more clever. He gradually builds a small fortune, and while it is the result of his own ingenuity and hard work, it can also be said that he would never have had the opportunity if it had not been for his father-in-law. Above all, Jacob enjoys the favor and blessing of God. And while his pursuit of God's purposes is sometimes misguided, it is to Jacob's credit that he never loses sight of what is best.

PRAYER: Help me this day to keep my eyes fixed on your will, O Lord, that my life may fulfill your purposes; to your glory. Amen.

GENESIS 31, 32, 33   *Week 3, Day 2*

*A*lmost all of us have some unfinished business in our lives, and the sooner we deal with it, the better off we'll be. Jacob had more than his share. These chapters report his handling of each matter.

First, there's his father-in-law, Laban. When Jacob sensed that trouble was brewing with his brothers-in-law, he fled the territory, but Laban soon caught up with him. In truth, both Jacob and Laban had poor records, and they settled matters in a rather tentative way, a truce of suspicion.

Chapter 32 records the story of Jacob's encounter with God, but it begins with Jacob's unfinished business with his brother, Esau. Over twenty years had gone by since Jacob had defrauded him and since Esau had vowed murderous revenge. Jacob apparently wants to make things right; but when he sends emissaries ahead, he learns that Esau is coming to meet him with four hundred men. Jacob organizes a diplomatic mission, but he is not at peace. That night he separates himself from every living person, only to find himself confronted by a Stranger.

Jacob and the Stranger wrestle through the night until at last Jacob wins by giving up. The Stranger gives Jacob a new name, *Israel,* the name that will ever after be that of his people.

Who was the Stranger? Centuries later Charles Wesley, putting himself in Jacob's place, said, " 'Tis Love! 'tis Love! Thou diedst for me." We aren't surprised that Jacob's meeting

18

the next day with Esau was successful. Having done business with God, he was ready to meet his brother.

PRAYER: Conquer my soul, O God, till I know your name is Love. Amen.

GENESIS 34, 35, 36; PSALM 20   *Week 3, Day 3*

*I*f you believe that the Bible is the story of God's dealings with our human race, as I do, you may wonder why chapter 34 is included. It is a primitive story, full of violence. It makes clear, however, that Israel was already committed to a higher level of sexual morality than the other nations, and that at least to a degree, there was more respect for women.

But it's also clear that they expressed their convictions in crude fashion, leaving Jacob in a perilous position. In this crisis Jacob returns to Bethel, with instructions to build an altar. It is as if the bad prospects were forcing him to re-examine his past, remembering his two major encounters with God, and to renew his vows. He remembers that God sustained him in other difficult times, and he turned to God again. It's good to be able to call back some experiences of mercy to carry one through a current crisis.

Now Benjamin is born, and the family of Israel is complete; here are the twelve tribes around which the nation's history will revolve for centuries.

The long list of Esau's family, constituting the nation of Edom, is not our favorite form of reading, but Genesis considers it essential to the story. As time goes by, the Edomites will appear again and again, generally in strife with Israel. So although Esau and Jacob are at peace (35:39), their descendants will dwell with the sword.

PRAYER: Grant me the grace, I pray, to hold deep convictions with a kindly spirit; to your praise. Amen.

GENESIS 37, 38; PSALM 21   *Week 3, Day 4*

*W*e human beings are a complex lot, and we weave strands of life that continually entangle us. Jacob was inclined, it seems, to love much but not wisely, so even as he had loved Rachel to Leah's hurt, now he loves Rachel's son Joseph to the resentment of his siblings and to Joseph's own pain. And Joseph, though very bright, is nevertheless not tactful enough to handle his dreams and his ambitions well. The smoldering resentment grows into disaster, and the teenager is sold into slavery. Jacob thus pays dearly for his favoritism. He will spend the next long years of his life mourning the son he thinks is dead, while in truth that son is preparing the way for his family's well-being. Probably much of our mourning comes from our ignorance. If we knew better how faithfully God is working behind the scenes, we would have more peace.

Not only does God work behind the scenes, but also the divine hand reworks many of our misshapen doings. So it is in the story of Judah and Tamar. Again, the story is told with candor; feelings and reputations are not protected. Judah denies his daughter-in-law the protection of the laws that were intended to provide for women, and Tamar uses a clever plan to make her case. Not much can be said for Judah's conduct, but at least this: he acknowledged his sin (38:26). The end of the story—God at work behind the scenes—comes in the Gospel of Matthew, when we discover that out of this incestuous relationship came a child who is in the line of the Messiah, our Lord Christ (Matt. 1:3).

PRAYER: Give me the faith to see you at work, O God, even in our human sins and shortcomings; in Jesus' name. Amen.

GENESIS 39, 40; PSALM 22   Week 3, Day 5

Joseph the dreamer must now see his dreams broken and delayed. At first all goes well: "The LORD was with Joseph, and he became a successful man" (39:2). But his very success and his being "handsome and good-looking" made him attractive to Potiphar's wife. Joseph is admirable in resisting her enticing, and his reasons are admirable: he feels a debt to his master and he knows that if he were to lie with his mistress it would be a "sin against God" (39:8, 9). He has obligations to both God and society, and he means to fulfill them.

But in doing so he loses his position and, even worse, is

thrown in prison. Doing what is right does not necessarily bring immediate reward. Perhaps not even on this earth, else what's a heaven for?

Even in prison Joseph's character and God's blessing combine for achievement; he is soon as trusted there as he was in Potiphar's house. A wise writer will say later that if people's ways please the Lord, even their enemies will be at peace with them (Prov. 16:7). Joseph seems to demonstrate the point, and when the opportunity comes to exercise his gift of insight through the dreams of his fellow prisoners, Joseph's future seems very hopeful.

But it is not to be so easy. "The chief cupbearer did not remember Joseph, but forgot him" (40:23). Sometimes faith shows itself best by our waiting.

PRAYER: If at times, O Lord, I am disappointed in life and in people, grant me the faith to hold steady; to your glory. Amen.

GENESIS 41, 42; PSALMS 23, 24   *Week 3, Day 6*

*A*fter two whole years" (41:1)! I imagine Joseph waiting almost momentarily after the cupbearer has left the prison; then, slowly, hope dies. But there is a time and a tide. If the cupbearer had told Pharaoh of Joseph immediately upon his return to his office, Joseph's name would have been filed under "applications received." But now Pharaoh is in need of just the talents Joseph has, and now the cupbearer remembers.

Joseph credits God with his gift of insight, as well he should and as well all of us should. Pharaoh sees more in Joseph than simply a diviner of dreams; he also has obvious administrative skills. The bright teenager who alienated his brothers with his dreams has now been matured by life's buffeting. He is prepared. And he has prospered. Rightly he names his second son, "God has made me fruitful in the land of my misfortunes" (41:52).

But the best evidence of Joseph's maturity is yet to be seen. It is sometimes easier to run an empire than to make peace with one's own family, and easier to execute orders than to forgive injuries. In the course of time Joseph is visited by his brothers. The teenager is now a grown man, dressed in the regal garb of an Egyptian ruler so his brothers don't recognize him. But he knows them. The situation is dramatically reversed from that dark day when they sold him into slavery. Now they are the suppliants and he is in command.

PRAYER: When I have moments of power, O Lord, help me use my strength with kindness and wisdom; in Jesus' name. Amen.

GENESIS 43, 44, 45   *Week 3, Day 7*

When you read these chapters, you realize why the Nobel-prize winning German author Thomas Mann felt driven to expand the story into a four-volume novel. What a plot: brothers sell their brother into slavery, then are dependent on him years later when he is in a position of absolute power; his father thinks his son long dead but now gets the unbelievable news that the boy is not only alive, but as successful as only that boy could have dreamed.

And what a tangle of emotions! Follow the brothers, from resentment to revenge to deception to fear. Or the father, from despair and grief, to fear of losing his other "special" son, to a fantasy of reunion. And Joseph, of course. Surely during his slave and prison days, and perhaps even more in his position of power, he must have contemplated revenge.

But the issue to the writer of Genesis is more than plot or human psychology. He sees God at work. Even through the ugliness of human jealousy and brutality, even in a motley course of heartbreaks and delay, God is working out the divine will. Joseph is so sure of it that he makes the point three times in one paragraph. The brothers are not to "be distressed" for what they did, because "God sent me before you to preserve life" (45:5), "God sent me before you to preserve for you a remnant on earth" (45:7), "So it was not you who sent me here, but God" (45:8). Joseph sees a far larger plot than his brothers ever dreamed.

PRAYER: May I have the faith, dear Savior, to see your hand at work in all the fortunes of my life! In the name of your Son. Amen.

*W*hen you see Jacob and his family setting out for Egypt, you are also laying the foundation for the book of Exodus. This move to Egypt is seen as a step in the making of "a great nation," and Jacob is assured that his family will return in time (46:4).

But the seeds of eventual trouble are already present. This family of seventy will become to the Egyptians a threatening nation; they follow an occupation that the Egyptians despise (46:34); and because of Joseph they are given "the best part of the land" (47:11), which in time will anger the native peoples.

Joseph's policies in 47:13-26 do not appeal to me, since they reduce the people to slavery, completely controlled by Pharaoh, but I am imposing the standards of another time; to the people of Joseph's day, he was a savior from starvation. And of course the tax he imposed—20 percent—would seem hospitable today, especially since it really was nothing other than rent on the land.

The blessing of Joseph's sons, Manasseh and Ephraim, brings them officially into Jacob's family. But they come, not as Jacob's grandsons, but as his sons, so that they will be listed among the tribes of Israel and Joseph's name will be removed (Num. 1:10, 32-35). Ephraim is preferred over Manasseh, following a consistent pattern in which the younger is chosen over the older (for example, Isaac and Ishmael, Jacob and Esau).

PRAYER: Lord, may I have faith to see you at work in all of life. Amen.

*J*acob's last words to his sons are not only "a suitable blessing" (49:28) but also a prediction of "days to come" (49:1). The most interesting, of course, is the section on Judah (49:8-12). It is this tribe from which King David eventually comes, and it is this tribe which later gives its name to all that remains of the people of Israel. And especially, it is from this tribe that the Messiah, Jesus, comes. Themes are established here that will reappear even into the New Testament.

Joseph's humane quality, his consistency of character, and his belief in God's purposes come through magnificently both in his love for his father and in his generosity toward his brothers. Though Joseph had told them years before that they should not be distressed over the evil they had done to him because it was part of God's purpose, nevertheless they are consumed with new fears now that their father is gone. They construct a story to convince Joseph, still not realizing that he needs no convincing. The shame of their long-ago deed still clouds their lives. After God and others have forgiven us, a harder task is to forgive ourselves.

"Am I in the place of God?" Joseph asks. Then, again, he reiterates what he said so long before: though your intentions may have been for evil, "God intended it for good" (50:20). That kind of faith gives all of life a quality of hope, dignity, and beauty.

PRAYER: Help me, O God, to believe that you can use even the darkest issues of life to my eventual good and to your honor. Amen.

EXODUS 1, 2; PSALMS 26, 27   *Week 4, Day 3*

When Jacob and his family came to Egypt, they were only the size of a good family reunion. As such they were welcome, particularly since one of their number, Joseph, was already established as a national hero. But when both Joseph and the generation that knew him died, and the family took on the proportions of a small city-state, their Egyptian neighbors began to fear them.

So the government set out to destroy Israel by killing each newborn baby boy. But the midwives frustrated their effort in general, and then one family in the house of Levi frustrated it in a particularly dramatic case. By faith and courage they saved the baby's life; then, by God's providence, the baby ended in Pharaoh's palace, adopted by his daughter. So it was that the king who intended to destroy all Israelite male babies ended up preserving the very one who would one day deliver the Israelites from slavery, a man named Moses.

But it was not going to be easy. Moses received the best of training in his setting of preferment, yet somehow kept a heart for his own people, and apparently a sense of justice, too. One day, while trying to protect an Israelite slave, Moses killed an Egyptian.

Just that suddenly the prince became a fugitive. He fled to Midian, where he could live in obscurity. There he became a shepherd, married, and started a family. End of the dream? Not with God.

PRAYER: Help me to see, dear Lord, that you are at work at all times and in all places, always and unfailingly. Thank you! Amen.

EXODUS 3, 4; PSALM 28   *Week 4, Day 4*

*A*s chapter 2 ended we learned that God saw the pain of the people (2:23-25); but how is deliverance to come? God's purposes are almost always achieved through persons. In this case the person is a likely/unlikely one, but this too is pretty typical of God's working. This man was miraculously saved as an infant and raised as a prince, but he had spent most of his adult life on the back side of a desert, tending his father-in-law's flock of sheep.

No wonder, then, that when God calls him, Moses has little self-confidence and quickly explains to God that he is not qualified; he has to be convinced and restored before he can be useful for any purpose. Yet see a marvel and an irony in this encounter. The marvel is that God allows the shepherd to argue with him, and the irony is that this man who says he is afraid to plead a case with Pharaoh is nevertheless bold to state his case before God.

And see the quality of God's patience. Instead of giving Moses an ultimatum ("Shape up and do it my way or else") or instead of simply overpowering him with divine reasoning, God cooperates with Moses' feelings of inadequacy and provides help through his brother, Aaron. "Two are better than one," a wise one said, "for if they fall, one will lift up the other" (Eccles. 4:9, 10). Moses and Aaron will have opportunity for such lifting.

PRAYER: Forgive me, Lord, when I argue with you; but remember that I am dust and that sometimes I feel very weak; in Jesus' name. Amen.

When Moses and Aaron come before Pharaoh in the name of the Lord, Pharaoh answers, "Who is the LORD that I should heed him . . . ? I do not know the LORD" (5:2). Pharaoh's answer is in the essential secular voice, one that denies any divine right except its own.

So Pharaoh flexed his muscle ("I'll show them who's king around here!"), and Moses found himself caught between a resentful people and the commands of the Lord. No wonder he pleaded, "Why did you ever send me?" (5:22). God reassures Moses, reminding him that the ancestral revelation to Abraham, Isaac, and Jacob was coming to an even more wonderful focus now, and that the covenant (one of the wondrous words of scripture) is indeed remembered. But the Israelites could not hear Moses "because of their broken spirit and their cruel slavery" (6:9). The harshness of life can make us dull to even heaven's assurance.

Now the grand dialogue begins between Pharaoh, on the hand of strength, and Moses and Aaron, on the side of weakness. Moses is warned that there will be a hardening of Pharaoh's heart, but even this warning is insufficient when the full degree of that hardening shows itself. The encounter begins with an almost playful show of power, Aaron's miraculous rod, a demonstration that Pharaoh's magicians easily imitate, though they are bested when Aaron's rod consumes theirs. When the water is changed to blood, however, we know the full battle is engaged.

PRAYER: Give me the grace, dear Lord, to stand with those who are broken in spirit by some slavery of life; in Christ. Amen.

The series of plagues follows a pattern of somewhat predictable disaster in the way each leads into another. The blood is followed by frogs in the land, and their rotting stench by gnats; then swarms of flies, followed by a plague of the livestock. So it goes, through boils, hail, locusts, and then thick darkness.

And always, a pendulum swinging in Pharaoh's soul. He repents, then rejects his own repentance. Sometimes the scripture reports that God hardened Pharaoh's heart, and at other times that Pharaoh himself hardened Pharaoh's heart. Which is it? And how do we reconcile the idea of God hardening someone's heart? Charles Wesley found it easy to understand:

> There needed, Lord, no act of thine,
> If Pharaoh had a heart like mine:
> One moment leave me but alone,
> And mine, alas, is turned to stone.

It seems to me there is always this fierce inner struggle between our self-will and the Voice that calls us. The Voice is sometimes pleading, sometimes insisting, sometimes fierce, but always wanting us. Destruction, as a last resort, is chosen by the victim, not by God.

The "darkness that can be felt" (10:21) is symbolic even while it is real, as it portrays the terror of the human soul that is absent from God and in rebellion against the Eternal.

PRAYER: Please give me a heart that is always tender toward you and your purposes, for my sake and yours; through Christ my Lord. Amen.

EXODUS 11, 12; PSALM 30   *Week 4, Day 7*

The Passover, Moses and Aaron understood, was to be "the beginning of months" (12:2). Many contemporary Jews who do not identify themselves as being religious nevertheless celebrate Passover; its roots are deep not only in their national heritage but also in the individual psyche. For the Egyptians it was a night of disaster and judgment, but for the Jews a night when they saw the power of God manifested on their behalf.

Thus it was a "day of remembrance" to be celebrated "throughout your generations" (12:14). A casual reader may find the many details tedious, but this exactness was intended to underline the gravity of this day above all days.

The Christian church, from its beginning, has found some of its roots in this same event. The first celebration of the sacrament of communion came in the setting of the Passover meal (Luke 22:14-18). Any number of details from Exodus 12 have carried over into the hymns and liturgical language of Christians. Most important of all, Jesus Christ is identified as our Passover Lamb (1 Cor. 5:7), the One who died that we might escape the eternal death angel.

I suspect that the Passover celebration is most poignant for those Jews who have a vivid sense of what God did for their ancestors in Egypt, just as Holy Communion means the most for those Christians who realize how profoundly they have been saved from sin. Those who know how much they have been forgiven are the most grateful for the divine gift.

PRAYER: Dear Lamb of God, may I never forget your death for me. Amen.

EXODUS 13, 14, 15   Week 5, Day 1

Since the Israelite firstborn were spared from the death angel, the people were to consecrate all their firstborn, both human and animal, to the Lord. This would be a reminder that the Lord had brought them "out of Egypt, from the house of slavery" (13:14). They were to be a covenant people, led by a safe route since they were not ready for war (13:17) and guided by the quiet, continuing miracle of cloud and fire.

But (like you and me) they were an obstinate lot. They rebelled as they faced the sea, contending that it would have been better to stay in Egypt than to die in the wilderness. How could they so quickly forget the power of the Lord from the Passover night? Most of us, if we reflect honestly upon our own journey, will understand. We so soon forget the pain of the slavery from which we have been saved and the glory and mercy of God in our deliverance.

But as they saw their pursuers destroyed, they joined Moses in singing a song of deliverance. Then Miriam, Moses' sister, picked up the theme. Tambourine in hand, she led the women in dancing and singing: "Sing to the LORD, for he has triumphed gloriously" (15:21). They were only three days down the road, however, when they not only forgot the songs they had sung with Moses and Miriam, they complained bitterly against Moses at their shortage of water. God used the occasion to add a new dimension to their covenant (15:25b, 26).

PRAYER: Give me a sanctified memory, I pray, so that when I am inclined to grumble against you, I will remember your mercy. Amen.

EXODUS 16, 17, 18   *Week 5, Day 2*

God provided food (16:35), water (17:6), and victory in battle (17:13). The people provided the grumbling. Each day seemed to require a new miracle if the people were to carry on, and always they seemed ready to return to Egypt where they "ate [their] fill" (16:3) and had plenty to drink (17:3). When I was seventeen a man named Herman Pencovic told me, "The Jews remembered the leeks and garlic of Egypt after they had forgotten the taskmasters and the making of bricks without straw." Most of us have just such a selective memory when we recall the good old days.

The visit by Jethro, Moses' father-in-law, is a special kind of bright spot in the midst of Israel's struggles. Wise as Moses may have been, he was using his time and energy poorly; leaders are often inclined that way because they see themselves as indispensable. Jethro gave Moses advice that was ingenious good sense: share the burden. From a religious point of view, Jethro might have been seen as a pagan; he was not one of the people of Israel. If Moses had been more narrow in his sympathies, he would have refused this counsel; after all, God had been speaking to him directly, so why should he listen to an outsider? But Moses was both wise enough and humble enough to learn—even from an in-law! Here's a lesson in common grace: God speaks to all his creation, to the degree we are willing to listen.

PRAYER: Dear Lord, help me to be ready to learn, no matter what channel or instrument you use to teach me; in our Savior's name. Amen.

EXODUS 19, 20; PSALMS 31, 32   *Week 5, Day 3*

Out in the wilderness there is a mountain called Sinai. It is not the tallest mountain in the world, but it may well be the best known. Israel had been on the road long enough to

29

know they needed the structure of law. Even the best and most careful drivers need a line to show which is their side of the road, and a sign to indicate who will stop at an intersection. Life together requires boundaries.

Although this law was to deal with the most practical issues, it was not ordinary; it was the gift of God. Moses made this clear by establishing restrictions of many kinds, so the people would understand that Sinai was holy ground.

The Ten Commandments come from a basis of God's right and our debt. So they begin, "I am the LORD your God, who brought you out of the land of Egypt, out of the house of slavery" (20:2). God has a right to our loyalty because of the deliverance we have received. The degree to which we are at peace with God's commands is probably directly related to our sense of his salvation.

The first four commandments regard our direct responsibility to God; the last five our duties to our fellow human beings; the fifth, the command to honor our parents, is a kind of bridge between them. But the responsibility to God comes first; as a philosopher has said, if there is no God, then anything goes.

PRAYER: Help me, I pray, to know with the psalmist that your word is a lamp to my feet and a light to my path; in Christ our Lord. Amen.

EXODUS 21, 22, 23   Week 5, Day 4

$\mathcal{I}$ am struck by the simplicity and directness of these laws, and by their mercy, too. If at times they seem severe, the severity is on the side of the injured. It seems almost taken for granted that there will be respect for truth; without it, witnesses are meaningless and the whole structure of the law collapses. Undergirding everything in these laws is a sense that life is lived under the hand of God. All justice and judgment is in the end dependent on this conviction and on the quality of life that comes from it.

There is a restraint on power. In a world where slavery was practiced, these laws limited the slave owner; if he broke a slave's tooth, the slave was set free in compensation for the tooth (21:27). At a time when women were subservient, protections were nevertheless provided (22:16, 17). Perhaps the most helpless in society were the aliens, but they were to be treated fairly because "you were aliens in the land of Egypt" (22:21). And as for the poor, lend to them and do not take interest; and if the surety for your loan is your neighbor's cloak, don't keep it at night, for "in what else shall that person sleep?" (22:25-27).

And above all, there shall be justice. You shall not side with a majority (23:2), nor take a bribe (23:8), nor shall you even in pity be partial to the poor (23:3). Your fairness shall extend to the land, allowing it to rest every seventh year (23:10, 11).

PRAYER: Give me regard, O Lord, for your commandments, so that I am fair to my fellow human beings and to all creation; in your name. Amen.

EXODUS 24, 25, 26   *Week 5, Day 5*

These chapters may bore a modern reader. Who cares, we ask, about the materials that went into the tabernacle or the details of the Ark of the Covenant with its table and lampstand and framework and curtains? Do these things matter to us today?

Actually, yes. Centuries later the writer of the New Testament Letter to the Hebrews will talk about these matters because he sees in them a foreshadowing of the new way of life in Jesus Christ. "This is a symbol of the present time" (Heb. 9:9). The Greek word that in this verse is translated "symbol" is usually translated "parable." Perhaps it will help if we will look upon these detailed descriptions as a physical parable of the glory and completeness that can be found in Christ.

So the Christian reader has an advantage over the ancient counterpart. The original reader knew the material was important because of the repeated command that it should be made "according to the pattern . . . which is being shown you on the mountain" (25:9, 40; 26:30). It is important for us because we have encountered the reality for which the original was only a shadow.

The intricate details of these chapters will also remind us that it is an awesome thing to appear before the Lord of the universe. Let it be done rightly and reverently, as befits such an engagement.

PRAYER: Lord of my life, give me a proper sense of your power and majesty, lest I become casual in your presence; to your glory. Amen.

EXODUS 27, 28, 29, 30   *Week 5, Day 6*

To read these chapters faithfully and effectively we have to move a distance into the world of the Jewish people. The altar represented so many things that ancient rabbis made each letter of the Hebrew name for *altar* the initial of a word, so the four letters would speak of forgiveness, merit, blessing, and life. The horn was a symbol of power and salvation; to take hold of the horns of the altar meant to lay claim on the power of God.

So, too, with the garments of the priests. The twelve stones on the breastplate, bearing the names of the twelve tribes of Israel, signified that the priest was always bearing the people before God in prayer; it is a quality that a parish pastor, at his or her best, would emulate. The priestly anointing was equally specific. Blood, the symbol of life, was touched to the ear of the priest, that it might be consecrated to hear God's word; to the hand, so he might perform properly the duties of the priesthood; and the foot, so that he would walk in righteousness (29:20). When he was sprinkled with blood, it reminded the people that atonement can be found for our sins, and when with oil, that there is light and joy in godliness (29:21).

And all of this, in the end, was that they should "know that I am the LORD their God, who brought them out of the land of Egypt that I might dwell among them; I am the LORD their God" (29:46).

PRAYER: May my worship always end, O God, in the recognition that you are the Lord of my life; to your honor. Amen.

EXODUS 31, 32, 33   *Week 5, Day 7*

The Hebrew scriptures look upon skilled craftsmanship as true wisdom; thus Bezalel and Oholiab are called by God and "filled . . . with divine spirit" (31:1-5). But talent is only as good as the use to which we put it. Even the best gifts of God can be made cheap and destructive. So it is that Aaron used his sacred office to collect gold from the people from which to make a golden calf. When Moses confronted him, Aaron first blamed the people ("They said to me, 'Make us gods'" [32:23]) without acknowledging his own abdication of leadership, then blamed circumstances ("I threw it into the fire, and out came this calf" [32:24]).

Moses, too, had a talent. It is too complex to be easily defined, but it is available at least in a measure to every child of God. Moses chose to stand between the people and God, pleading their cause to God, and pleading God's cause to the people. His commitment is so intense that he challenges God to blot his own name from the divine record if the people are to be rejected (32:32).

Moses' prayer is effective: "The LORD said to Moses, 'I will do the very thing that you have asked'" (33:17). Yet even so, Moses was not granted the favor of seeing God's face. The ultimate reward of those who exercise Moses' gift is that they will see God's will accomplished in the world and will see a body of people (or a single individual) restored to communion with God.

PRAYER: Lord, help me know such concern for the welfare of others that I will plead their cause faithfully before you; in Christ. Amen.

EXODUS 34, 35, 36   *Week 6, Day 1*

*E*xodus 34 is a chapter of the second chance. Moses is privileged to return to the mountain to receive a new set of the tables of the law, to replace those that were broken. Moses confesses that his people are "stiff-necked," but asks that God "take us for your inheritance" (34:9). The covenant is renewed, with a solemn warning about the perils that lie ahead. Israel will have the power to conquer the nations they will one day face, but they must guard against taking on the evil practices of those people.

It's interesting to see what matters are emphasized here.

Idols—a reminder that their recent disaster came at this issue. And remember the festival of unleavened bread (34:18); this will remind them of their deliverance from slavery. Remember, too, the obligation of the firstborn; a reminder of the climaxing plague. And the sabbath (34:21-24), because this is the unique symbol of God's people. Moses came from this encounter with God with a face that shone too brilliantly to be viewed.

Then there is the story of talent and of willingness. What a beautiful combination! Neither is fully adequate without the other. The two craftsmen, Bezalel and Oholiab, were joined by "everyone whose heart was stirred to come to do the work" (36:2). A freewill offering was received, with response so great that "the people were restrained from bringing" more (36:6). What a happy quality of commitment!

PRAYER: I want my heart to be so devoted to you that I can hardly contain my desire to give; to your glory. Amen.

EXODUS 37, 38, 39, 40   *Week 6, Day 2*

A great entertainer once said that he became an overnight success after twenty years of hard work. Most of life's best achievements are the product of tedium. It may be devoted and even inspired tedium, as in the case of Bezalel and Oholiab, and it will almost surely be crowned from time to time with feelings of achievement. And yes, for one who loves what he or she is doing, even the tedium has a kind of glory. Nevertheless, routine and discipline are inevitable factors in any true accomplishment.

That's something of the lesson of these chapters. Step by step the workers produced the tabernacle, its furnishings and the garments of the servers. When they were finished it could be said that they "had done all of the work just as the LORD had commanded Moses" (39:42). Now Moses could anoint and consecrate each item, and he, too, "did everything just as the LORD had commanded him" (40:16).

Then God placed a special seal of approval upon the project. The cloud that symbolized God's presence covered the tent of meeting, "and the glory of the LORD filled the tabernacle" (40:34). The glory was so great that, for a time, not even

Moses could enter the building. Let this be a word to all who prepare and teach Sunday school lessons, all who earnestly serve on committees, all who write sermons and sing in church choirs: do so with dedication and God will visit with glory.

PRAYER: I ask not for a glory that I cannot endure, but for that which will draw me nearer to yourself; in Jesus' name. Amen.

LEVITICUS 1, 2, 3   *Week 6, Day 3*

The tribe of Levi became the spiritual leaders of the nation. As such, they lost their tribal identity; their place among the twelve was now taken by the dividing of Joseph's descendants into the tribes of Ephraim and Manasseh. The Levites were to find their portion in the Lord rather than in a unit of land.

This book is largely a guide for the Levites in their work, but as such it mattered to all of Israel—perhaps in the same way the Constitution of the United States matters to all its citizens, even though it is the particular responsibility of the courts.

This is especially true for those of us who believe in the Protestant doctrine of the priesthood of all believers. Not that we are instructed by the details of conduct at the altar of sacrifice or proper methods of preparing animals for burning, but in the spirit and commitment with which the Levites were expected to do their work.

A grain offering, for instance, was to "be of choice flour"; and if one brought an animal before the Lord, it should be "one without blemish" (2:1; 3:1). God is to receive the first fruits (2:14), not the leftovers and not what is not good enough for the commercial market. If I sing, I will give my best at the church, preparing as earnestly as if it were for a secular concert; whatever I do, it shall be an offering that will be a "pleasing odor to the Lord" (1:7).

PRAYER: Let me be your priest, O Lord, offering my life and my daily duties as my sacrifice of love to you; in your name I pray. Amen.

*T*he blood sacrifices of ancient Israel are usually offensive to our modern sensitivities. But they help us understand the seriousness of sin. Dietrich Bonhoeffer warned against "cheap grace"; all of us are susceptible to such a disposition, especially in a time when society seems to suggest that "anything goes." Leviticus makes clear, by its system of sacrifices, that sin is an affront to God. This, even beyond what our misdeeds do to others and to our own bodies and psyches, is why we must treat sin seriously. Yes, Leviticus has something to teach us.

A lovely provision is made for those who are poor. "If you cannot afford a sheep, you shall bring to the LORD . . . two turtledoves or two pigeons" (5:7); and "if you cannot afford two turtledoves or two pigeons, you shall bring . . . one-tenth of an ephah of choice flour" (5:11). But while provision is made for economic limitations, everyone is expected to bring something. No one is exempt from the recognition of sin or from dealing with it.

What is our responsibility to the persons we may have harmed? When an Israelite defrauded or deceived a neighbor, the law required that they "repay the principal amount and add one-fifth to it" (6:5); but then the guilty party must also bring to the priest a guilt offering to clear the soul before God. Our sins have both a horizontal and a vertical dimension; we deal with them before God and whatever injured party.

PRAYER: I am sometimes casual about the wrong I have done; thank you for reminding me of my blood-guilt; and save me, through your Son. Amen.

*I*srael was called to be a holy people—that is, a people separated to God and to God's purposes. But if there is to be a holy people, a particular burden rests upon those who are called to lead to holiness. Thus the ceremony is long and complex, with details that may easily seem tedious to us.

But the end of the matter is *cleansing*. Those who would serve God must be God's clean people, and the physical and ritual events merely emphasize the issue of spiritual purity. "It will take seven days to ordain you," Moses warns (8:33). The scriptures often use numbers in a symbolic way, to make some significant point. Seven is the number of completeness or perfection, so the seven-day ceremony conveys the idea of a completed act of dedication and a finished holiness.

The consummation of it all is found in 9:22-24, in the blessing of the people. When Moses and Aaron come out of the tent of meeting (the tabernacle) to bless the people, "the glory of the Lord" appears. The writer of Leviticus recalls it as such an awesome sight that the people shout and fall on their faces.

We shout at sporting events, and applaud and sometimes even call "bravo" at an opera or a concert, but we do not often feel such excitement at the presence of God, and even less often do we show it. It may be, again, that Leviticus has something to say to us.

PRAYER: When I serve, O Lord, let it be with purity of heart; and when I worship, let it be with holy excitement; in Jesus' name. Amen.

LEVITICUS 10, 11; PSALMS 33, 34   *Week 6, Day 6*

*T*he teaching of chapters 8 and 9 is dramatically demonstrated in this story of Nadab and Abihu. As Aaron's sons, they were in the highest ranks of the priesthood, yet somehow the awesome responsibility hadn't fully gotten to them. They violated their office by offering "unholy fire," and they died. Aaron, who it seems had himself erred far more seriously in the making of the golden calf, "was silent," and the people were instructed not to mourn.

Nadab and Abihu's misconduct apparently sprang from their being intoxicated (10:8-11). If it is hazardous to drive a high-powered engine after drinking, how much more, Aaron's sons proved, to deal with holy things with less than our best ability.

The subject of clean and unclean foods may seem mundane after the Nadab and Abihu story, but for the writer of Leviticus they are all of a piece. Holiness is an issue not only while ministering in the tabernacle but in all of life. The rules were pragmatic. Maintaining health and sanitation in a desert world, among essentially nomadic peoples, was not simple. Every precaution had to be taken. Many foods that can be safely prepared in our time were a hazard in that time and setting.

The spiritual issue of dietary regulations became an issue early in the Christian church, especially as non-Jews came into the fellowship. The discussion arises often in the book of Acts.

PRAYER: Help me, I pray, to treat all of life with a sense of awe, lest I thoughtlessly handle holy things in a common way. Amen.

LEVITICUS 12, 13; PSALM 35   *Week 6, Day 7*

*R*eligion at its best involves all of life; a healthy spirit fed by a healthy mind dwelling in a healthy body. The New Testament tells us that our bodies are the temple of the Holy Spirit (1 Cor. 6:19). The laws of Leviticus teach us the same thing in another way by their often intricate rules for care of the body and for sanitation. These rules tell us, tacitly yet forcefully, that our bodies are holy.

In the ancient world the term *leprosy* covered a wide range of diseases, from simple and curable to the most fearful. Many of these skin diseases were infectious, so extreme precautions were taken. These Jewish sanitary rules were far in advance of the rest of the world. Some Western medical practices didn't catch up with them until the middle of the last century.

We are coming increasingly to understand that a profound tie exists between the health of the soul and the health of the body. It is significant that the tribe of Levi was responsible for both. They led the nation in worship and they watched over its health. "Glorify God in your body," Paul said (1 Cor. 6:20). Other things being equal, our bodies have their best chance for health when our spiritual lives are healthy. The Sunday morning jogger would do better to join in the adoration of God, and the worshiper should celebrate divine adoration with a body that has been treated with holy respect.

PRAYER: Help me, O Lord, to treat my body as your temple,

so that it may be blessed with your fullness of health; in Jesus' name. Amen.

LEVITICUS 14, 15; PSALM 36   *Week 7, Day 1*

*R*abbis taught that the command for holiness had both a positive and a negative aspect. The positive is the Imitation of God. The negative means withdrawing from that which is impure and abominable. So Rabbi Pinchas ben Yair said, "Heedfulness leads to cleanness; cleanness to purity; purity to holiness; holiness to humility; humility to dread of sin; dread of sin to saintliness; saintliness to the possession of the Holy Spirit." Such, surely, is the mood of these chapters. Their lengthy, patient list of regulations having to do with leprous diseases and with bodily discharges should be seen as the efforts of a people to avoid anything that might defile them. And they remind us again that there is often a close link between physical and spiritual defiling.

So many of the conditions of temporary uncleanness were "until the evening" (15:18, 19, 21, and so on). For the Hebrews, the new day began when the sun went down. Persons who had been unclean for a day could retire at night with a sense of purity; they began their new day at sunset with a sense of freshness and peace. When the Apostle said, "Do not let the sun go down on your anger" (Eph. 4:26), he was working on the same principle. The mind and spirit, as much as the body, ought to be clean as we begin a new day by entering the sleep that will have so much to do with how the following morning will be experienced.

PRAYER: I want all of my person—body, mind, and spirit—to be clean in your holy sight, that I may truly please you. Amen.

LEVITICUS 16, 17, 18   *Week 7, Day 2*

*W*hat does the grandeur of the day of atonement have to do with the food we eat or with our sexual relations? A very great deal, if we take our walk with God seriously. The way this passage moves from the sublimely spiritual to what we might consider cultic and then to the physical dramatizes how the Jewish Law (and our continuing faith) sees life as a whole. The line between the sacred and the secular is not so sharp as our logic might want to make it.

The most fascinating creature in the atonement experience is the scapegoat, Azazel. The sins of the people are laid on it and it is led out "into the wilderness." The scene reminds me of Psalm 103:12, when the psalmist notes that God has removed our transgressions "as far as the east is from the west," and also of the New Testament writer who, in probable reference to this ceremony, says that Jesus "suffered outside the city gate" (Heb. 13:12).

The code of sexual conduct is specifically to be other than what "they do in the land of Egypt [and] in the land of Canaan" (18:3). The conduct of those peoples caused the land to be "defiled" so that at last its inhabitants would be "vomited out" (18:25). The people of Israel were to have a different standard, because of their relationship to God and their regard for the bodies God had given them. No doubt much of the popular culture of our times (which can easily engulf us) is equally repugnant to God's standards.

PRAYER: Jesus, Savior, I lay on you the burdens of shame I cannot bear; take them far from me, I pray; to your glory. Amen.

LEVITICUS 19, 20, 21; PSALM 37   *Week 7, Day 3*

*A*s we said before, to be holy is to be different from those around us. But it is very difficult to live in the midst of a culture without taking on much of its style and standards. Chapters 19 and 20 deal with that problem. Some of the issues may sound trivial to us, but for the Israelites they were marks of distinction; if they became too much like their neighbors in these matters, they might easily slip over into their patterns of ethical conduct, too.

Other laws are fascinating for their practical social sensitivity. When reaping a harvest, leave some for the poor and the alien (19:11)—perhaps the only time Israelites were asked to be careless in their work! "You shall not keep for yourself the wages of a laborer until morning" (19:13). Why not? Because in an economy of day laborers, many lived from one day's pay to the next, and if the wages were held back, a family was left hungry for the night. Do not "revile the deaf or put a stumbling block before the blind" (19:14); that is, don't take advantage of someone's limitations. In judgment, "you shall not be partial to the poor or defer to the great" (19:15)—a standard we still find it hard to fulfill even in a modern legal system. And "rise before the aged, and defer to the old" (19:32).

And the basis for all these commands: Because "I am the LORD your God, who brought you out of the land of Egypt" (19:36).

PRAYER: You have brought me from my own kind of bondage, gracious Lord, so I gladly acknowledge your right to my devotion. Amen.

LEVITICUS 22, 23, 24   *Week 7, Day 4*

*E*very day is sacred in its own right, but we need special occasions in the calendars of our lives that give a lift to life and that help to center our focus. The several festivals performed that function for Israel. For while there were many laws that reminded them of their differentness, these festivals gave a certain beauty and glory to their role.

Three of the celebrations had to do with nature. The Israelites were an agricultural people, so it was natural for their lives to revolve around seedtime and harvest. Most of us aren't as conscious of our dependence on nature, because we live more removed from its rhythms; but now and then an earthquake, a flood, or a tornado reminds us that as surely as ever we are dependent on nature.

Only the day of atonement called for fasting; others were in a more celebrative mood. Several were intended to remind the people of the power of God in their nation's history and of the loyalty that was therefore owed to God. The festival of booths, in particular, recalled that they had lived in booths when they escaped from the land of Egypt.

But while these occasions came scattered through the year as annual events, there was always the seventh day of the week with its sabbath. As an ancient rabbi said, "More than

Israel kept the sabbath, the sabbath has kept Israel." It is God's gift of rest and dignity for those who will receive and observe it.

PRAYER: Thank you, Lord, for days of rest, awe, and laughter. Amen.

LEVITIUS 25, 26, 27   *Week 7, Day 5*

*I*f the sabbath is a gift to us, it is meant also to be a gift to nature. Every seventh year the land was to lie fallow. Whatever came of the unpruned vine or the untended field could be eaten, but there was to be a rest for the land. Here was a simple method of soil conservation long before it became a science. And here was a reminder of our obligation to nature. The land is blessed or cursed according to the quality of our stewardship. In a sense, the land is helpless beneath us; we determine its fate. But it will have the last word. If we do not treat it with care, it will get the *really* last word.

As we noticed earlier, seven was one of the significant numbers for the Hebrew people. After seven sevens of years, there would be a year of jubilee. "It shall be holy to you: you shall eat only what the field itself produces" (25:12). More than that, there shall be a reordering of the economy: debts are cancelled, and those who have sold themselves or their families into slavery are set free.

What a festival! "You shall have the trumpet sounded loud" (25:9) to announce the beginning of this year. Charles Wesley wrote a hymn around this chapter, applying it to our redemption in Christ.

> Ye who have sold for nought
> your heritage above
> Shall have it back unbought,
> the gift of Jesus' love:
> The year of jubilee is come!
> The year of jubilee is come!
> Return, ye ransomed sinners, home.

PRAYER: Help me to make this year, this very year, a jubilee of glad and holy living; and help me to share it well with others. Amen.

42

*T*he book of Numbers gets its title from the first census of Israel, which is contained here. If it were titled for its most significant event, however, a cynic might well call it the Book of Retreat, because it is in Numbers that we read the sad story of the Israelites coming within reach of their land of promise, then retreating into their fears. But more of that later.

There is a sense of family lineage among many ancient peoples which we in America seem to have lost until recently. The Israelites are told to make a census in clans, by ancestral houses, so the people will know their origins. I think this was also part of a movement to establish their pride. A people who have lived in slavery for over four centuries need to know that they have proud roots of heritage.

What we mentioned earlier about Joseph is now established: Joseph is phased out, and his descendants are named through Ephraim and Manasseh (1:32-35). The tribe of Levi shall not be enrolled, but shall have responsibility for the tabernacle (1:48-53).

The people are set up in orderly fashion, with three tribes to north, south, east, and west. At the center of the encampment is Levi with the tent of meeting. The place of worship is at the center of life. The Levites have their role "as substitutes for all the firstborn among the Israelites . . . ; [they] shall be mine. I am the LORD" (3:45).

PRAYER: Let me be a Levite, Lord, remembering that whatever I have and whatever I gain is yours—as I am; in Jesus' name. Amen.

NUMBERS 4, 5, 6   *Week 7, Day 7*

*C*lergy sometimes complain that they have to do all sorts of routine tasks unrelated to preaching and pastoral care. If so, they are in the biblical tradition. Part of the calling of the Levites was to assemble and disassemble the tabernacle as the Israelites moved from place to place. It wasn't glamorous work but it was essential and, from the scriptural point of view, it was holy—like cooking a church supper.

The process for settling a marital suspicion is known as trial by ordeal. It was to be used in instances when suspicion was felt but there was no evidence. In a male-dominated culture, it was probably a woman's best defense against a jealous husband.

Chapter 6 is a bright spot in this book. One admires the nazirites for their desire to dedicate themselves to a special pursuit of God. It is the kind of commitment some make during Lent. It's easy to discredit such acts as meaningless or superficial, but if they are performed earnestly they have a positive effect. God honors the seeking heart, and probably the discipline is good for our character. *Like Black Hole of Calcutta*

The blessing with which this chapter ends is a good model not only for benedictions but for our general life-style. These beautiful words sent persons on their way under the glow of faith and hope. In a world where people seem so easily to curse and damn others, we ought to be ones who bless. Thus, in some measure, we help God's kingdom to come.

PRAYER: Help me this day to bring blessing to someone by a word of love and grace, spoken in your name and in your Spirit. Amen.

NUMBERS 7, 8; PSALM 39   *Week 8, Day 1*

*M*ost of us would confess, after reading chapter 7, that we would have been content if the writer had settled for the summary at the end rather than giving us the detailed, identical lists, which take up 83 verses. Rabbinical commentators felt that repetition was intended to show the stately solemnity that marked these gifts, and also to indicate that none of the princes wanted to outrank the others but that by their identical gifts they would show unity and harmony of spirit. According to tradition, Nahshon was chosen to lead the way because when the Israelites were pursued by the Egyptians at the Red Sea, the tribes hesitated to enter the waters, and while each urged the other, Nahshon plunged in, fearlessly trusting God.

I like also to feel that this repetitious list shows that each gift matters to God, and that each one—even if identical!—is singular in heaven's eyes. Each gift is a product of some person's devotion, and each is given with the mark of the spirit of that individual. Therefore, each has its own glory and its own limitations.

Some stories need to be retold. When the Levites are con- secrated to service, we are again reminded (8:14-19) that they are a special people because they take the place of the first- born. But special as they are, they still must be cleansed and presented with a particular offering. Serving God is an awe- some calling, whatever the level, whatever the task.

PRAYER: I give myself anew to you this day, O God. I am this one-of-a-kind person, and I want to be yours; in Jesus' name. Amen.

NUMBERS 9, 10; PSALM 40   *Week 8, Day 2*

I never cease to marvel at the way biblical religion bal- ances the spiritual and the commonplace. These chap- ters offer two examples. The first has to do with what may seem to us a picayunish question, because we can't fully sense the exalted significance of the Passover festival. But some Israelites were worried; what if some unavoidable circumstance prevented their participating in this once-in-a-year event?

Moses felt the gravity of the question and respected the earnestness of the inquirers. His answer preserved the sanctity of the occasion while also caring for the concern of the indi- vidual.

The other instance has to do with divine guidance. Israel was led by a cloud that hovered over the tabernacle by day and by "the appearance of fire" by night. They trusted this provision implicitly, whether moving frequently or at long intervals. Yet when Moses' brother-in-law, Hobab, was going to leave, Moses pleaded with him to stay because he needed Hobab's special skills: "You know where we should camp in the wilderness, and you will serve as eyes for us" (10:31).

Some might assume that direct divine guidance was enough. Moses recognized that God uses human beings. Spiri- tual as he was and accustomed as he was to dealing with God directly, he nevertheless was ready to seek human assistance. God has not left us alone in this world, and we ought not to act as if he had. Our cloud and fire may be a person.

PRAYER: Help me see your goodness in both the extraordinary and the commonplace, and to hear your voice through others. Amen.

NUMBERS 11, 12; PSALMS 41, 42   *Week 8, Day 3*

*W*e expect so much from some experiences—adulthood, marriage, career, for instance—that when we come upon the hard places we may not deal with them well. So it was with Israel and their freedom. There had been a certain kind of security in slavery that was missing in freedom, and Israel responded with murmuring.

This time their murmuring got the best of Moses. "Why have you treated your servant so badly?" he challenged God (11:11). When God promised a miracle, Moses answered in the fashion of the disciples when they found themselves with a hungry multitude (Luke 9:12-17). Although he had seen God's provision in the past, his faith was a bit low just now.

But the more I see of Moses, the more I respect him. When God offers a remedy with a committee of seventy who will receive some of Moses' spirit, Moses doesn't cling to his power. And when Eldad and Medad begin to prophesy, Joshua is jealous for Moses, but Moses wishes only that "all the LORD's people were prophets" (11:29). Then Moses is attacked by his own kin, Aaron and Miriam, and still he keeps a right spirit. When judgment falls on Miriam (since she alone was punished, it seems she led the way in this rebellion) and she is smitten with leprosy, Moses pleads to God on her behalf. Moses shows himself to be human enough but remarkably strong in an often thankless job. + *changed Jehovah's*

PRAYER: If I, like Israel, complain of my life, hold me back *mind* from such murmuring as would destroy me; in Jesus' name. Amen.

twice

NUMBERS 13, 14, 15   *Week 8, Day 4*

*T*he church committee is at least as old as this story in Numbers 13. The plan was good: get one representative from each tribe to search out the land and bring back a report. And they seem to have done their work well. But col-

46

lected data is no better than the committee that interprets it, and in this case a large majority saw the data negatively. They confessed readily that it was a good land, flowing with milk and honey. But the towns were fortified, the people strong. How strong? "To ourselves we seemed like grasshoppers, and so we seemed to them" (13:32). The sequence in their analysis is right, of course; when we see ourselves as grasshoppers, others will soon see us the same way.

Ten people felt that way. But Caleb spoke for himself and Joshua: "Let us go up . . . we are well able" (13:30). The difference in their points of view came from an intangible factor, as it so often does. Caleb and Joshua were confident of God's help: "the LORD is with us; do not fear them" (14:9).

But the nation believed the negative report, not simply because it came from the majority, but because it is almost always easier to retreat than to move forward. So the Lord declared that none of that adult generation except Caleb and Joshua would enter the promised land. This is a rule of life; those who live in doubt, despair, and reluctance are sure to miss the best that God has for them.

PRAYER: Save me, O Lord, from seeing myself as a grasshopper. I want to enter into your promised land! In Jesus' name. Amen.

NUMBERS 16, 17, 18   *Week 8, Day 5*

*F*ew things are so intoxicating as power. Three Levites, who already enjoyed a position of influence, decided they wanted more. Their argument seemed logical; "all the congregation," they said, "are holy" (16:3). But in their grasping for power they failed to recognize that though all were holy, all didn't have the same calling.

Moses' confrontation with the rebels was quick and decisive. But his troubles didn't end there. Although the people were terrified by the destruction that came, they returned the next day to challenge Moses and Aaron again. Obviously the rebellion within the community was very deep and broad.

Once again Moses became an intercessor for the people. His patience with their "stiff-necked and rebellious ways" is impressive. Again, the problems reflected both the political and spiritual immaturity of a people who were enjoying their first taste of freedom.

Now a new test is developed. Where the rights of Aaron's line were demonstrated previously in an act of judgment-violence, now the proof comes in a demonstration of fruitfulness. Aaron's rod buds and bears almonds. It is a fitting symbol. The best evidence of our place in the purpose of God is the fruitfulness of our lives. Ultimately, a demonstration of power only angers others so that they return later to make their case, whereas the fruits of life are persuasive.

PRAYER: I want to be one of your fruitful persons, so others will find strength and sustenance in my life; in Jesus' name. Amen.

NUMBERS 19, 20; PSALMS 43, 44   *Week 8, Day 6*

*T*his book of Numbers mixes law and action indiscriminately, as if to say that the whole business of life is the business of law and that it touches life at every point. That seems logical, in light of the conduct of the people. They are murmurers and rebels. Again and again they find some reason to question the leadership of Moses or to complain against God. From our distance, this seems strange. We think they ought to feel profound gratitude to Moses for his tireless leadership and to God for their deliverance from slavery. But our spiritual memories are often short. Even miracles, like the encounter at the Red Sea, are forgotten or at least pushed aside when frustration sets in.

This time the issue was water. That was a valid concern, surely, but the people handled it in what seems to have been their customary fashion: "Why have you brought us up out of Egypt to this wretched place?" (20:5). This time Moses loses his patience. Instructed by God to speak to the rock, instead he impatiently strikes it, twice. Both he and Aaron are held responsible for this act, which was an expression of unbelief. Neither was allowed to enter the promised land, though Moses will later have opportunity to see it from afar. But Aaron's ministry has now come to an end. In a dramatic changing of the guard, his garments are passed on to his son, Eleazar. Life goes on.

PRAYER: Am I inclined to use my freedom for complaint and rebellion? If so, correct me and restore me, for your name's sake. Amen.

NUMBERS 21; PSALMS 45, 46   *Week 8, Day 7*

on some skewed scales

Grumbling is a deadly sin. We don't usually recognize that. It is an expression of unhappiness—sometimes with ourselves, sometimes with others, and sometimes with God—and it springs from our unbelief. Its deadly quality shows itself in this dramatic story, where the grumbling of the people brings a plague of deadly serpents. *we got born unsure which gods exist.*

The particular form of judgment may appropriately remind us of the serpent in Eden, for he did his work by a grumbling against God. The remedy for Israel is a brazen serpent, which is posted in the center of the community; any who look upon it are healed. *Again, many died. Kids too?*

This brazen serpent reappears twice in the biblical story. Apparently the people kept it as a religious memento; and as happens with such items, the object itself came to be seen as a source of power. Generations later, when King Hezekiah began his religious reforms, he saw that the people were using this bronze serpent as an object of worship, so he broke it in pieces (2 Kings 18:4). *All angels knew. Why did so many go nuts?*

The Gospel of John uses the brazen serpent as an introduction to the most beloved verse in the Bible, making it a symbol of Jesus' crucifixion. "And just as Moses lifted up the serpent in the wilderness, so must the Son of Man be lifted up, that whoever believes in him may have eternal life" (John 3:14, 15). Jesus became the embodiment of sin so that those who look to him might be saved.

PRAYER: Help me, dear Savior, to see that however great my sins may be, you have graciously provided a remedy; in Jesus' name. Amen.

NUMBERS 22, 23, 24   *Week 9, Day 1*

The ultimate battlefield of history is the individual human soul. There is the same deployment of forces, the same advancing and retreating, and at last the same satisfaction of victory or shame of defeat.

Rarely do we get a clearer account of such a struggle than we have in this story of Balaam. It is, of course, the story of a conflict between two nations, but as it happens—and as is so often the case in the affairs of state and world—it is settled within the confines of one human soul. What goes on in Balaam's heart eventually affects a whole people.

Balaam is a talented, gifted human being, able to commune with God in an extraordinary way. At first he answers God rightly, but he tips his hand early in a conversation with Balak's servants when he says, "Although Balak were to give me his house full of silver and gold, I could not go beyond the command of the LORD my God" (22:18). I don't think he knew it, but he was announcing his price; Balak now knew he was susceptible to an offer.

So we watch the pendulum of the soul swing, and we smile at times at the way Balak tries to get a curse upon Israel, only to see Balaam offer another blessing. It looks as if this strange man is on the right track, but unfortunately he is too clever for his own good.

PRAYER: Help me, O Lord, to keep my values straight so that I never trade the eternal for the transient; in Jesus' name. Amen.

NUMBERS 25, 26, 27   Week 9, Day 2

When we left the battle of the soul yesterday it appeared Balaam had won, for he was blessing Israel, just as God had commanded him to do. Now we learn differently, though we don't get the details until later. What Balaam could not do through cursing he did through his counsel. He obeyed the letter of God's command on his life but violated the spirit.

Balaam sensed that the men of Israel could be led astray by the attractiveness of the Moabite women (25:1, 31:16), and Balak followed his counsel. Balaam, not able to curse Israel, found a way for Israel to curse itself. It was a devastating sin, not only for its sexual infidelity but also because it meant violating what was then so important to Israel, her ethnic purity.

The New Testament book of Jude will refer to this sin, and will correctly identify Balaam's error: greed (Jude 11).

But there are bright elements in today's reading. For one, we learn that in spite of Korah's sin, his sons do not die; indeed, they must have come to some kind of redemption, because later they author a number of psalms. The daughters of Zelophehad (27:1-11) make a notable early instance of establishing women's legal rights. And provision is now made for a successor to Moses, the man Joshua. He has been Moses' right-hand aide for years and—even more important—he is "a man in whom is the spirit" (27:18). God's servants go, but the work of God goes on. There will be life after Moses.

PRAYER: Sometimes, Lord, like Balaam I stay within the letter of the law even as my heart goes outside it. Save me, I pray. Amen.

NUMBERS 28, 29, 30, 31   *Week 9, Day 3*

*A*s we have seen before, life has its holy, memorable occasions. They add luster to life and direction, too, and the biblical writers want to be sure they are not neglected. The Israelites, with a routine life-style in a world that seemed never to change, needed such occasions to lift their eyes to the divine; you and I, sometimes almost drowned in an endless sea of sound, activity, and clamor, need these times to lift us from the trivial and the transitory to the eternal.

It isn't always easy for us to put ourselves in the place of the Israelites in their wilderness wanderings. When we read the rules concerning women and their relationship to husbands and fathers, our modern sensibilities are offended; and when we see the violence of Israel's vengeance against the Midianites, that offense is heightened. But we need to remember that it is always easy, in another time and place, to say, "They shouldn't have been like that"; as a matter of fact, future generations will no doubt pass such judgments on us. No generation really has a right to impose its standards or its solutions on the actions of another because each generation has to cope with its problems with the equipment at hand. We can hardly imagine the struggles of maintaining order in a nomadic wilderness, so we're probably no more qualified to say what they should have done than they would be to offer advice on dealing with air pollution, nuclear holocaust, and urban crime.

PRAYER: Give me the grace, O God, to be a faithful steward of the times in which I live, demanding as they are; in Christ's name. Amen.

NUMBERS 32, 33, 34 *Week 9, Day 4*

*I*f you find the data in these chapters so tedious that you wonder why they are in the Scriptures, you are not the first to have such feelings. Those long-ago persons known as the Early Church Fathers apparently had the same concerns. They concluded that the details of the journey were intended for our instruction, as symbolic of the steps by which Christians leave sin and advance from virtue to virtue, until they come at last to their final abode in God's eternal home. Does that help you appreciate these chapters more?

Nevertheless, there are also some practical lessons of character to be learned. I admire Moses' wisdom and firmness in dealing with the tribes who decided to have their inheritance on the other side of the Jordan, and his adaptability, too. As a young man I thought that if I made one wrong decision, the rest of my life would be ruined; I've come since to learn that God works patiently with what we give him, even when the pieces do not fit easily into a coherent whole, just as accommodations were made for the tribes that wanted to alter the original plans. God's laws are strict, but God's character is gracious.

The warning of 33:55 seems harsh to our ears, but as the history of Israel unfolds we will see that it was not without foundation. Our problem is still the same. If we become comfortable with an ungodly life-style, it will eventually corrupt and destroy us.

PRAYER: It is better, dear Lord, that I learn from the experience of the Israelites than from my own errors. Please? Amen.

NUMBERS 35, 36; PSALM 47 *Week 9, Day 5*

*T*he Levites, as I have mentioned before, had no inheritance of land; their inheritance was the Lord. They were given forty-eight cities in which they could live, but as residents rather than owners. Among those cities were the six cities of refuge. In a culture where family vengeance was practiced, these cities provided safety until fair judgment could be had, and afterward if the person was innocent. It was a wonderfully simple and effective plan for its time and place, and it was appropriate that the Levites were the keepers of this security.

Wouldn't it be wonderful, in our day, if there were some sort of refuge where we could be protected against character assassins until all the facts were in? At one time or another, all of us would have occasion to run to such a refuge, if it existed.

In any event, we Christians ought to fill such a role. Taking the Levites as our pattern, we should protect and sustain those persons whom life is treating badly, whether they be victims of something so vast as political injustice or as ever-present as the "slings and arrows of outrageous fortune." Every human being has times when he or she wishes there were a place to run and hide, not out of cowardice but out of necessity. Such a refuge is available in prayer, of course, but I'm sure God intends for us to become a physical and active place, in heaven's stead, for those who are pursued by destruction.

PRAYER: Help me, O God, to provide shelter for those who are victims—by fault or faultless—in the struggle of life; in Christ. Amen.

DEUTERONOMY 1, 2, 3; PSALM 48   *Week 9, Day 6*

S ome things need to be said twice. The book of Deuteronomy, which gets its name from two Greek words meaning "second law," fills that role. It is presented as a kind of valedictory address by Moses, as he bids farewell to the people he has led for forty years and tries to prepare them for the new land they are about to enter.

He begins by reviewing their history. Philosophers say we should study history in order to learn from it. No doubt this is part of Moses' intention, but there is more than that. For Israel, history was the story of their encounter with God, so to review history was to recall God's involvement in their lives.

Even so, Moses reminds the people of the sharing of leadership (1:9), and of the crucial decision their ancestors made to turn back at Kadesh-barnea. That decision led to a generation of wandering in the wilderness before at last there could be victories over Sihon and Og—victories that would be celebrated often in song (Psalm 136).

In all of this the people are reminded of the faithfulness of God and also of their own erratic ways. As we read the account, we get a strong feeling that the history of Israel is the history of every person who sets out for God's promised land. Every spiritual biography has its uneven path between victory and defeat, good judgment and stupidity. And in it all, whether in Israel's story or ours, God is at work.

PRAYER: Give me the humility and the attentiveness, O God, to learn from the past, so I can make a better future; in Jesus' name. Amen.

DEUTERONOMY 4, 5; PSALM 49   *Week 9, Day 7*

*T*he laws of God are not arbitrary restraints, but directions to a fulfilled life. So Moses warns Israel that they must give heed to the statutes he is teaching "so that you may live to enter and occupy the land that the LORD, the God of your ancestors, is giving you" (4:1). As an introduction to the laws, Moses reminds the people of the miracles God has done on their behalf. What other great nation, he challenges, has a God so near to be called upon, and what other has a law as helpful as the one he is about to review (4:7, 8)?

But with all that God has done for Israel—bringing them "out of the iron-smelter . . . of Egypt" to be God's own people (4:20) and making them a nation "by a mighty hand and an outstretched arm" (4:34)—there is nevertheless the danger that their descendants will go astray when they "become complacent in the land" (4:25). Our spiritual memories tend to be very short. Yesterday's miracle easily becomes today's non-event.

The commandments in chapter 5 are in the same order and possess essentially the same content as recorded in Exodus 20. It is interesting that the laws of measurable conduct (murder, adultery, theft, false witness) are stated directly, without commentary, while those that have to do with the more subtle

54

issues of our minds (the sabbath and coveting) are spelled out with specifics.

PRAYER: I want to remember, O Lord, that your laws are for my benefit, and that my best happiness is in loyal obedience; in Christ. Amen.

DEUTERONOMY 6, 7, 8   *Week 10, Day 1*

*I*t could well be argued that Deuteronomy 6 is the most important chapter of the Old Testament, because of the *shema*, verse 4: "Hear, O Israel: The LORD is our God, the LORD alone." Judaism identifies this sentence as the center of Jewish thought, upon which all other Jewish belief turns. No wonder, then, that the people are commanded to keep this word in their hearts, recite it to their children, talk about it, and make it an emblem on forehead and doorpost (6:7-9). There is a passion in this command that we should make our own.

There's a toughness about chapter 7, reminding us that love has demands. But there's a wonder in love, too, and verses 7 and 8 celebrate it when they say, essentially, "God loves you because he loves you." Logic can find no further explanation. Here is a precursor (as in other places in the Hebrew scriptures) of what the New Testament will call *grace*.

Moses assures the people that victories and blessings await them: prosperity in their work, health of body, and conquest of even their most fearsome enemies. But with all of these favors, there is a peril. In that new land, having "eaten your fill" and when "all that you have is multiplied" (8:12, 13) it will be very easy to forget "the Lord your God who brought you out of the land of Egypt, out of the house of slavery" (8:14). How could they be so ungrateful, we wonder, until we look carefully at some of our own experiences with God.

PRAYER: In days of prosperity, let me never forget you. Amen.

DEUTERONOMY 9, 10, 11   *Week 10, Day 2*

A poet speaks of "the prophet's righteous scorn." This is the quality we feel in these chapters. One senses

Moses' wrath even over the stretch of the centuries and through the printed page. He remembers how he pleaded with God for this people, and he is determined that his efforts shall not have been in vain. He understands our human capacity for self-adulation. These people who "have been rebellious against the LORD from the day [they] came out of the land of Egypt" (9:7) are likely someday to think, "It is because of my righteousness that the LORD has brought me in to occupy this land" (9:4). We human beings have an astonishing ability to rationalize our past wanderings once we are on track for a brief time.

When the spies researched the land a generation before, they warned that it was a land that would eat its inhabitants. A greater hazard now faces the people, that they will be devoured by unbelief, compromise, and idolatry. Moses gives instructions that are almost fierce in their intensity, to be sure they will keep their purity. It's all up to them: a blessing and a curse has been set before them, depending on whether or not they obey the commandments of the Lord.

You and I live in a pagan world, too. But for us, the enemy is more subtle and not so obviously threatening. Like the Israelites, we're constantly in danger of compromising our souls.

PRAYER: Make me sensitive, O Lord, to the subtle matters that would destroy me, and draw me close to your purposes; in Christ my Lord. Amen

DEUTERONOMY 12, 13, 14; PSALM 50   *Week 10, Day 3*

*F*or a time like ours, when the key words are *pluralism* and *broad-mindedness*, chapters 12 and 13 may seem harsh and narrow-minded. But we need to hear the message. There is a point at which breadth means not only shallowness but also an absence of content and character. Israel lived among practices that were abominable in the way they debased both ethics and morality; to cooperate with such practices would eventually bring disaster. We should seek to understand other points of view and even to see what we can learn from them, but we should also hold fast to the integrity of our beliefs.

The problem is particularly complicated when it arises within the family (13:6-11) because there is a clash of loyalties. Jesus dealt with a comparable issue in his call for full discipleship (Matt. 10:34-39). The physical severity of Deuteronomy is not there, of course, but the issue is the same. It is a hard word, and we shouldn't be too quick in brushing it aside or in taming it to fit our thinking.

The laws regarding clean and unclean foods were meant to protect the health of the people, which was surely important. They were also to underline the fact that the Israelites were separate from the nations around them. Consider how hard it was for Simon Peter to leave these dietary regulations when a vision used them as a sign that Gentiles were to be welcomed into the church (Acts 10:9-16).

PRAYER: Help me, I pray, to have a breadth of mind toward those who are now different from me, and a singleness of commitment to you. Amen.

DEUTERONOMY 15, 16, 17   *Week 10, Day 4*

God was calling the Israelites into a way of life in which worship and ethics would dominate. Instead of accumulating endlessly, getting ever more to pass on to one's heirs, there were to be regular opportunities for starting again with a clean slate. This would assure that there would be "no one in need among you" (15:4). But it was not a naively optimistic approach; it was built on the hard realization that "there will never cease to be some in need on the earth" (15:11).

Such a program could succeed, of course, only in a nation or a community bound together by a common religious commitment. It is at this point that economics, ethics, and worship come together. Properly, then, there is again a review of several major religious festivals; these occasions were the spiritual power undergirding the political and economic structure. Our values need to be lifted up on occasions of sacred celebration.

The day would come when Israel would want a king. But he must remain close to the people in his life-style, not accumulating silver, gold, horses, and wives. Above all, he is to be a student of God's law, having it near at hand so he can "read

57

in it all the days of his life"—not simply to accumulate knowledge or as an act of piety, but "so that he may learn to fear the LORD his God" and follow God's path (17:19). Ideal? Yes. Attainable? Yes. Did Israel have it often? No.

PRAYER: Help me, O Lord, to be a source of light in a pluralistic and secular society, to your glory and to human gain; in Christ. Amen.

DEUTERONOMY 18, 19, 20   *Week 10, Day 5*

*T*he poet Robert Frost said that good fences make good neighbors. Laws are such fences. They make it easier for people to live together in harmony. So the tribe of Levi shall know what portions of the sacrifices are theirs (18:1-8), there are specific regulations regarding the cities of refuge (19:1-13) and careful limitations on the use of witnesses (19:15-21). And especially, the ancient boundaries shall be respected, not only because to move a marker is a theft from your neighbor, but because the land is, ultimately, the Lord's (19:14).

We usually think of Moses as a great lawgiver and political leader, but he is identified here as a prophet (18:15-22)—that is, he was one who spoke for God. This is what made his leadership unique. Thereafter there would be national leaders and there would be prophets, but with the possible exception of David, the two were not again combined, at least not on a continuing basis.

Are you troubled that the Old Testament gives rules for warfare and encouragement for Israel in times when their enemies outnumbered or outpowered them (20:1-20)? The Bible is a wonderfully realistic book. It not only holds up ideals for perfection, as in the Sermon on the Mount and 1 Corinthians 13, but also gives pragmatic insights for living in a less than perfect world. War was as commonplace in that ancient world as the baseball season in ours, and the people had to know how to live with it.

PRAYER: Give me, I pray, a faith that is pragmatically tough, so I will know how to cope with life when it is short of your will. Amen.

DEUTERONOMY 21, 22, 23; PSALM 51 *Week 10, Day 6*

Religious people are sometimes accused of being so heavenly-minded they're of no earthly use. No such accusation can be made against the rules laid out in Deuteronomy. They are wonderfully down to earth—so much so that they may at times seem quaint to people far removed from a relatively simple, primitive society. It doesn't take too much imagination to adapt many of the rules to life in the twentieth century.

There is a severity to the laws—as in, for instance, the issue of a rebellious son (21:18)—because this is a nomadic society where order is a crucial issue. But there is also great care for those who may be at a disadvantage, such as the woman taken captive in war (21:10) or the firstborn who is the son of an unloved wife (21:15). And there is practical neighborliness, if an ox or sheep has strayed or a donkey or ox has fallen into a ditch (22:1-4); and there is a kind of pre-liability law (22:8), not simply to protect one from a lawsuit but because if there were an accident you would "have bloodguilt on your house" (22:8). Neighbors can feel free to eat one another's produce in passing; in their ancient culture this was not theft. But to take a container or put in a sickle was (23:24, 25).

All of these commandments, both small and great, rest on the same foundation: the responsibility to "the Lord your God." If God is truly paramount in our lives, right conduct must follow. Like ending blood libel on Jews

PRAYER: Dear Lord, may I always remember that you are an issue in every detail of my life, great and small; in Jesus' name. Amen.

goh, Deuteronomy 21 + Judges 21 need VERY careful reading! + Exodus quickly 21

DEUTERONOMY 24, 25, 26 *Week 10, Day 7*

Someone has said that a society can be judged by the way it treats those who are least able to defend or care for themselves. So many of the commands in Deuteronomy are for the protection of the poor or the alien. When you collect for a loan, you wait outside for the pledge (24:10, 11), thus respecting the dignity of the borrower; and if the pledge is a

Some poor & some alien

poor man's garment, you return it to him in the evening because it is his only nighttime covering (24:12, 13). So, too, you pay wages at sunset so the day laborer has food for his family (24:14, 15). You extend justice to the alien because "Remember that you were a slave in Egypt" (24:17, 18). You purposely leave some food behind when you harvest, so the poor can glean on your property (24:19-22). If you will so live, "it will be to your credit before the LORD" (24:13).

Personal honesty also rests in godly belief. You have honest weights and honest measures because "all who act dishonestly are abhorrent to the LORD your God" (25:13-16).

If an Israelite heard the law rightly, all of life had a divine glory about it. The harvest time was more than simply an issue of abundance; it was a reminder of the One who had given this land to their ancestors when they were slaves (26:1-15). With the tithe of the harvest one is able to bless the "aliens, the orphans, and the widows" (26:13); thus a person's resources become a quality of mercy rather than just wealth.

PRAYER: O Lord, help me see that what I have is yours and that I am privileged in being able to share it with others; in Christ. Amen.

DEUTERONOMY 27, 28, 29   Week 11, Day 1

*W*hen we're about to enter unexplored land, whether a new school, a new job, or a marriage, we need a ritual of entrance. Some are simple and unstructured; but usually the more significant the event, the more solemn the ritual. As Israel prepared to enter their new homeland, they stood on the slopes of Gerizim and Ebal while the Levites stood in the valley between, pronouncing first a blessing toward Gerizim and then a doom toward Ebal. A Jewish commentator calls it the most imposing, solemn, and impressive event conceived for such an occasion. With each blessing and curse, the people were to say *Amen* to indicate their agreement with the contract. Only the curses are listed here; rabbis say that the blessings were negations of the dooms.

The same theme is carried forward in chapter 28, but this

time by a listing of blessings and curses without a list of the commands. The message of doom is longer than the promise of blessings. Perhaps this is because we human beings seem to be moved more by threats than by promises of favor. At the least, the Israelites had to confess that they were properly and vigorously warned!

But in spite of the sometimes threatening language, the call is to the good life. If the Israelites miss, it will be because "you did not serve the Lord your God joyfully and with gladness of heart" (28:47). In Egypt they had been slaves; here they were to be co-workers with God.

PRAYER: Father, make me wise enough to know that blessings and curses are built into life, and that the choice is mine; in Christ. Amen.

DEUTERONOMY 30, 31, 32   Week 11, Day 2

*I*f the mixture of life's blessings and troubles seems fearful, it is because we have forgotten God's rule in the whole process. If we will learn from the fortunes and misfortunes and will "return to the LORD, . . . then the LORD your God will restore your fortunes" (30:2, 3). Mercy is woven into all the fabric of life, even into those sections which seem at the moment to be ugly.

The lawgiver becomes an evangelist as he nears the end of his speech. "See, I have set before you today life and prosperity, death and adversity. . . . Choose life . . . , loving the LORD your God, obeying him, and holding fast to him" (30:15, 19, 20). There could hardly be a more impassioned call to the altar of decision.

But now it is time for the changing of the guard. No matter how often Israel rebelled against Moses' leadership, they must now have felt very uneasy at the prospect of continuing without him. But they have a grand assurance: "The LORD your God himself will cross over before you. . . . Joshua also will cross over before you" (31:3). They can enjoy the same confidence they knew before, because again God is with them, working through a visible leader. Moses seems for a moment to strike a bitter note ("I know well how rebellious and stubborn you are" [31:27]), but he seems nevertheless to be confident they will learn: "Take to heart all the words that I am giving . . . you today" (32:46). Well—we shall see!

PRAYER: Help me, O Lord, to choose well today, and every day. Amen.

DEUTERONOMY 33, 34; PSALMS 52, 53 *Week 11, Day 3*

*L*ike the patriarchs before him, Moses pronounced blessings as he died. In his case, however, he was blessing not simply his own descendants, but an entire nation, tribe by tribe.

What a beautiful way to die! But if we are to die with a blessing on our lips, we'll have to get in practice early. Ordinarily we are, in our old age and in our dying, what we have been in earlier years, only written larger.

One could say that Moses spent the first two-thirds of his life preparing to lead Israel—first through formal education in the courts of Egypt and then in a character seminar on the backside of the desert—and the last third of his life providing that leadership. The days of leadership were anything but tranquil, and at times Moses was impatient with the people. But he never ceased to love them and to plead for them. Now, ready to die, he reminds them what a fortunate people they are:

> "Happy are you, O Israel! Who is like you,
> a people saved by the LORD" (33:29).

Moses was not a perfect man. At times he fell into self-pity, and he wasn't above blaming Israel for his problems. He became impatient to a point that he lost his opportunity to enter the land of promise. Yet there was no one like him. He saw the Lord, and did God's will (34:10).

PRAYER: I'm not expecting to be a Moses, dear Lord, but I want to be true to you in my place, in my time; in Jesus' name. Amen.

JOSHUA 1, 2, 3 *Week 11, Day 4*

*T*he Wesley brothers said that the Lord buries his servants but that the Lord's work goes on. Moses is dead; and now Joshua, Moses' assistant, will carry on. He is assured that

God will be with him as with Moses, and he must therefore be "strong and very courageous" and "act in accordance with all the law. . . . Meditate on it day and night" (1:7, 8).

Sometimes the Lord surprises us by the people he employs. One would hardly expect a prostitute to be the key human figure in the invasion of Jericho—and one certainly wouldn't expect her to become part of the lineage of the messiah (Matt. 1:5) nor heralded as an example of both faith (Heb. 11:31) and works (James 2:25). But perhaps that's because we become so absorbed with outward appearances while God looks at the heart. Rahab, plying a rough trade in a pagan city, nevertheless had such a capacity for God that she would put her life on the line for what she was coming to believe.

Forty years earlier, ten of the twelve spies melted in fear before the inhabitants of the land, but now the two-man scouting party reports that "the LORD has given all the land into our hands" (2:24). But first the people must sanctify themselves (3:5) to be ready for the conquest; and before they can see God's power at the Jordan River, they must step forward in faith (3:15, 16).

PRAYER: Give me the grace, I pray, to see the potential you have invested in every human being, including those I might scorn. Amen.

JOSHUA 4, 5, 6   *Week 11, Day 5*

*W*e need devices to help our spiritual memory even more surely than we do to assist the everyday secular process. A new generation will forget the faithfulness of God to their ancestors unless there is something to help them. So the Israelites built a mound of twelve stones (4:1-9) to recall God's faithfulness—just as we celebrate the sacrament of holy communion to recall our Lord's sacrifice (Luke 22:19).

But the memory of the past is not enough; each new generation must have its own commitments. As the saying puts it, God has no grandchildren. So this new generation must be circumcised, as evidence that they, too, are God's covenant people (6:2-7).

And now, the victory at Jericho. Symbolism is present in the priests leading the way, blowing the rams' horns before the Lord, with the Ark of the Covenant following. It is there also in the use of numbers: seven priests because seven is the number of completeness or perfection; then, six days of marching but with the victory on the seventh day, the customary day of rest, as if to say that this triumph is God's doing, not theirs. And at last a shout, an act of faith.

Some will explain the Jericho story with the data of physics; some will see it as a miracle needing no explanation; still others will interpret it symbolically. But for Israel, it was evidence God was with them.

PRAYER: I have my Jerichos now and then, dear Lord; break their walls before me, I pray; in Jesus' name. Amen.

JOSHUA 7, 8, 9; PSALM 54   *Achan*   *Week 11, Day 6*

When life goes bad, a first inclination is to give in to despair, perhaps even to the point of thinking all is lost. That's what Joshua did after the defeat at Ai. But it was no time for wailing. God said, "Stand up! . . . Israel has sinned" (7:10, 11). It was a time to think and then to get at the root of their problems.

The remedy was a fierce one. Achan was destroyed, with his family, who were seen as party to his theft. And then on to an even more fierce chapter as Israel wiped out the city of Ai: "For Joshua did not draw back his hand . . . until he had utterly destroyed all the inhabitants of Ai" (8:26).

I will not ask that we agree with all that happens in this often bloody book, but only that we seek to put ourselves into the times and to understand something of the setting. The people Israel must be a holy people, altogether different from the nations around them, so purity is enforced vigorously. As for Jericho, Ai, and the others still to come, they were seen as part of a culture whose iniquity had come to the full and upon whom judgment must now fall—and Israel is the instrument of judgment.

On the other hand, see an act of integrity in the case of the Gibeonites. They deceived Israel, but because Israel had sworn a solemn oath, they kept it, even though they could easily have justified doing otherwise.

PRAYER: When I am inclined to despair, help me first to see

64

where I may have erred, and help me to deal with my mistake; in Christ. Amen. *Vs Stoning of family!*

JOSHUA 10, 11, 12 *Week 11, Day 7*

Joshua 10:4 / Free Will

*W*hat difference does it make today that millennia ago several scores of city-states, with kings whose names are hardly a speck in history, were defeated by Israel? To a scholar, it means one more small piece in the knowledge of the ancient world, the kind of information that, added to some archaeological finding, becomes a segment in the human story.

But for Israel the importance is far more than the data of history. It is the stuff, eventually, of hymns of praise to God, with each name a reminder that "the LORD fought for Israel" (10:14, 42). Religion for the Israelites was no theoretical study; it dealt with specifics of names, dates, and battles. And when the event was marked by what seemed to be the cooperation of nature itself, the victory was all the more memorable.

When we are far removed from the circumstances, we may not be especially empathetic with a testimony about a God who marches with a nation's armies. For that matter, a comfortably middle-class person today may not appreciate the emotional witness of a ghetto mother who says God sent the relief check just in time. But when one lives in the midst of some kind of oppression or peril, whether political, economic, physical, or emotional, and the answer comes in good time—well, the story looks different from that position. Then one wants not so much to analyze as to sing.

PRAYER: Give me a heart, O God, for the rejoicing of others. Amen.

JOSHUA 13, 14, 15 *Week 12, Day 1*

*I*n the midst of what might seem a rather tedious geography lesson, we are re-introduced to that doughty man of faith, Caleb. As he looks back on the events forty-five years before, he sees the report that was then controversial as nothing other than good sense: "I brought him an honest report"

(14:8). When one views life with faith, one sees a logic in the data that another might miss.

His zeal has not been diminished by the years. He has grown old victoriously. "I am still as strong today as I was on the day that Moses sent me" (14:11). So much so that he wants to take on another challenge: show me the Anakim and their fortified cities "and I shall drive them out, as the LORD said" (14:12). Faith gives a zest for life. For Caleb life has always been a matter of advancing, not retreating.

It seems his daughter Achsah was made of the same stuff. When he gave her to the man who would attack a certain city (it seems Caleb wanted a son-in-law of his own kind!) and Othniel claimed her, Achsah dared to ask for more. What good is land in the Negeb without a spring of water? she asks. So Caleb gave her upper and lower springs—more, I think, than she sought. Himself a person of vigor, he was proud to see his daughter take hold of what life proffered and reach out for still more. And that, too, is the style of faith.

PRAYER: Sometimes I sell you short, O Lord, by selling myself short. Give me a grand zeal for life, I pray; in Jesus' name. Amen.

JOSHUA 16, 17, 18   Week 12, Day 2

When a baseball, football, or basketball season is about to begin, you'll hear a coach say of a particular player, "The position is his to lose." That is, in the competition for a position, this person is already considered the winner; if he doesn't get it, it's his own fault.

That's the way Joshua deals with the tribe of Joseph and later with seven other tribes in the apportioning of land. Joseph—that is, Ephraim and Manasseh—complain that they haven't been given a portion in comparison with their size and strength, and Joshua answers, "If you are a numerous people, go up to the forest, and clear ground there for yourselves" (17:15). It's theirs if they will go and get it!

So, too, there were seven tribes "whose inheritance had not yet been apportioned." It seems they were sitting back, waiting for something good to happen to them. Joshua asked, "How long will you be slack about going in and taking possession of the land the LORD, the God of your ancestors, has given you?" (18:3). He instructed them to send a delegation to write out a description of the land and its boundaries, and he promised that he would divide it. Then, however, it would be their responsibility to get it. So it is with the promises and blessings of God. They're there for us, but we have to take hold of them.

PRAYER: I wonder, O Lord, how many blessings I have missed because I didn't "rise up to take the land"? Help me, I pray; in Christ. Amen.

JOSHUA 19, 20, 21; PSALM 55   *Week 12, Day 3*

*A*t this point in its history, Israel was a theocracy—a nation ruled by God. When the territory was divided among the tribes, it happened therefore "at Shiloh before the LORD, at the entrance of the tent of meeting" (19:51). As with all of Israel's experiences, it was a religious event. As a theocracy, all of their history was sacred history.

So, too, when the dividing of the land was complete, the writer reminds us that Israel had received everything the Lord had promised and that now they would enjoy "rest on every side"; again, just as it had been promised. "Not one of all the good promises that the LORD had made to the house of Israel had failed" (21:45).

But perhaps you still ask yourself why you should have bothered to read these several chapters which list in such detail the division of the lands, especially when they seem repetitious and overly precise. In a sense, the answer is like climbing Mount Everest: because they're there. That is, they're part of the Bible. It's true that Jesus never quoted from them in the Gospels, nor did Paul in his epistles. They don't have the quality of the Psalms or of Isaiah. They do, however, belong to the sacred canon, and in reading these portions we come to a more intimate sense of knowing the people of Israel.

PRAYER: Help me to know, dear Savior, that your promises to me are as sacred as those made to Israel. I can count on you; in Christ. Amen.

*W*hen John Wesley warned the early Methodist movement against "solitary religion," he was reflecting both Old and New Testament teaching. Israel understood that it could not maintain its spiritual purity and strength if it became divided, so when it appeared that Reuben, Gad, and Manasseh were isolating themselves, the other tribes responded with alarm (22:1-34). In the same mood, Joshua appealed to the people to maintain their racial unity lest they lose their spiritual unity and commitment (23:1-13). They were to be the people of God, corporately as well as individually.

Joshua's farewell is a challenge, as impassioned in its own way as was that of Moses before him. He reminds the people again that God has worked miracles on their behalf in bringing them out of slavery to the land of promise. So now, "choose this day whom you will serve . . . ; but as for me and my household, we will serve the LORD" (24:15).

We are tempted, as was Israel, to have a comfortable religion, without too many demands and with a casualness that allows us to go in and out as our mood directs. But gracious as God is, he will not be mocked. There is a time when we must say, "As for me, I will serve the Lord." And we say it not only once, in a moment of climactic decision, but daily, sometimes hourly, through hundreds of little choices.

PRAYER: Forgive me, dear Lord, if sometimes I treat you in casual fashion, forgetting your majesty and honor; in Christ's name. Amen.

JUDGES 1, 2, 3   Week 12, Day 5

*I*t is always difficult to live up to our occasions of high decision. Perhaps no book of the Bible makes that point more directly than Judges. The people worshiped the Lord as long as there were those who could recall the miracles of the days of Joshua (1:7), but then came another generation "who did not know the LORD" (2:10).

The problem was no doubt accentuated by the weakness of

the political structure under the judges. But all through this book the plot line is the same; 2:18, 19 summarizes it perfectly. When a judge, raised up by God, delivers the people from the hand of their enemies, the people serve the Lord— usually as long as that judge lives. But as soon as the judge dies (and sometimes before) "they would relapse . . . , following other gods" (2:19). And despite all the warnings of Moses and Joshua, and all of the peoples' earnest vows of purity, they soon intermarried with the foreign peoples living among them and began to take on their pagan religious practices.

So we begin a series of fascinating but essentially tragic stories. The lead characters change—Othniel, Ehud, Shamgar— but the plot remains the same. The people forget God until they are in trouble; then they repent and God sends a deliverer; but as soon as their fortunes are secure, once again they forget God, and the whole dreary scenario repeats itself.

PRAYER: I'd rather not have to repeat my poorest lessons, O Lord; help me, I pray, to learn well the first time; in Jesus' name. Amen.

JUDGES 4, 5; PSALMS 56, 57   *Week 12, Day 6*

*H*ow does one explain a woman like Deborah? At a time when everything about the culture fenced women in, how is it that this woman was both a prophetess and a judge in Israel? She was obviously tremendously gifted and she was courageous. She dared to challenge Barak to lead the troops, and when he answered that he would do so only if she would go with him, she let him know that the victory would come through the hand of a woman. Perhaps credit should also be given to Barak, for his readiness to accept leadership under such circumstances.

The troops of Israel were wonderfully victorious, but the climactic blow came through the hand of a woman who was not even an Israelite. As is often the case through the Old Testament scriptures (one thinks immediately of Rahab and much later of Cyrus, king of Persia), an outsider becomes an instrument of God to help the people of God.

Not all of Israel did as well. When Deborah and Barak joined for their victory duet, they noted that some of the tribes—Reuben, Dan, Asher, Zebulon, and Naphtali—all held back. But where they failed, nature itself was enlisted on Israel's side:

"The stars fought from heaven,
from their courses they fought against Sisera.
The torrent Kishon swept them away" (5:20, 21).

It was a great day of victory, and it brought peace for forty years.

PRAYER: I want to stand with you, O Lord, in the battles between right and wrong; give me always the courage of high convictions. Amen.

JUDGES 6, 7, 8   *Week 12, Day 7*

Gideon is one of God's unlikely servants. When he was called, he protested that his clan was the weakest in his tribe and "I am the least in my family" (6:15). He fulfilled his first assignment of leadership, but he did it by night "because he was too afraid . . . to do it by day" (6:27). And when God called him to further action, he asked for a sign, and then a second sign (6:36-40).

But once he got started, there was no stopping him. He dared even to cut his army to ridiculously small proportions in obedience to God's command, and he led them to victory in one of the most memorable Old Testament stories.

Power and success are heady stuff, however, and Gideon didn't handle them well. When the people asked Gideon to establish a family dynasty, he refused, insisting that only the Lord would rule Israel (8:23). But then he collected gold from the people and made an ornamental garment, which became to the people a graven image—the very evil from which Gideon had first been called to deliver Israel. "It became a snare to Gideon and to his family" (8:27), and no doubt it prepared the way for the worship of Baal, which was revived soon after his death. The people soon forgot both God and the house of Gideon (8:34, 35). There is usually a close tie between our gratitude to people and our gratitude to the Lord God. Forgetting one, we're likely to forget the other.

70

PRAYER: Help me, I pray, to remember your kind works in my life, and also those persons through whom your kindness is extended. Amen.

JUDGES 9, 10, 11   *Week 13, Day 1*

Not all of the judges were powerful or dramatic figures. Some, like Tolah and Jair (10:1-5), and later Ibzan, Elon, and Abdon (12:8-15), are disposed of in just a few lines. And as far as Jotham was concerned, his half-brother, Abimelech, ought to have been in the same category. In a masterful parable, Jotham identified Abimelech's main qualification as his availability. Unfortunately, Jotham's parable sometimes seems equally appropriate to the political scene in our own times.

And then there is Jephthah. In his life, achievement and tragedy are inextricably intertwined. He was born in a setting of shame, the product of his father's relationship with a prostitute. He was brought into his father's home, but in time this proved an impossible situation and his half-brothers forced him out. One wonders how much Jephthah's drive for success was a result of his feelings of rejection. In any event, in time he is asked to lead Israel against the Ammonites. With an admirable sense of statesmanship, he tries first to negotiate peacefully, but without success.

With his passion to win, Jephthah vowed to God that for victory he would sacrifice whatever came from his door to greet him on his return. It was a rash vow, appropriate to the pagan religions around him but not to Israel's faith. The price turned out to be his daughter; and intense as he was, he didn't see the grace that would have allowed the vow to be altered.

PRAYER: If I make a vow, O God, let me see your grace. Amen.

JUDGES 12, 13, 14   *Week 13, Day 2*

The powerful leadership of Jephthah was followed by three judges who are remembered only marginally, for the size of their families. Along the way Israel again wandered from God's plan and found itself once more captive to the Philistines. That brings us to perhaps the most dramatic and the most unpredictable of the judges, Samson.

Like several other key biblical personalities, Samson was chosen by God from before his birth. In his case, he was also put under a special commitment as a nazirite, a person separated and consecrated to God (Num. 6:1-21). A particular factor in Samson's separation was that a razor should never come to his head.

The heroes in the early part of this story are Samson's parents. When their quiet, pastoral lives are interrupted by a heavenly visitor, they courteously offer hospitality; and when they discover the true nature of their guest, they're sure their lives are gone (14:22). They maintain their portion of the nazirite vow in preparation for Samson's birth; and they must surely have watched with awe and uncertainty as their son began not only to mature but to be touched by the Spirit of God. It couldn't have been easy being Samson's parents.

The first dramatic event in his life brings together what will prove to be the continuing issues of his life—his extraordinary physical prowess and his distressing lack of moral restraint.

PRAYER: O Lord, I marvel again at your readiness to use unlikely people. I guess I'm unlikely, too, in my way. Please use me. Amen.

JUDGES 15, 16; PSALMS 58, 59   *Week 13, Day 3*

From all that we're told in Judges, Samson was anything but a conventional leader. He was not a statesman, nor was he a true military leader; in a sense, he was a kind of one-man wrecking crew. Yet he was probably just what Israel needed at the time. A people who had been physically and psychologically dominated for over a generation must have found a whole new self-image in each new Samson episode. One can imagine the glee with which the stories of his bizarre victories were passed from village to village. A more conventional leader could never have made such an impact on the pride of the Israelites—nor proved such an embarrassment to the Philistines.

But at last, Samson's weakness destroyed him. Erratic as he was, he nevertheless kept his nazirite vow until one day when Delilah's attractiveness and pleading broke him down. But of course this would not have happened if Samson had not put himself constantly in the path of temptation. If we insist on walking at the edge of peril, we will eventually fall over. So it was with Samson.

Samson's story ends, however, with an act of grace. After he was blinded and humiliated by his enemies and forced to work like an animal, "the hair of his head began to grow again" (16:22)—a symbolic way of saying that he will have another chance. When the opportunity came, Samson conquered more at his death than in his life (16:30).

PRAYER: Lord, teach me something that Samson learned too late: to keep a wide distance between myself and temptation; in Christ. Amen.

JUDGES 17, 18, 19   *Week 13, Day 4*

J had a teacher long ago who said that the book of Judges was the story of Israel's Wild West days. He took that theme from these words: "In those days there was no king in Israel; all the people did what was right in their own eyes" (17:6)—a verse that appears not only at this point but also as the conclusion to the book, as if to say that we will understand the crude and violent history only if we see that this was a people who had no structured restraints.

The story of the plundering delegation from Dan which robbed Micah of both his idol and his priest demonstrates a world where people were taking the law into their own hands (chap. 18), and the brutal story of the Levite and his concubine (chap. 19) makes the point even more forcefully. The Levite used a ghastly object lesson to tell the people that such conduct had never before occurred in Israel (19:30). The people were shocked, but as we shall see, they didn't allow the shock to bring about any continuing moral change.

It's quite possible that the book of Judges was trying by this recital of outrageous conduct to indicate how badly the nation needed a king, since the phrase "there was no king in Israel" occurs several times. But with Levites selling themselves to highest bidders and idols taking the place of true worship, they needed most of all a new birth of faith in the Lord God.

PRAYER: Some days, dear Lord, our culture seems as unrestrained as in the times of the judges. Make me an instrument of peace. Amen.

JUDGES 20, 21; PSALM 60   *Week 13, Day 5*

*I*t is usually said that World War I began with a single assassin's bullet. Here a bloody civil war begins with the irresponsible behavior of a raping party of young bullies, and the failure of their own people to discipline them. It is a tragic story of thousands of lives being lost to no good purpose.

But now the united tribes find themselves caught between their own stubbornness—that they will not allow their daughters to marry Benjaminites—and their loyalty to the totality of their nation ("why has it come to pass that today there should be one tribe lacking in Israel?" [21:3]). They "had compassion for Benjamin their kin" (21:6), but their solution was an act of violence on a neighboring people and then a kidnapping at a festival; and in all of this, of course, the women involved were treated simply as objects of plunder. And all because of a failure on Benjamin's part to deal with evil in their midst, and a stubborn insistence on the rectitude of a vow (21:18).

Probably Hollywood could make a musical of the story, in a kind of massive *Seven Brides for Seven Brothers*, but it's still a sad story. These were frontier days, indeed, in which people responded to issues with tribal loyalties and misapplied commitments, though always with a very real earnestness. And of course it's easier for us to judge them from a distance than to find solutions to the troubles of our day.

PRAYER: Dear Lord, when I see how others deal with their problems, give me charity; and in my own problems, give me wisdom; in Christ. Amen.

74

S omeone long ago told me that the book of Ruth is God's silver lining to the book of Judges. Certainly when we left Judges yesterday, the mood was heavy and foreboding; but as Ruth opens, the prospects seem even more dim, for "there was a famine in the land" (1:1). So great a famine, in fact, that Elimelech and Naomi and their two sons took a solution that was almost unthinkable; they migrated to Moab, a nation so hated by the Jews that a Moabite was not to be accepted into the assembly of the Lord "even to the tenth generation" (Deut. 23:3).

Misfortune continued. Elimelech died, then the sons married Moabite girls (again, unthinkable), and then they died. But now a ray of very special light, as a Moabite girl, Ruth, pledges dramatic loyalty to her mother-in-law. Leaving her homeland, she goes with Naomi to what promises to be a hostile environment.

And there the light of beauty grows. Ruth catches the eye of the aged Boaz, and with her mother-in-law's counsel, receives his pledge of love. When the baby is born, the women of the community think of it as Naomi's child, while telling her that her daughter-in-law (Moabite though she may be) is "more to you than seven sons" (4:15).

But there's more. The closing genealogical lines reveal that this child will be an ancestor of Israel's greatest king, David—which means that later he will be in the line of the messiah (Matt. 1:5, 6).

PRAYER: As I finish this reading, O Lord, I marvel at your grace, even in the midst of hard times. Thanks be to your name! Amen.

T he scene in Israel was gloomy as the book of Judges ended, but God was at work backstage. So far backstage that only the person of great faith would believe that anything was happening, and only a future generation would see the proof. Now we have a family scene in the household of

Elkanah and his two wives, one of whom, Hannah, has been unable to bear children. As she cries out to God in her distress, her prayer is answered, with more ramifications than she could ever have dreamed. She prayed for a child; in answer to her prayer, a watershed leader was born to Israel.

Her son, Samuel, was dedicated to God from before his birth and was given to service in the house of the Lord, under Eli. He arrived at a crucial time. Though Eli was a good and honorable man, his sons were not following his example: "they had no regard for the LORD or for the duties of the priests" (2:12, 13). Meanwhile young Samuel grew "both in stature and in favor with the LORD and with the people" (2:26), until one night he received a message from God for Eli. Samuel was afraid to deliver the harsh word (I think God rarely trusts messages of judgment to anyone who enjoys delivering them), but Eli insisted on knowing; and when Samuel reported, Eli showed the depth of his character by accepting the message graciously. So it was that in tumultuous days God was at work in ways that no one at the moment would ever have recognized.

PRAYER: I am tremendously reassured, O Lord, by the knowledge that you are at work in my life and in our world at this very moment. Amen.

1 SAMUEL 4, 5, 6   Week 14, Day 1

The focal point—one might even say the hero—of these chapters is not a person but an object, the ark of the covenant. For Israel, it was visible evidence of their covenant with God and of God's commitment to be with them and preserve them. But it was never meant to be a magic object, and, unfortunately, Israel came to reduce it to such. Having lost a battle with the Philistines, they concluded that if only they would carry the ark with them, they would win. It would be their magic charm.

Instead they lost, and lost horribly, with Eli's two sons killed in the battle and the ark taken hostage. To understand how crucial the ark was in Israel's thinking, notice that it was the news of the ark, more than the death of his sons, that caused Eli to collapse (4:18), and that it was the loss of the ark that made the dying widow name her child Ichabod ("the glory has departed") because Israel's glory was gone when the ark was captured (4:22).

The Philistines quickly concluded that the ark was more than they had bargained for. But isn't it interesting that though the God of the ark seemed more powerful than their god, Dagon, they didn't choose to forsake Dagon? They tried to appease the God of the Israelites, but they didn't convert. When religion lacks moral power and is reduced to magic, it becomes simply a contest of excitements. Israel herself needed now to restore moral content to what had become a debased faith.

PRAYER: Dear Lord, give me a sense of deep reverence and awe, but save me from easy superstition; in Jesus' name. Amen.

1 SAMUEL 7, 8, 9   *Week 14, Day 2*

Samuel, groomed from before birth to lead Israel, now steps forward to bring the king of moral renewal the nation so badly needed. He called for total commitment to God, then brought the people together so he could pray for them (7:3-6). So he led Israel through most of the years of his life.

But it's sad and also perplexing to note that his sons did not follow in his commitment to righteousness (8:1-3). Although a godly home is the best guarantee of a godly next generation, even the best of parents are sometimes disappointed in the course their children pursue. In the end, each individual must choose for himself or herself.

So the people pressed for a king. Samuel took it personally (as indeed he might, in light of the failure of his sons), but God assured him that the change was deeper than a personal one. They wanted to be like the other nations, and they were unmoved by Samuel's anxious warnings (8:19-22).

The choice was a good one. That Saul later failed so tragically doesn't diminish the quality with which he began; like many others since, Saul was changed by the blandishments of power. But at the outset he was not only industrious and physically prepossessing, he also had great humility. When Samuel identified him as Israel's hope, he seemed genuinely surprised that he, of all people, should have been chosen.

PRAYER: As leaders come and go, dear Lord, help me keep my eyes fixed hard on you and your purposes; for Christ's sake. Amen.

1 SAMUEL 10, 11, 12; PSALM 61   *Week 14, Day 3*

*I*f you know the end of Saul's story, it's hard to begin it without sorrow. He makes such a grand start. As he leaves Samuel, he receives a new heart from God, and is filled with the Spirit (10:9-13), and he returns to his home without any pretensions of his new office. He is so reluctant to claim power that when Samuel wants to present him as king, he is hiding in the baggage (10:22).

This humility continues into the early period of his leadership. Apparently he continued farming rather than moving into any governmental office, because when the first national crisis arose, he "was coming from the field behind the oxen" (11:5). His first conflict was an impressive triumph, so his supporters wanted him to put to death those "worthless fellows" who had "despised him" when he was named king (10:27), but Saul turned the people's attention to God: "No one shall be put to death this day, for today the LORD has brought deliverance to Israel" (11:13).

I'm not sure I like Samuel's farewell address, because it seems to undercut Saul. Nevertheless it is true that the people have sinned in seeking to have a king, and Samuel reminds them of their transgression. But he also reassures them that all is not lost; they are still God's people and he will still pray for them. A particular sin, even a great one, does not cut people off from God—not if they still want God.

PRAYER: Dear Lord, when I see Saul's good beginning and know that in time he lost his way, I ask you to watch over me all my days. Amen.

1 SAMUEL 13, 14, 15   *Week 14, Day 4*

*N*othing is so intoxicating as power. Any kind of power: parent, teacher, pastor, foreman, mayor, president. Any time we are in a position of influence over another person, or several persons, we run the risk of becoming intoxicated with power. And if our office is one that carries some measure of prestige, the peril is all the greater.

King Saul's story is a series of power-tests. When Samuel was slow in coming to offer sacrifices and "the people began to slip away from Saul" (13:8), he usurped the priestly office, reaching far beyond his role. In the heat of a crucial battle, he made a rash, even arrogant, rule, which his son Jonathan didn't hear; and although Jonathan was the hero of the day, Saul vowed to kill him until the people intervened (chap. 14). Then, in the case of the Amalekites, there was an act of direct disobedience to Samuel, his spiritual advisor and his primary link to the will of God for Israel. And with it all, Saul—who once had hid in the baggage to avoid honor—now had built a monument in his own honor (15:12). But worst of all (and this is a particular danger when we come to feel our own importance), he developed an inability to take full responsibility for his sin. He wanted to be forgiven and he confessed that he had sinned, but as he confessed he shifted the responsibility: "I feared the people and obeyed their voice" (15:24). A confession that denies responsibility is a poor foundation for a new start.

PRAYER: When I have sinned, O Lord, help me face myself, acknowledge my fault, and seek with you to start again; in Jesus' name. Amen.

1 SAMUEL 16, 17, 18   *Week 14, Day 5*

*O*ne of the recurring motifs of the biblical story is God's practice of employing unlikely persons. We have seen several instances already; now the principle is spelled out for Samuel. Saul's role is coming to an end, so Samuel is sent to the household of Jesse to anoint Saul's eventual successor. Samuel is impressed with Jesse's oldest son, Eliab, and assumes this is the chosen one, but the Lord reminds him that the person's stature and appearance don't really count: "mortals . . . look on the outward appearance, but the LORD looks on the heart" (16:7).

So it is that David, the shepherd boy from Bethlehem, enters the story. It is not that David was undesirable; "he was ruddy, and had beautiful eyes, and was handsome" (16:12).

But he was the youngest of the family, probably still in his teens, and was tending the flocks. He was no novice, however. When he visited the camp of Israel, where the army was cowed before the challenge of Goliath, he listened attentively to the rewards that would be given to the one who conquered Goliath (17:25, 26) and threw out his challenge in defense of the honor of God.

He won gloriously, and thus became a national hero. He married Saul's daughter, Michal, and gained the undying friendship of Saul's son Jonathan. But he also got the jealousy and the seeds of enmity of Saul, who began to see this young man as his rival.

PRAYER: Give me the grace, I pray, to see people for what they are, beyond outward appearance and possessions and position; in Christ. Amen.

1 SAMUEL 19, 20, 21, 22   Week 14, Day 6

*D*avid has been anointed king of Israel, but now he must live like a fugitive from justice. Anyone who becomes his friend gains the immediate enmity of Saul. This includes Saul's own children—Michal, who deceives on David's behalf (19:8-17), and Jonathan, who appeals for just treatment for David and endangers his life by doing so (20:30-34). The priests of Nob innocently befriend David, and pay when their whole community is wiped out by Saul.

It was said that an evil spirit was upon Saul. In the most basic sense, this was true. Saul was allowing himself to be consumed by a spirit of envy and of fear. As a result, he fled all rational conduct and became obsessed with only one subject: that his position and power were in danger of being taken over by David. Anything that so possesses an otherwise rational person, causing the person not only to forsake all reason but also to alienate those who are dearest to him, is an evil spirit, indeed.

There's nothing terribly mysterious about such a development. It is probably more commonplace than we know. It may be that we have, ourselves, played on the edge of such madness because it often starts at a relatively rational level and an apparently harmless one, and only as time goes by does it become all-consuming. If allowed to go unchecked, it will destroy joy, life, and at last, the soul.

PRAYER: Save me, O Lord, from being so absorbed in myself that I try to make all of life revolve around me; in Christ's name. Amen.

1 SAMUEL 23, 24, 25   Week 14, Day 7

Meanwhile David, though a fugitive, is victorious. He delivers the city of Keilah from the Philistines (23:1-5), and when Saul comes with troops to capture him, Saul himself is drawn away by a military mission. He wins, too, in the incident with Nabal.

But far more important, David is victorious within his own soul. He has a perfect opportunity to destroy Saul—so perfect that his aides tell him that the Lord has delivered Saul into his hands. It would have been easy to draw such a conclusion, especially since he had already been chosen by God to succeed Saul. David, however, was profoundly convinced that he must not touch "the Lord's anointed" (24:10). Saul was in his position by divine appointment, and David reasoned that only God could alter that appointment. He did not even see himself as an instrument of God's action, perhaps because he realized that his own motives in the matter were too easily prejudiced. Saul wept when he realized that David had spared his life, and he pledged good faith to David. But the evil that was consuming Saul was too great for this good feeling to last.

David could easily have sinned in the case of Nabal. Probably he would have done so if it had not been for the wisdom of the woman Abigail. After Nabal's death, David realized how close he had come to doing great wrong. He thanked God for sparing him, but Abigail was God's assistant in the process.

PRAYER: Thank you, Father, for holding me back from hurting others. Amen.

1 SAMUEL 26, 27, 28   Week 15, Day 1

As we expected, Saul pursues David again, in spite of his penitent pledge; he is a possessed man, and pledges and honor go the way of all rational issues. Again, David refuses to take advantage of his opportunity to destroy Saul: "The LORD forbid that I should raise my hand against the LORD's anointed" (26:11).

Not that David was perfect. His relationship with King Achish is very pragmatic and self-serving, and he seems to think little of deceiving a man who obviously trusts him. But in the issue of Saul, at what was the core of David's life, he kept the faith.

Meanwhile Saul becomes an increasingly pathetic figure. He needs guidance in his kingship; and with Samuel gone, he is at a loss, especially since he receives no answer from God or from the customary channels of divine communication. At last he turns to a medium, even though he himself has previously outlawed them. The woman to whom he goes is apparently startled by her own success in raising the spirit of Samuel. Samuel offers not solace but a more desolate picture, telling Saul that the Lord has become his enemy.

Now Saul falls in terror, destroyed by his own ambition and seemingly forsaken by God. Whatever her character, the medium becomes at this point a source of mercy for Saul, offering him common sense, food, and a measure of sensitive kindness.

PRAYER: Dear Lord, when I see someone who seems beaten by life and forsaken, make me a messenger of your love; in Jesus' name. Amen.

1 SAMUEL 29, 30, 31   Week 15, Day 2

*D*avid himself is passing through a series of trials at this time. He is rejected by the commanders of the Philistine army, and leaves with a measure of fear for his life. Then the people of Ziklag turn on him, threatening to stone him (30:6). But there is a profound difference between David's circumstances and Saul's. Saul was without divine sustenance, "But David strengthened himself in the LORD his God" (30:6). In one of the psalms attributed to David he cries, "Do not take your holy spirit from me" (51:11). One can endure any of life's buffeting if only there is the assurance that God is still at hand.

82

But for Saul, the end has come. His three sons, including Jonathan, are killed in battle, and Saul himself is shot by an archer. With ethnic and religious pride, he calls upon his armor-bearer to take what remains of his life, so that "these uncircumcised" will not be able to make sport of him.

One cannot come to the end of Saul's story without feeling deep sorrow for the tragedy of his life. He had so much going for him at the outset, including the anointing of God's spirit and a very real humility. But he wasted his resources in a fascination with power and then with fear of one he perceived to be his rival; for whenever one becomes absorbed with power, he or she will inevitably, eventually become obsessed with threats, real and imagined, of losing that power.

PRAYER: Like David, O Lord, I would pray: whatever may happen, take not your Holy Spirit from me; in Jesus' name. Amen.

2 SAMUEL 1, 2, 3; PSALM 62   *Week 15, Day 3*

Now the anointing that David received as a boy in Bethlehem has become effective; he is the king of Israel. In truth, most of the tribes will not swing their loyalty to him for another seven years, but there can be no doubt now about the eventual outcome.

These chapters offer us a mixture of heroism and violence and sometimes both in the same instance. They are unvarnished reports, largely without comment; what you see is what you get. The Bible acknowledges us as we are: raw material—sometimes exceedingly raw!—with which God works. Such is the stuff with which heaven must achieve its goals.

So we see David's extraordinary loyalty to Saul and Jonathan, even in their death, but his harsh treatment of the Amalekite messenger (1:1-16). The elegy for the two men is a masterpiece of human affection, and David's treatment of the people of Jabesh-gilead translates the poetry into deeds. But the violence of the times re-appears in the senseless army games at the pool of Gibeon, where young life is made very cheap (2:12-16). And when Abner defects to David over sexual accusations and palace intrigue (3:6-11), the story line is a little like a contemporary tabloid.

Abner is a fascinating character. He tries to spare young Asahel's life, knowing he has him overmatched, but he is a tough negotiator and promises David he will bring round the reluctant tribes. Yet wise as he is, he dies "as a fool dies" (3:33), neglecting simple caution.

PRAYER: Heavenly Father, our world seems still to be a mixture of kindness and violence; help me always to be on the side of good. Amen.

2 SAMUEL 4, 5, 6   Week 15, Day 4

*I*s it ever proper to use evil means to reach a good end? David didn't think so, so when two young men assassinated Ishbaal in order to clear the way for David to take leadership of all the tribes, he responded with the same anger he had shown seven years before at the news of Saul's and Jonathan's deaths (4:5-12). In this matter, there was no gray area in David's thinking.

Now he began to solidify his power. Along the way, something special seems to have happened in his thinking, apparently when Hiram was building him a house in the new capital of Jerusalem. The writer puts it this way: "David then perceived that the LORD had established him king over Israel" (5:12). Life has such moments, long after formal procedures are past, when one at last "feels" what the document says.

But the best was yet to come. Israel could never feel she was fully the nation she was intended to be as long as the ark of the covenant was in enemy hands. Winning it back from the Philistines was only half the struggle, however; getting it safely to Jerusalem proved more difficult. A certain reverence was required, and poor Uzzah apparently failed it. But when at last the ark entered Jerusalem, David led the way, dancing "before the LORD with all his might" (6:14). His wife Michal was offended by his conduct; perhaps as a king's daughter she had always seen David as a crude shepherd, but especially she seemed to lack the spiritual depth that could sense the glory of a high and holy occasion.

PRAYER: Grant me the freedom, O Lord, of a dancing heart. Amen.

*T*he Bible is a book of covenants. We acknowledge that fact each time we refer to the Old and New Testaments (Covenants), but we rarely consider the wonder that is implicit in such an idea—that the God of the universe would enter a contractual agreement with members of his creation. In chapter 7 the covenant relationship enters a new phase as God responds to David's desire to build a house of worship by telling him that his throne "shall be established forever" (7:16). This covenant will later have continuing significance for Christians as they see it fulfilled in Jesus Christ.

Next to seeking after God, perhaps what David does best is to wage war. So he defeats the Philistines, Moabites, and King Hadadezer of Zobah—"the LORD gave victory to David wherever he went" (8:6). And with it all, he "administered justice and equity to all his people" (8:15). David seemed to have an almost fierce sense of justice, and his people trusted him.

At last that sense of justice expressed itself in fulfilling the vow he had made to Jonathan so many years before. "Is there still anyone left of the house of Saul to whom I may show kindness for Jonathan's sake?" (9:1). Mephibosheth was located, a son who had been crippled years before during the days following Saul's and Jonathan's deaths (4:4). David now repays an old debt of friendship, providing a place for Mephibosheth at the royal table all the days of his life (9:10).

PRAYER: Remind me today, O Lord, of any old debt of kindness that I ought to repay, and help me to pursue it; in Jesus' name. Amen.

2 SAMUEL 10, 11, 12; PSALM 63   *Week 15, Day 6*

*D*avid the public figure continues to pile victory on victory, sometimes in battle and sometimes through diplomacy, including diplomacy which was rejected (10:1-19). But in his private life, David was not doing as well. He had accumulated a large family of wives and concubines (5:13-16), a fact that would eventually be a source of trouble; but now he erred even more dramatically.

It happened in an idle moment, when from his rooftop he saw Bathsheba, the wife of Uriah, bathing. Instead of turning from the temptation ("flee" is the word Paul used [1 Cor. 6:18 KJV]), he pursued it, adding sin upon sin—adultery, deception, murder.

It looked as if he were getting by with his crimes, but "the thing that David had done displeased the LORD" (11:27). In pagan empires the king might be a law unto himself, but not in Israel. The prophet Nathan delivers God's judgment. I'm sure it was a painful assignment, partly because Nathan loved David and perhaps also because he may have wondered if David had become so captive to the power syndrome that he might not readily receive a message of judgment.

But David accepted the judgment and repented. Here we see why David, the decidedly imperfect man, is nevertheless a person after God's own heart. Since we humans sin, we had better know how to repent. David did. And God, in mercy, grants a new chance—Solomon (12:24, 25).

PRAYER: Since I know not how to be perfect in my living, O Lord, teach me how to be perfect in my repenting; for Christ's sake. Amen.

2 SAMUEL 13, 14, 15   Week 15, Day 7

But the problems of David's private life have not ended. The seeds of trouble that were sown in his many marriages now begin coming to fruit in the tangled relationships of his children. First there is the rape of Tamar by her half-brother Amnon, then, two years later, Absalom's murder of Amnon in his sister's revenge.

Absalom may well have been the most able of David's sons, and apparently he was something of his father's favorite. Now they were alienated by the murder, but at last through Joab's artful intervention, Absalom returns to Jerusalem. But still a distance remains between the men, largely at David's end. Perhaps this is an instance where David cannot find a middle ground between his sense of legal rightness and personal caring, and since both those elements are so strong in his nature, the tension is fierce.

Now Absalom begins a campaign. Handsome ("from the sole of his foot to the crown of his head there was no blemish in him" [14:25]), clever, aggressive, he orchestrated a program that would have done a modern political public relations firm proud. Slowly and steadily he won to himself numbers of those persons who were easily convinced that they were suffering injustice; he "stole the hearts of the people of Israel" (15:6). Then he brought together some members of his father's staff, and when the time was ripe, announced a coup, driving his father out.

PRAYER: Help us to see, O Lord, that when we fail those who are closest to us, the harm may in time reach far into the human family. Amen.

2 SAMUEL 16, 17, 18   *Week 16, Day 1*

*H*ow ironical that David, who once fled from Saul, now must flee from his own son! In light of David's great capacity for human affection, it is especially sad that some of his most serious political problems arose in the setting of his personal relationships.

He retreats from his beloved capital and is strengthened soon by Ziba, the servant of Mephibosheth. Then he is cursed by Shimei, a distant relative of Saul who probably had waited for years for a chance to pour out his hatred on David. When a person is in retreat he not only finds out who his friends are, he also discovers some people who have awaited the day they can speak a bitter word.

Meanwhile the political brain trusts are at work, in Ahithophel and Hushai. In spite of Ahithophel's prestige, Hushai's counsel—false advice, intended to aid David—wins, and the weight begins to go David's way.

Again David is caught between public policy and personal affection. "Deal gently for my sake with the young man Absalom," he appeals (18:5). But Joab is a tough-minded man with no room for sentiment or even for his king's orders, and when the opportunity comes he takes Absalom's life. It is ironical, of course, that Absalom's fall is because of his greatest pride, his wondrous head of hair. The revolt is over, but for David it was a bitter victory. He had lost his son.

PRAYER: Give mercy, I pray, for those persons in public life who are torn between personal loyalties and the general good; in Christ. Amen.

*J*oab, still the tough-minded politician, sees David court-ing even greater danger in his mourning for Absalom; and he was right, of course, in noting that David seemed to be moved by "love of those who hate you and . . . hatred of those who love you" (19:6).

So David took command of himself and of his kingdom and acted both wisely and compassionately. He granted mercy to Shimei (though he will revoke it on his deathbed), and did the best he could with the confusing reports from Ziba and Mephibosheth.

The rising controversy between Judah and the ten north-ern tribes is a rumbling that will become a full storm in the days of David's grandson, Rehoboam. But Sheba's effort is pre-mature, and David is too strong to overthrow, even after the Absalom incident. And of course David has Joab on his side—the kind of man you may not always want with you but whom you surely don't want against you. When the writer says of his killing of Amasa, "he did not strike a second blow" (20:10), he has given us a succinct summary of the decisive-ness with which Joab did his work.

The vengeance granted to the people of Gibeon is a kind of civic fulfillment of the eye-for-an-eye, life-for-a-life rule. It also illustrates the sense of community that so characterized ancient peoples. A family or an extended family was both blessed and held guilty as a unit.

PRAYER: Make our nation sensitive, I pray, to decisions of the present generation which may burden succeeding ones; in Christ. Amen.

*S*ince David is the sweet singer of Israel, it is appropriate that the heart of his story should conclude with a song—

one that is also found in Psalm 18. Some of the lines reflect David's experience as we have read it. When he says,

> "In my distress I called upon the LORD;
> to my God I called" (22:7),

we think of any number of instances that might have inspired such words. But when he says that "the LORD rewarded me according to my righteousness; . . . from his statutes I did not turn aside" (22:21, 23), we're not so sure. In any event, it is a great song of faith—and who am I to question another person's testimony?

We wish David's story might end with his song, but there is another deed to be done. David takes a census of the people. Joab, a hard man but full of insight, senses that his king is numbering the people for ego reasons. Perhaps it is because David feels his powers slipping from him as he recognizes that he is no longer the mighty warrior or the dominating leader. Whatever the motivation that makes him susceptible to temptation, he does wrong. He repents, but his people suffer. We human beings are bound up together in the bundle of life; when we do good, others are blessed, and when we sin, many suffer. No one lives to himself or herself, least of all a nation's ruler.

PRAYER: Help me, dear Lord, to end my days singing your praise, rather than stepping over into paths of harm; in Jesus' name. Amen.

---

1 KINGS 1, 2, 3   *Week 16, Day 4*

The old order passes, but not without some last gasps of distress. Once again David pays the price of his many marriages and his mixed-up family. This time it is Adonijah, a son whom David had "never at any time displeased . . . by asking, 'Why have you done thus and so?'" (1:6)—that is, a spoiled child. Not surprisingly, he sees himself succeeding his father. David keeps faith with Bathsheba and with what he perceives the will of God to be, and makes Solomon his successor. But Adonijah doesn't give up easily. Clever as well as handsome, he enlists—of all people—Solomon's mother to plead his cause in a subtle move. Solomon sees through the plan, and Adonijah pays with his life.

This time Joab threw his influence in the wrong direction, supporting Adonijah's cause. When Solomon orders his execution, he recalls that Joab has been a bloody man; now his blood comes back on his own head (2:33). Having lived by the sword, he dies by it.

Much to his credit, Solomon realizes that the post he has inherited is too big for him. "Who can govern," he cries, "this your great people?" (3:9). Given an opportunity to have what he will, Solomon asks for "an understanding mind to govern your people" (3:9). His request was itself an act of wisdom. Having asked unselfishly, he is assured by God that he will receive not only that which he has requested, but all the other favors he might easily have sought.

PRAYER: Give me the wisdom, O God, to seek your best, knowing that if I do, other things will follow—and if not, they don't matter. Amen.

1 KINGS 4, 5, 6   Week 16, Day 5

The writer is anxious for us to know the magnificence of Solomon's life-style (4:20-28); we've come a long way from the early days of Saul, when he, as king, could be found following his oxen. Which goes to show that expanding government is not something our century invented.

Solomon's wisdom, which "surpassed the wisdom of all the people of the east" (4:30), is measured not only by his writings, but by his knowledge of nature (4:33). This reflects a world that lived closer to nature than does ours, and whose idea of wisdom was far more basic.

Solomon sets out early to do the assignment especially given him by his father, the building of the temple. King Hiram is a proud associate in the effort. It is significant, of course, that the date given as the beginning of construction is numbered from the time the Israelites "came out of the land of Egypt" (6:1). The exodus was their beginning as a nation; it was for them "the beginning of days."

The detail of building that fascinates me most is the provision that all of the stone work shall be finished at the quarry, "so that neither hammer nor ax nor any tool of iron was heard in the temple while it was being built" (6:7). There was to be a kind of reverent silence in the project. And Solomon is reminded that the purpose of this building is that the people will keep all the commandments so that God, in turn, can "dwell among the children of Israel" (6:13).

PRAYER: Dear Lord, help me to build the temple of my soul with all of the intricate care Israel invested in its physical temple. Amen.

1 KINGS 7, 8, 9; PSALM 65   *Week 16, Day 6*

*I*n his latter days, Solomon ceases to be the person he started out to be. I think the decline may have begun between 6:38 and 7:1, when we learn that Solomon spent seven years building the house of the Lord and thirteen years building his own house. If so, there is an application to all our lives.

Solomon's prayer at the dedication of the house of the Lord could be a model for all dedicatory prayers. It begins with a recognition of the glory of God, and acknowledges that no house is worthy of the Lord: "Even heaven and the highest heaven cannot contain you, much less this house that I have built!" (8:27). It portrays God's house as a place where forgiveness can be sought (8:31, 32), and where the nation can turn in times of defeat (8:33, 34) or when there is drought, famine, or plague (8:35-40). There is gracious provision for the "foreigner [who] comes and prays toward this house" (8:42). And above all, a petition for times when we have sinned against the Lord—"for there is no one who does not sin" (8:46). And with it all, the remembrance that this is the One who "brought our ancestors out of Egypt" (8:53).

Whatever claim can be made for the wisdom of Solomon in his wise sayings, his remarkable decisions, his vast knowledge and learning, I will honor him above all for this, his prayer at the hour of dedication. In this moment, Israel was at her best: her king was her intercessor.

PRAYER: Week after week, as I enter houses dedicated to your name and glory, help me to sense the sacredness of the place; in Christ. Amen.

*A*s the knowledge of Solomon's wisdom spread, at last it reached the Queen of Sheba. She traveled a great distance in a time when travel was slow in order to "test him with hard questions" (10:1), and when she saw all the grandeur of his house and the excellence of his administration, she confessed that it exceeded even what she had heard (10:7).

But our most telling weaknesses seem often to be hidden in our strengths. Wise as he was, Solomon sinned grievously—and if we may say it, foolishly. He "loved many foreign women" (11:1), though he knew that they would incline his heart to follow their gods (11:2). As he grew old, his heart was turned by his wives to their gods "and his heart was not true to the LORD his God as was the heart of his father David" (11:4). As an old man he wanders from one pagan altar to another, following his wives. It is a tragic, pathetic sight.

As a result, enemies arose, such as Hadad and Rezon (11:14-25). But the worst would come in the days of his son Rehoboam, through the hand of one of his own servants, Jeroboam. The prophet Ahijah told Jeroboam of the role he was to fill, taking ten of Israel's tribes with him. When Solomon heard of the coming judgment of God via Jeroboam, he sought to kill him. Now we know how far from wisdom Solomon has gone, when we see him trying to subvert the judgment of God by destroying the prophet of judgment! Thus ended Solomon's reign of forty years.

PRAYER: Let me never forget, O Lord, that no wisdom is greater than that which keeps me close to you and your purposes; in Jesus' name. Amen.

*T*he problems that began in the latter years of Solomon's reign now reach full proportions under Rehoboam. Rejecting a chance to win the loyalty of the northern tribes, he chooses instead to reject them completely. At this point the nation divides, never to be reunited. The ten northern tribes will hereafter be known as Israel, while the two southern tribes, Judah and Benjamin (plus the no-count tribe of Levi), will be known as Judah.

Israel's cause is just and Jeroboam is a God-ordained leader, but he almost immediately takes a wrong turn. He feels that if the people have to go to Jerusalem (capital of Judah) for their major religious festivals, he will not be able to hold their allegiance; so he turns to the familiar golden calf and, with a good eye for merchandising, places one in the northern extremity at Dan, and the other to the far south in Bethel. Somehow Jeroboam couldn't trust the God who raised him to power.

During the sickness of his son, Jeroboam made a tentative move toward God, but only for purposes of help, not for a change of life and direction. After twenty-two years as king he died, an adequate administrator but not a spiritual leader. Meanwhile, Rehoboam was doing no better in Judah. He "did what was evil in the sight of the LORD" so that the people "committed all the abominations of the nations that the LORD drove out before the people of Israel" (14:22, 24).

PRAYER: Help us, O Lord, in times of political change, to keep our eyes fixed steadily on you and your purposes; for Christ's sake. Amen.

1 KINGS 15, 16; PSALM 67   *Week 17, Day 2*

*T*his book and the three that follow, 2 Kings and 1 and 2 Chronicles, offer a rather relentless panorama of national tragedy, slipping back and forth between Israel and Judah in a way that can be both confusing and tedious to a casual reader. Nevertheless, some messages become clear. For one, Judah's story is often relieved and redeemed, sometimes for a generation or more, by good kings; but Israel never has a good king. Not one. Also, notice that the quality of the rulers, as far as the biblical writers are concerned, is judged not by our usual contemporary standards; that is, not by their building programs, their legislation, or their economic policies, but by this measure alone: whether the heart is right with God.

In these chapters we see the first of a number of intermittent wars between Judah and Israel—civil wars, we might call them, since they are really one people. In Judah we are introduced to Rehoboam's successor, Abijam, whose short reign is especially evil, then Asa, whose heart "was true to the LORD all his days" (15:14), forty-one good years.

In Israel, meanwhile, Nadab succeeds his father but for only two years before he is overthrown by Baasha, who leads Israel for twenty-one evil years. His son, Elah, reigns only two years when one of his officers, Zimri, assassinates him and takes his throne. Zimri has just seven violent days and is replaced by Omri, who in twelve years "did more evil than all who were before him" (16:25). And still worse, Ahab is coming.

PRAYER: In evil times, O Lord, help me remember your mercy. Amen. *As I'll always*
2 Samuel 24, matey

1 KINGS 17, 18; PSALMS 68, 69   *Week 17, Day 3*

Ahab and Jezebel are very bad news, but they are not all of the story. Quite out of nowhere (except the purposes of God) comes Elijah the Tishbite, one of the most remarkable characters in the scriptures. We don't know how long he was in God's process of preparation or the nature of his training, but he appears with a bang and only once slips into a whimper.

While drought—announced by Elijah—is over the land, he lives first by the care of ravens, then by the kindness of the widow of Zarephath, for whom he works a miracle at the time of her deepest need. And then he challenges King Ahab (and even more directly, Queen Jezebel, whose prophets are brought to the showdown).

The scene at Mount Carmel is dramatic and, like much good drama, shot through with humor. Elijah mocks the prophets of Baal and Asherah unmercifully, with scathing sarcasm; then, when it is clear they have failed, he calls the people to come closer to him while he repairs "the altar of the LORD that had been thrown down" (18:30). He builds in the symbolism of the tribes, reminding the people of their heritage, which had grown so dim in years of wicked leadership; then heightens the drama by covering the area with water before calling down the fire. With vengeance he destroys the false prophets, then—without seeing a cloud in the sky—promises King Ahab that rain is on the way.

PRAYER: I want always to remember, O Lord, that whatever the headlines may be, you are at work, finding some Elijah; in Christ. Amen.

1 KINGS 19, 20; PSALM 70   *Week 17, Day 4*

$\mathcal{H}$aving won such a momentous victory, Elijah suffers post-triumph exhaustion. Fearless before hundreds of false prophets while a nation looks on, now he flees before Jezebel's threats. God does not chide him or rouse him with superficial encouragements; he gives him sleep, a meal, still more sleep and still another meal; then on to a cave, where Elijah reminds God how zealous he has been, how little good it has done, and how he is all alone in the battle.

God's answer is both mystical and practical. On the mystical side, Elijah experiences the power of God in wind, earthquake, and fire and then in a "sound of sheer silence" (19:12). Again God asks Elijah what he is doing in retreat, and again Elijah offers his litany of despair. Now God outlines some practical details: he is to anoint new kings for Aram and for Israel and a prophet—Elisha—who will eventually succeed him. And then, a correction of Elijah's factual data: he had argued that he was entirely alone in his battle for God, but God's records show there are "seven thousand in Israel, all the knees that have not bowed to Baal" (19:18). So Elijah offered his brusque call to Elisha, and a new prophetic chapter begins.

Meanwhile, Aram is attacking Samaria, headquarters of Israel. God blesses Israel's defense in spite of Ahab's disregard for his faith heritage. But even when blessed, Ahab fails to fulfill God's purposes.

PRAYER: When I am tired, O God, give me the kindness you gave Elijah, restoring me by rest, food, and a revelation of yourself. Amen.

1 KINGS 21, 22; PSALM 71   *Week 17, Day 5*

$\mathcal{T}$he confrontation between King Ahab and Naboth might seem hardly a footnote in some national histories, but it is given a place of significance here. The incident demonstrates that in Israel, the king was under the same law as were the people. Jezebel, with her pagan heritage, didn't understand this; as a person of action, she took the law into her own hands, using her queenly power.

But the writer wants us to know that she will not get by with such conduct. The Hebrew scriptures insist that there is order and justice in our universe; this theme finds expression in the deeds of history, the prayers of the Psalms, and the declarations of the prophets. In many different ways they remind us that judgment will fall on those who do wrong; there is a moral core to the universe, and we can depend on it.

There is also, however, a way of escape: *repentance*. Even the declarations of the prophets are subject to change if the objects of judgment are willing to change. When Ahab repents, wicked as he was, God postponed the judgment that had been announced (21:27-29).

We meet the prophet Micaiah only briefly (22:13-28), and wish we knew him better. He is a man of courageous convictions; one wonders how many others like him were pleading the cause of righteousness during the period of the kings without ever finding a place in the sacred history. Meanwhile, Judah's good king Jehoshaphat dies, and Ahab is succeeded briefly by a son, Ahaziah, who follows in his parents' footsteps.

PRAYER: Let me never forget that you are at work in your world. Amen.

2 KINGS 1, 2, 3; PSALM 72   *Week 17, Day 6*

*E*lisha knows that he is to succeed Elijah, but he intends to be more than a poor carbon. When Elijah asks him to stay behind, he refuses to do so, and when other prophets warn him that he will soon lose his mentor (and that he may as well therefore go his own way), again Elisha will not be dissuaded from his commitment.

His persistence pays off. Elijah asks what he wants, and Elisha boldly states it: "Please let me inherit a double share of your spirit" (2:9). As soon as Elijah disappears, Elisha puts his new role to the test: "Where is the LORD, the God of Elijah?" (2:14)—that is, now show me that I have what I've asked for!

He gets his evidence, plus the witness of the other prophets (2:15).

Elijah was one of a kind (as we all are, though not usually so dramatically), so it's hard to compare his ministry and Elisha's. In sheer number of pages and listing of miracles, Elisha seems, indeed, to have gotten a double share of Elijah's power. If so, he demonstrates the value of faithfulness. I don't think he had the strong personality or the forceful leadership qualities of Elijah, but he was committed enough to God that he left what must have been a rather well-to-do home in order to follow Elijah and to serve him in a humble role. It is by that modest identity that he is recommended to King Jehoshaphat: "Elisha . . . who used to pour water on the hands of Elijah" (3:11).

PRAYER: May I always remember, O Lord, that any service done in your name is a high privilege, including the pouring of water. Amen.

2 KINGS 4, 5; PSALM 73   *Week 17, Day 7*

*L*ike Elijah before him, Elisha seems sometimes to be so severe in his commitments as to be unapproachable. But here we see his tender side. He is a caring man as he deals with the poverty-stricken widow. The supply of oil lasts as long as there are vessels to contain it. The lesson? We might get more from God and from life if we expected more.

And then, the Shunammite woman, who extends continuing hospitality to Elisha and his servant so Elisha seeks to do a kindness in return. It is a very great favor, the birth of a son. But even life's miracles are subject to the normal passage of time, which in this instance brought illness and death. Elisha shows not only great sensitivity in his concern for the woman, but also persistence in getting an answer for her. I like the Elisha I see here.

He's in his crusty mode in the Naaman story. Naaman is afflicted with leprosy, but an Israelite slave girl offers hope in a prophet back home. When Naaman arrives in the glory of a Middle Eastern procession, he expects a fitting reception. Instead, Elisha sends word by a servant that he should bathe in the Jordan seven times. Naaman is offended; they have better rivers back home, and besides, he expected a bit of a ceremony. But a wise servant gently urges him to give it a try, and he is healed. Hail the heroes: an Israelite maid, a sensible servant, and the Jordan River. Paul might say that the cross is like the Jordan: foolishness until you give its power a try (1 Cor. 1:18-25).

PRAYER: Dear Lord, may I never belittle the power of your grace. Amen.

2 KINGS 6, 7, 8   Week 18, Day 1

Perhaps the loveliest thing about the miracle stories clustered around Elisha is that they show God involved in all the issues of life, ranging from recovering a lost, borrowed ax head to extraordinary military triumphs. There are noble moments, as when Elisha delivers an army to Samaria. When the king asks, "Shall I kill them?" Elisha instead orders him to give them food and drink and let them return home. For a time, at least, it brought peace between the nations (6:20-23). There's also nobility in the four lepers who stumble upon untold wealth in the deserted Aramean camp. At first they begin collecting loot, until they confess to one another, "What we are doing is wrong. This is a day of good news" (7:9). Good news and good fortune are to be shared, not hoarded.

Elisha's servant, Gehazi, also behaves honorably in helping the Shunammite woman. Here the miracle comes through more conventional means, as a king changes his mind as the result of what seems on the surface to be coincidental good timing.

We're given a glimpse of the tender side of Elisha as he weeps at the prospect of what Hazael will do to the people of Israel after he becomes king. Hazael denies indignantly that he could ever be so base, but he returns home to inaugurate his new career with an act of just such shamelessness. Was he intentionally deceiving Elisha when he pleaded innocence of character, or didn't he know his own depths?

PRAYER: My little world waits for small miracles of human thoughtfulness; make me your channel of favor, I pray; in Jesus' name. Amen.

'Zeal

This time Jehovah used of proxy

*P*erhaps if you had your way, some of these stories of human brutality wouldn't be in the scriptures. But the Bible is utterly honest in its portrayal of us human beings. It doesn't glorify our violence or intrigue, just as it never relates sexual misconduct in a way that is likely to titillate, but neither does it pretend that we are above such conduct, nor does it even apologize for it. It holds up the data and leaves it to us to draw conclusions on the basis of the ethical teachings found elsewhere in the law, the prophets, and the New Testament.

So Jehu, who "drives like a maniac" (9:20), becomes an instrument of judgment *very violent* and he fills the role with a passion. He sees himself as a reformer when he destroys Joram (9:22), and when he wipes out the family of Ahab it is with the cry, "see my zeal for the LORD" (10:16); and in the same mood he massacres the followers of Baal (10:18-27). But physical destruction is always easier than inner renewal; "Jehu was not careful to follow the law of the LORD . . . with all his heart" (10:31). Nevertheless, perhaps he comes as close as any king of the northern tribes to being good, by the prophet's judgment.

In Judah, a new day comes when Athaliah contrives to succeed her son, Ahaziah, following his death in battle. She tries to kill all the royal family to make the throne secure for herself, but an infant son of Ahaziah, Joash, is hidden for more than six years while Athaliah reigns. Then, led by the priest Jehoiada, seven-year-old Joash is made king.

PRAYER: In my sometimes violent world, let me make a difference. Amen.

*J*oash (or Jehoash) is to be remembered for repairing the temple in Jerusalem. It is perhaps an even greater thing to restore what has fallen than to build anew, because particular patience and delicacy are required. After years of waiting for the priests to use accumulated gifts to begin repairs, Joash took things in his own hands and developed a special means of fund-raising. One occasionally finds a contemporary church with a "Joash Box" for anonymous offerings. Joash pleased the Lord through all his forty-year reign, but died at the hand of servants.

His son Amaziah also pleased God; "he did what was right in the sight of the LORD, yet not like his ancestor David" (14:3). David, whatever the failures of his private life, continues to be the standard by which all his successors are measured. Amaziah had military ambitions, however, and they eventually led him into a disastrous war with Israel; he was not wise enough to take the advice of Israel's king to "be content with your glory, and stay at home" (14:10).

Israel's kings, meanwhile, continue in their sorry pattern. Jehoahaz, Jehoash, and Jeroboam II all suffer the same judgment: they follow the sins of Jeroboam son of Nebat (13:2, 11; 14:24). It is as if the writer sees them afflicted with a spiritual malady that passes on from generation to generation, almost as if they were seeking to imitate their regal ancestor. The prophet Elisha dies, but we hear of a new prophetic voice, Jonah (14:25). The word of the Lord goes on.

PRAYER: Help me to see that you are never without a witness. Amen.

2 KINGS 15, 16, 17   *Week 18, Day 4*

*F*or some reason this writer says little about King Azariah (Uzziah), though he reigned fifty-two years. We will learn more of him in the Chronicles and also in the prophet Isaiah. Both he and Jotham are generally good, except for their allowing sacrifices at the high places, the unappointed altars in Judah. But Ahaz is another matter. He "walked in the way of the kings of Israel," even to the point of taking on practices of the pagan nations around him (16:3, 4).

But the main burden of these chapters is the fall of Israel. There is a dreary run of short reigns (Zechariah, Shallum, Pekahiah) and of empires set up on assassinations (Pekah, Hoshea). But mostly we sense doom in the air, not only in the instability of Israel's throne but more ominously in the rising power of Assyria. Menahem buys time from King Pul of Assyria (15:19, 20), but one knows this is only a stopgap measure.

During Pekah's reign Assyria invades several areas, carrying off numbers of people; then disaster comes in the ninth year of Hoshea's reign, when the land is overcome by the Assyrians, the mightiest war machine of their time. This invasion is dated at 722 B.C., and for all practical purposes it marks the end of the ten northern tribes. Their identity is slowly lost through intermarriage, so that today they are often popularly referred to as "the ten lost tribes of Israel." And it happened because "the people of Israel had sinned against the LORD their God" (17:7) and stubbornly resisted the warnings of every prophet (17:13, 14).

PRAYER: Make me sensitive in my time, O Lord, to your warnings. Amen.

2 KINGS 18, 19, 20   *Week 18, Day 5*

*A*fter coping with the intrigues, assassinations, and at last invasion in the closing days of Israel's story, it's good to think about King Hezekiah. The writer says simply that "there was no one like him among all the kings of Judah" (18:5) in his faithfulness to the Lord.

Not that the times were easy. When Israel was invaded, Hezekiah had to know that Judah was also at peril, and in time King Sennacherib of Assyria came. He engaged in a propaganda war, to break the morale of the people, insisting on the one hand that no other gods had been able to stand against him (18:33, 34) and, on the other, that the Lord had sent him to defeat Judah (18:25).

When Sennacherib sent a declaration of war, Hezekiah "went up to the house of the LORD and spread it before the LORD" (19:14) and prayed. He was then assured by the prophet Isaiah (a wonderful person to have on your side!) that God would defeat the Assyrians. Not only were they dramatically defeated, Sennacherib himself was killed by his sons while—of all things—he was in the house of his god Nisroch (19:37).

Some time later Hezekiah became ill and received word

that he should set his house in order, because he was not going to recover. Again he prayed, turning his face to the wall, and Isaiah told him that God would add fifteen years to his life. In those years, unfortunately, he erred by showing his wealth to envoys from Babylon. Thus Babylon in time will do what Assyria could not—invade Judah.

PRAYER: Help me, O Lord, to use answered prayers only to good. Amen.

2 KINGS 21, 22, 23; PSALM 75   Week 18, Day 6

*M*anasseh, Hezekiah's son, tipped the scales to evil as far as his father had tipped them for good. It is as if he set out to counter all the good his father had done. He led the people into "the abominable practices of the nations that the LORD drove out before the people of Israel" (21:2), until at last he "misled them to do more evil" than those nations (21:9). It was a long reign, fifty-five years, and then his son, Amon, followed the same course for two years, walking "in all the ways in which his father walked" (21:21).

Amon was killed by his servants and was succeeded by his eight-year-old son, Josiah, who eventually became a king "who turned to the LORD with all his heart, with all his soul, and with all his might" (23:25). During his reign the high priest Hilkiah stumbled upon the book of the law in the house of the Lord (22:8). It was probably the book of Deuteronomy; one wonders how a document of such value was ever mislaid, but of course almost anything could have happened in the fifty-seven years of Manasseh and Amon.

The prophetess Huldah urged a penitent return to God's law, and Josiah led the way. He instituted a massive cleansing of the religious practices of the country and then a celebration of the passover such as no one had kept "since the days of the judges" (23:22). He died in battle, but only after leading his nation back to God.

PRAYER: Grant your mercy this day on those for whom your word is as much hidden as when it was lost in days long ago; in Christ. Amen.

And now another curtain is about to fall. It will come down somewhat fitfully, but in the end we will see Judah fall into captivity, just as we saw with Israel more than a century before. The decline begins with the three-month reign of Jehoahaz, then eleven years under Jehoiakim during which the Babylonians, under King Nebuchadnezzar, make their first invasion. At first Jehoiakim pledges servitude, but in time he rebels. At his death his son Jehoiachin takes over, but only for three months before he has to surrender to Babylon. This time Babylon carries away not only the accumulated treasures of the centuries, but also "the men of valor," officials and warriors, artisans and smiths, leaving behind only "the poorest people of the land" (24:14, 16). The king of Babylon made Zedekiah, Jehoiachin's uncle, the puppet king over what remained in Judah (24:17, 18).

In time Zedekiah foolishly tried to rebel. The remnant still in Jerusalem suffered greatly under a Babylonian siege, and Zedekiah himself was mercilessly cut down. Years later Jehoiachin was released by a benevolent Babylonian king so that he could dine for the rest of his life in the king's presence (25:27-30), but Judah was now a captive people.

The writers of 2 Kings are consistent. They believed in the justice of God, that sin brings inevitable tragedy, whether it be the sin of individuals or of rulers; and it never occurred to them to think that Judah and Israel, though God's chosen people, should be exempt.

PRAYER: Thank you, Father, for a universe in which there is a moral order. Help me to trust you in the working of that order; in Christ. Amen.

1 CHRONICLES 1, 2, 3   *Week 19, Day 1*

For a modern reader, these chapters—and several yet to come—are as exciting as reading a telephone directory, and with hard-to-pronounce names at that. But several things need to be said. The records were more than simple genealogical pride; it was an expression of their sense of being the covenant people of God, and it was particularly significant for members of the tribe of Levi, to establish their right to serve at the altar.

One is impressed, too, that though the Israelites had strong convictions about their role as God's unique people, they did not isolate themselves from the rest of the human race. The Chronicles record begins, not with Abraham or Jacob, but with Adam; and so, too, the "other lines" of the family are identified, such as the descendants of Ishmael and of Esau.

But especially, let it be noted that the Bible cares about people. We are important enough to be mentioned by name, one by one. To demonstrate our worth in God's sight, Jesus said that "even the hairs of your head are all counted" (Matt. 10:30). In light of such a belief, surely names are consequential. In the biblical world, names were usually given on the basis of some special individual significance; and for that matter, still today a person's name is a sacred possession. When the long lists of Chronicles are tedious, pause to thank God that biblical faith bothers to mention names. Individuals matter.

PRAYER: I thank you for my name; for me, it is special. Amen.

1 CHRONICLES 4, 5; PSALM 77   *Week 19, Day 2*

*T*here are occasional jewels hidden in these genealogical listings, some of them a kind of historical footnote and sometimes the making of a theological point. I pause, for example, at the mention of sons born to "Bithiah, daughter of Pharaoh, whom Mered married" (4:17), wondering how it was that a daughter of Pharaoh married an Israelite who was simply one of the company. Was she a faith-convert, or was it romance?

The chronicler is also an exhorter when he reminds us that several of the tribes won because "they cried to God in the battle, and he granted their entreaty" (5:20); on the other hand, some "mighty warriors, famous men, heads of their clans . . . transgressed against the God of their ancestors, and prostituted themselves to the gods of the . . . land" (5:24, 25).

I especially like Jabez, with his two-verse biography (4:9-10). He brought particular pain at his birth, so that his mother named him Sorrowful. That's not a pleasant name to carry through life, reminding you and all who meet you that you have been the source of sorrow to another. A name like that could give a person all kinds of complexes! Instead, Jabez was challenged by it. He asked God to bless him and enlarge his borders and "that you would keep me from hurt and harm." And the happy fact is, "God granted what he asked." Jabez saw no reason for suffering to continue and grow. He thought better of God and life, and he was right.

PRAYER: When I am inclined, O Lord, to let some discouragement be fastened to my life and outlook, remind me of Jabez; in Christ. Amen.

1 CHRONICLES 6, 7; PSALMS 78, 79   *Week 19, Day 3*

*T*here's more than one reason to call David the sweet singer of Israel. Not only is he credited with writing so many psalms, he obviously encouraged music, as indicated by his naming a number of persons to be "in charge of the service of song in the house of the LORD" (6:31). All of us who appreciate sacred music can be thankful for the emphasis David gave it.

The phrase that appears repeatedly in 6:66-81, "with its pasture lands," reminds us that, unlike American farmers, these people often lived in a village or city and maintained pasture land outside the town, just as centuries of other civilizations have done in subsistence farming. Such a structure provided security and community.

Remember our friend Zelophehad, who had only daughters, and whose daughters made a successful plea for their inheritance? We're reminded of them again in this record (7:15). We're reminded, too, unfortunately, that people sometimes won't forget unpleasant facts about us. When the Chronicler gives Manasseh's record he notes that Asriel was born to Manasseh's "Aramean concubine" (7:14). She did not have the status of a wife, though she surely fulfilled the functions and perhaps more, and she was also an outsider. One often hears such references in daily conversations: "That's the baby that was conceived before they were married," or, "He married out of his class, you know." Lord, save us!

1 CHRONICLES 8, 9; PSALM 80   *Week 19, Day 4*

*O*nce again the chronicler is both a theologian and a prophet, while letting us know why the genealogies are so important. We realize (9:1) that this book was written after Judah had returned from the Babylonian captivity and that the records were significant for establishing family lines as the people set out to re-establish their nation. And of course the whole historical record in Chronicles is important to a people whose identity might so easily have been lost during two generations of captivity away from their homeland.

But in any event, the writer wants us to know that "Judah was taken into exile in Babylon because of their unfaithfulness" (9:1). If some future generation were to conclude that it was only a matter of political movements and military power, the chronicler has made the record clear: Judah's troubles have a spiritual origin, in her failure to keep faith with the Lord God.

And since that's the case, the eventual rebuilding of the nation (of which we will read, in time, in Ezra and Nehemiah) will depend very much on the leadership that the Levites will give. So we are reminded of certain of their duties. The chief gatekeepers (a role the psalmist would have cherished [Ps. 84:10]) are important because they must open the temple each morning; and important, too, are those who watch over the "holy utensils" (9:29) and those who make the flat cakes and bread (9:31, 32). For all that happens in God's house has its glory.

PRAYER: Remind me, O Lord, that whatever I do for you matters. Amen.

1 CHRONICLES 10, 11, 12   *Week 19, Day 5*

*W*e return now to sacred history, the record of the dealings of God and the people of Israel. The period covered is the same as that in much of 1 and 2 Kings, but the particular writers have their own points of emphasis.

Most of us probably wonder at times why David, imperfect as he was, was nevertheless a person after God's own heart. A major insight comes by way of contrast with Saul. The chronicler summarizes the tragedy of Saul's story by reminding us that "Saul died for his unfaithfulness; he was unfaithful to the LORD in that he did not keep the command of the LORD; moreover, he had consulted a medium, seeking guidance, and did not seek guidance from the LORD" (10:13, 14). David did just the opposite. When he failed God, he sought heaven in repentance, readily changing his ways and starting anew. He sought not simply to avoid penalties, but to bring his life into conformity with what he perceived God's purposes to be. In our walk with God, the issue is not our falling down, but our getting up again; it is not our sins, grievous though they may be, but our readiness to turn from them and follow God's way.

But David was not alone in his achievement. He drew to himself a great number of men of valor (among them, Uriah the Hittite [11:41]). They "kept coming to David to help him, until there was a great army, like an army of God" (12:22). At his best, he meant them to be that.

PRAYER: I learn many things, O Lord, from the lives of your saints, but especially this: when I fail, I will repent, and try again. Amen.

---

1 CHRONICLES 13, 14, 15; PSALM 81   *Week 19, Day 6*

We do well to look again at some of the qualities of David's life that made him appealing in God's sight. As David addressed himself to the nation, he reminded the people of the importance of the ark of God, and of the fact that the nation "did not turn to it in the days of Saul" (13:3). The worship of God and the glory of God were primary issues to David. However uncertain his course may sometimes have been, his basic commitment was unerring; and it is for that reason that he was able, again and again, to find his way back to God.

He became angry with God for what he felt was an injustice against one of his soldiers, Uzza, so that he "was afraid of God that day" (13:11, 12). But again he showed the ability to correct himself. When he tried again to bring the ark to Jerusalem, he asked the priests to be the carriers, acknowledging that the tragedy that occurred the first time came "because we did not give it proper care" (15:13); this time the Levites will carry it "as Moses had commanded" (15:15). Whatever else might be said about the incident, I am impressed by David's readiness to learn from what he felt were his mistakes in the past. Life is a long learning process. That's why saints grow slowly.

And again we note the unbridled joy David found in his walk with God. He had a "leaping and dancing" faith, which Michal not only could not understand, but also despised. I wish, instead, she had watched and learned.

PRAYER: My pilgrimage with you is so long and sometimes faltering; help me, O God, to keep learning and following; in Christ. Amen.

1 CHRONICLES 16, 17, 18   *Week 19, Day 7*

*B*iblical religion has more of a celebrative quality than we sometimes seem to realize. Thus when the people come to Jerusalem to rejoice in the return of the ark, David distributes "to every person in Israel"—man and woman alike—to each a loaf of bread, a portion of meat, and a cake of raisins" (16:3). It was a wondrous kind of communion service, so to speak. One can imagine the awe and joy the people felt as they returned to their homes to enjoy the foods David had distributed as his expression of joy in the presence of God.

As the chronicler recalls David's victories, he notes that "the LORD gave victory to David wherever he went" (18:6, 13). David, in turn, "administered justice and equity to all his people" (18:14); and when he came home, in ancient military fashion, with the spoils of battle, he chose to dedicate them to the Lord (18:8, 11) rather than look upon them as his own possession. The movie *Chariots of Fire*, the story of a dramatic portion of the 1924 Olympics, comes to a climax when Eric Liddell, the devout Scottish athlete, refused to run in the qualifying race for his specialty because it came on a Sunday and to run would violate his faith. He was finally assigned to an unfamiliar length (400 meters). As the movie portrays it, a competitor gave Liddell a message as the race began. In truth it was given him that day by the team masseur. It read, "In the old book it says, 'He that honors me I will honor.'" Liddell believed it that day. I think David lived by the same rule.

PRAYER: I want, dear Lord, to honor you in all I do; in Christ. Amen.

1 CHRONICLES 19, 20, 21   *Week 20, Day 1*

*T*he chronicler begins chapter 20 exactly as 1 Samuel 11 begins the story of David's sin with Bathsheba, but he chooses to omit that story. Instead, he tells us of the splendor of David's crown; perhaps that was a grievous sin, too, though surely not of the proportions of his crime with Bathsheba.

But he is unsparing in the story of David's numbering of the people of Israel. It seems clear that David's goal was personal exaltation, and that Joab saw through it. Joab, as we have noted before, was not always an exemplary man, but he had the best skill of a military leader in seeing to the heart of an issue. Why number the people, he asked; "are they not, my lord the king, all of them my lord's servants?" (21:3). He sensed, too, that the whole nation would suffer for David's sin, as indeed they did. *Why, 70,000 died, tsee 2 Samuel 24*

David responded in what was the faithful pattern of his life, by acknowledging his sin: "I have done very foolishly" (21:8). His choice of words is appropriate; among other things, sin is inevitably stupid. It sometimes looks clever or expedient on the surface, but in the long run—and sometimes even in the short one—it is stupid. As much as he was able, David tried to pay the penalty for his wrongdoing. When Ornan volunteered to give David the site for his sacrifice, David answered, "I will not . . . offer burnt offerings that cost me nothing" (21:24). This, too, is an accepting of life's penalties, and it is instructive.

PRAYER: When I err, Lord, let me confess it, and pay; in Christ. Amen.

David asked if Jehovah is merciful pre plague, was He?

*D*avid isn't allowed to build the house of the Lord because he has "shed so much blood" in God's sight (22:8); for although war seems to be taken for granted in the Hebrew scriptures and seems even to be sanctioned by God, it was clearly not the preferred way to go. Thus Solomon (whose name in Hebrew is a cognate of *shalom*) will be a man of peace.

But David isn't going to leave his beloved project without his mark on it. With the older generation's natural skepticism about the judgment and ability of the young ("My son Solomon is young and inexperienced . . . ; I will therefore make preparation" [22:5]), David makes extensive preparation, not only in providing materials but also in setting up administrative structures for the temple (23:2-23). Now that the Levites no longer need to carry the tabernacle and its equipment, they must be organized for the care of the new temple. David was obviously an able administrator, and he wanted to be sure that this matter which was nearest to his heart was done perfectly. And like many administrators, especially an older one, he felt he was the best equipped to do that.

But in all these details, one senses David's great love for God and for God's dwelling place. His passion was more than the manner of a perfectionist; he had an awe of the glory of God, as he had experienced it over the rough and ready years of his life, and he wanted this new house of God to be worthy of such exceeding glory.

PRAYER: I see many houses of worship, so none is unique as was David's; nevertheless, give me the same sense of awe; in your name. Amen.

I once watched a woman doing needlepoint. It seemed so painstaking, so tedious; every stitch was precise. But she was reveling in it, because it was a wedding gift for her son and daughter-in-law. I have something of that feeling about David as I read the list of musicians and gatekeepers for the temple. It is a detailed listing of the people who were to make worship effective in the new house, and what might seem tedious detail to us must have seemed beautiful to him—"something beautiful for God."

One of the musicians is Heman, who had been blessed with fourteen sons and three daughters, all of them "under the direction of their father for the music in the house of the LORD" (25:5, 6). It's interesting to come upon this reference to him, since he is identified as author of one of the psalms.

As a young pastor, I often became frustrated with the burden of administration, until one day I realized that *administration* and *minister* are almost identical words—and that, properly done and rightly dedicated to God, administration is a ministry. David and the chronicler could have told me as much long before. It is clear that they saw the list of officers, military leaders, and tribal leaders as people who were fulfilling a calling before the Lord. They were to be "men of ability . . . for everything pertaining to God and for . . . the king" (26:32).

PRAYER: Dear Lord, help me do routine tasks with a sense of glory until all I do is made beautiful for you; in Jesus' name. Amen.

1 CHRONICLES 28, 29; PSALM 83   *Week 20, Day 4*

*A*s David passes the kingdom to his son, his major theme is the building of the temple. A critic might suggest that this is simply the emphasis of the chronicler, but David's enthusiasm for this project is consistent with his lifelong pattern. He was a person after God's own heart because he pursued God all of his days. Probably nothing was dearer to him than the building of the temple, and not being able to do so was no doubt the biggest disappointment of his life.

His vision for the temple is that it "will not be for mortals but for the LORD God" (29:1). Here is an issue for every church architect and every building committee. Obviously a church must be built in such a way as to meet human needs in the worship of God, but David was moved by the high conviction that it must always be seen as a house to the glory of God.

And the people caught his spirit, so that "with single mind they . . . offered freely to the LORD" (29:9). In receiving the gifts David acknowledged that everything they had given "comes from your hand and is all your own" (29:16). It was a day to remember as the people "ate and drank before the LORD . . . with great joy" (29:22).

The chronicler lets us leave David on this high note, without giving us the story of Adonijah's rebellion (1 Kings 1) and the struggles of succession. Like every historian, he chooses what to use and what to omit.

PRAYER: Renew my sense of awe at the glory of your house. Amen.

2 CHRONICLES 1, 2, 3   Week 20, Day 5

Solomon knew what his position required, and he sought it. He was wise enough to realize that he was not capable of ruling "this great people of yours" (1:10), so he asked for the required wisdom. In these days when we are often told that our massive cities are ungovernable and that no person is really capable of bringing together all the reins of administration for complex modern government, one wishes that candidates for office might catch Solomon's spirit.

When Solomon's wish is granted, he is told that he will also receive "possessions, wealth, honor" (1:11); and something in us says, "Of course!" Because if Solomon is equipped to do his work really well, all these other gifts—and many more—will come as by-products of his success. In seeking the best for his people, Solomon unconsciously was getting the best for himself. And there's a parable in that, of course.

Someone has said that among earthly gifts, no person is more fortunate than the one who discovers the work he or she loves most to do, then finds that he possesses the gifts to do it really well. Unfortunately some do not recognize their good fortune even when they have it in hand. As Shakespeare said:

> Desiring this man's art, and that man's scope,
> With what I most enjoy contented least. (Sonnet xxix)

Much to Solomon's credit, he knew what he needed—and God gave it.

PRAYER: Help me, O Lord, to find my place before you, then grant me, please, the heart and skills to do my work truly well; in Jesus' name. Amen.

2 CHRONICLES 4, 5, 6, 7   *Week 20, Day 6*

*I*f you're like me, you may be uneasy with all the wealth that is built into the temple (4:7-22); gold seems a common commodity! Some qualifying words should be spoken. Remember that this was the only house of worship in the nation; all the investment of worship was in this place. Remember, too, that their society and their faith made full provision for the poor.

And of course grandeur was of the essence of the temple, because it was meant to reflect the glory of God; simplicity had its place elsewhere, but here the aim was magnificence. I'm afraid we can easily use the ornateness of the temple to distract us from our contemporary sins. Our generation pours its wealth into massive government buildings, spectacular shopping malls, and cathedral-like entertainment centers, all of which we pretty much take for granted.

We discussed Solomon's wonderful prayer earlier, but let's pause now to see the foundation on which the prayer and the divine-human relationship are based. As Solomon completes the prayer, and the glory of God is revealed, the priests bow to the ground and give thanks, extolling God's goodness and saying, "for his steadfast love endures forever" (7:3). That phrase is a recurring motif of Old Testament worship. It is the Hebrew *hesed*, which is a precursor of grace. To understand it is to realize God's enduring love for Israel.

PRAYER: Thank you, Lord, for your steadfast love toward me. Amen.

2 CHRONICLES 8, 9; PSALM 84   *Week 20, Day 7*

*T*he human mind has wondrous powers, one of the most troublesome of which is its ability to rationalize. For political reasons, Solomon marries Pharaoh's daughter, just as he married into several other royal families, thus cementing his relationships with a number of countries. But he feels there would be something inappropriate about having the daughter of a pagan king in the house of his father David, because there was a special holiness to that house, since the ark of the Lord had been there (8:11). What a careful line Solomon drew, being uncomfortable with his wife inhabiting a house where the ark of God had been but being untroubled with her inhabiting his own life! What tangled webs of inconsistencies we are!

The chronicler is less critical of Solomon than is the writer of Kings. He tells us of his meeting with the Queen of Sheba and of his great wealth; he was so blessed that he "excelled all the kings of the earth in riches and in wisdom" (9:22). We read that he had four thousand stalls for his horses and twelve thousand horses, and we recall that Deuteronomy had warned that Israel's king should never "acquire many horses for himself" nor should he "acquire many wives for himself" (Deut. 17:16, 17). And then one is troubled that with all that is said about Solomon's achievements and his wealth, we read almost nothing, after the temple dedication, of his communion with God. And that's where the biography grows sad.

PRAYER: Help me, O Lord, as I live in a world of human success and material possessions, to keep my soul focused on you; in Christ. Amen.

2 CHRONICLES 10, 11, 12   *Week 21, Day 1*

J think it would be difficult to grow up as the son or daughter of a king and retain one's personal equilibrium. That may give us a bit more sympathy with Rehoboam as we see him deal so poorly with Jeroboam and his delegation. Rehoboam was accustomed to the feeling of power and he liked it, so when his young counselors urged him to throw his weight around, he did it—and he lost the northern tribes.

He began to rebuild his power. He was encouraged by the loyalty of the Levites and perhaps especially by the fact that some of the more devout among the northern tribes came to Judah in order to be able more surely to fulfill their religious vows (11:13-16). But then it appears that Rehoboam's pride reasserted itself, for "when the rule of Rehoboam was estab-

114

lished and he grew strong, he abandoned the law of the LORD" (12:1). Defeat at the hands of Egypt brought him back, especially as the prophet Shemaiah told Rehoboam and his advisors that God was displeased with their conduct. So they humbled themselves before God (12:6) and escaped a measure of loss.

There's something pathetic in the faded grandeur described in 12:9-12. When the king of Egypt carried away the shields of gold, Rehoboam replaced them with shields of bronze; but still they made a kind of grand processional each day, as if the glory had not really departed. Perhaps they were making the best of a bad scene.

PRAYER: When I repent, dear Lord, and experience your mercy, give me the character to live up to my words of regret; in Jesus' name. Amen.

2 CHRONICLES 13, 14, 15   *Week 21, Day 2*

*W*e know from our earlier reading that Asa was a king who "did what was good and right in the sight of the Lord," but the chronicler gives us two insights into the quality of his faith. After enjoying peace for ten years, he found himself facing the massive military strength of Zerah the Ethiopian. It seemed quite clear he could never win, but he made his case before God. "O LORD, there is no difference for you between helping the mighty and the weak" (14:11). It was the kind of faith young Jonathan expressed generations earlier (1 Sam. 14:6) when he reasoned that God can save by many or by few. Someone has said that "one with God is a majority." Asa seemed to believe that.

After Asa won so handily against the Ethiopians, his soul may well have been in danger. Success is a dangerous potion. In any event the prophet Azariah came to Asa with a message that had in it both assurance and warning, and with it an urging to "take courage." Asa did just that. He "put away the abominable idols," which were still everywhere in the land, and then "he repaired the altar of the LORD that was in front of the vestibule of the house of the LORD" (15:8).

A number of action verbs follow: They sacrificed to the Lord (15:11), they entered into a covenant (15:12), and they took an oath (15:14). Nothing passive about this commitment! In fact Asa went so far as to remove his mother from office because of her idolatry (15:16).

PRAYER: Give me a faith in you, O Lord, which shows itself in solid commitments and faithful actions; in Jesus' name. Amen.

2 CHRONICLES 16, 17, 18; PSALM 85   *Week 21, Day 3*

*A*sa was a good man and a good king, but like anyone who has grown accustomed to power, he didn't like to be crossed. That meant trouble, because there were prophets in Judah and Israel, and it was the business of prophets to cross people, including kings, if they violated the will of the Lord. When Asa made an alliance with Benhadad of Aram without seeking counsel from the Lord, the seer Hanai told him he had done wrong; he ought to have trusted in the Lord God who empowered him to fight the Ethiopians. Instead of repenting, as his ancestor David did when the prophet Nathan came to him, Asa threw the prophet in prison, and in his rage even inflicted cruelties on some of his people (16:10). Still worse, Asa didn't seek God even when personal distress came his way. It's a sorry end to what had been a very good life (16:12).

The prophet Micaiah ran into the same kind of resistance in witnessing to King Ahab of Israel. "I hate him," Ahab said, "for he never prophesies anything favorable about me" (18:7). Apparently it never occurred to Ahab to change his ways in order to get a favorable message; instead, he just became angry with the messenger. Micaiah's position was especially difficult because there were prophets available who were ready to give whatever report the king wanted. It wasn't easy to be a prophet in Judah or Israel, even though these nations presumably were God's covenant people. Sometimes, you see, they found the covenant troublesome.

PRAYER: When I receive a message that upsets me, help me to seek you penitently rather than resenting the messenger; in Christ. Amen.

*W*hat do you do with bad news? When Jehoshaphat was told that the armies of Edom were marching against his people, he "set himself to seek the LORD, and proclaimed a fast" (20:3). Then in the assembly of the people he reasoned with God, reminding him of the way his ancestors had dealt with Edom. He confessed that he and his people were "powerless against this great multitude. . . . We do not know what to do, but our eyes are on you" (20:12).

His answer came through Jahaziel, a Levite, as the spirit of God came upon him. It was a message of good cheer: "Do not fear or be dismayed at this great multitude; for the battle is not yours but God's" (20:15). In this case a Levite acted as a prophet. Usually the priests and Levites filled more of a structured, institutional role, while the prophets acted in apparently irregular, spontaneous fashion; but occasionally Levites also acted as prophets, as in this case.

The battle that followed was extraordinary. A company of singers, "in holy splendor," preceded the army, singing their traditional hymn of faith:

"Give thanks to the LORD,
    for his steadfast love endures forever" (20:21).

We're not surprised that they returned to Jerusalem with joy, victorious. We're only sorry that twice (19:1-3; 20:35-37) Jehoshaphat missed God's leading, and that his son Jehoram followed the wrong examples.

PRAYER: In times of conflict, help me to lean on you, O Lord. Amen.

*J*udah experienced evil days under not only Jehoram but also during the long reign of Ahaziah and then the bloody coup of Queen Athaliah. But some good people were at work behind the scenes, especially Jehoshabeath, who endangered her own life to save the baby Joash, then protected him for nearly seven years until her husband, Jehoiada the priest, was able to place Joash on the throne.

He was only a boy at the time, but under the influence of Jehoiada he did all the right things. Most notably, he led the way both spiritually and administratively in the restoration of the temple.

But apparently he was not a very strong person. When Jehoiada died, Joash came under the influence of advisors who caused him to abandon the house of God, the very place he had worked so hard to repair, and to raise up places of idol worship. When Jehoiada's son, Zechariah (Luke 11:51), stood to challenge his evil, Joash "did not remember the kindness that Jehoiada . . . had shown him" (24:22) and killed Zechariah.

It isn't our business to pass judgment on Joash or anyone else, but to the degree that we can learn from their lives, we should. It appears that Joash, who was influenced for good by Jehoiada, was just as easily influenced toward evil once Jehoiada was gone. Perhaps Joash never fully got a faith of his own, or, getting it, neglected it under the pressures and expediencies of office. In any event, it's a sad ending.

PRAYER: Help me, dear Savior, to run the race with faithfulness to the very end, never stopping until I am finally with you; in Christ. Amen.

2 CHRONICLES 25, 26; PSALMS 86, 87   *Week 21, Day 6*

*A*maziah was a good king but not really good enough. As the New International Version puts it, "He did what was right in the eyes of the LORD, but not wholeheartedly" (25:2). That doesn't suffice for a faith which commands, "You shall love the LORD your God with all your heart, and with all your soul, and with all your might" (Deut. 6:5). We're not surprised, then, when he brings back the gods of the people of Seir after he has defeated them, and worships these gods. A prophet asks him, quite logically, "Why have you resorted to a people's gods who could not deliver their own people from your hand?" (25:15), but we're inclined to do illogical things when we follow God with only half a heart. I think Amaziah recognized the truth of the prophet's logic, for it angered him to the point that he threatened his life (25:16).

Uzziah, on the other hand, was good but not long enough. He came to the throne as a sixteen-year-old, and he did what was right in the sight of the Lord, aided by the instruction of Zechariah, "who instructed him in the fear of God" (26:5). But as we have noted before in the stories of the kings (and in experiences closer to home, too), power is a peril. "When he had become strong he grew proud, to his destruction" (26:16). He usurped the office of the priests and was smitten with some form of leprosy. Because of the Hebrew laws of isolation for lepers, he remained in a separate house from then until the day of his death.

PRAYER: Give me a love for you, dear Lord, which is both deep and long, so that I will follow you all the days of my life; in Christ. Amen.

2 CHRONICLES 27, 28; PSALM 88   *Week 21, Day 7*

S ometimes we learn from the bad examples of others. Perhaps that was the case with Jotham, son of Uzziah. The chronicler says that he did what was right in the sight of the Lord just as his father, Uzziah, had done, except that "he did not invade the temple of the LORD" (27:2). He repaired the temple and built cities and forts, and won battles, too; he "became strong because he ordered his ways before the LORD his God" (27:6).

But if Jotham learned from his father's mistakes, his son Ahaz did not learn from Jotham's admirable example. It is not that he was indifferent to God; he was outright hostile, following the example of the kings of the northern tribes rather than the sometime goodness of his own predecessors in Judah. It seems almost as if he went in search of evil practices, making images for Baal, making his sons pass through fire in the manner of the pagan peoples, and offering sacrifices "under every green tree" (28:4).

At last he came to a time of distress. Trouble drives many people to God and to a re-evaluation of their way of life, but not Ahaz. He simply became "yet more faithless to the LORD" (28:22). Finding new gods among the people of Aram, making altars to false gods "in every corner of Jerusalem" (28:24), his life ended in such shame that the people chose not to bury him among his fellow kings.

PRAYER: As I compare the stories of those who followed you

and those who denied you, I am more than ever persuaded to give you my all. Amen.

2 Chronicles 29, 30, 31, 32   *Week 22, Day 1*

*W*hat do we do with the sins of our ancestors? It is quite easy to bewail them and it may satisfy the ego to do so, but no real good is accomplished. Hezekiah repented by turning Judah in a new way, beginning with a great housecleaning in the temple (29:16-19), then restoring temple worship. The chronicler notes that "the thing had come about suddenly" (29:36), but I expect this was because Hezekiah was so much in earnest. In fact, he would not even let the religious calendar stand in his way. When there was not time enough to sanctify the priests before the traditional Passover date, they celebrated at a different time (30:1-4); and what they had in mind was so exciting they did their best to bring in all their kin from Israel, though not many accepted (30:10, 11). Some who came hadn't followed the established preliminaries, but Hezekiah prayed God would accept them "even though not in accordance with the sanctuary's rules of cleanness" (30:19). Then Hezekiah cleaned out the accumulated pagan shrines, and reorganized the priesthood.

When the chronicler says that he did these things "with all his heart" (31:21), we can believe it. His was no woeful shaking of the head about the past, but a vigorous beginning again. No wonder, then, that he was able to face the threatened invasion from Assyria, including a high-powered propaganda war. We're sorry Hezekiah's heart became proud in the midst of these achievements, but glad that even then he was good enough to turn back once more to God (32:25, 26).

Prayer: Give me the courage, dear Lord, to clear away the past. Amen.

2 Chronicles 33, 34; Psalm 89   *Week 22, Day 2*

*W*hat perversity is there in human nature that Manasseh would want to overturn all the good his father Hezekiah had done? He was only twelve years old when his father died, so he had no remembrance of how bad things had been before his father's reform, yet surely people must have told him. Perhaps it is simply that some of us insist on learning our lessons the hard way, from our own painful experience. In time, "bound . . . with fetters" by the Babylonians, Manasseh "humbled himself greatly before the God of his ancestors" and God restored him. "Then Manasseh knew that the LORD indeed was God" (33:11-13). From that time on, he served God faithfully.

Amon, his son, didn't do so well. He didn't get time to learn from experience, because after only two evil years he was killed by his servants. That's the trouble with learning by experience; sometimes we don't get to finish the course.

But Amon's son, Josiah, did well. Only eight years old when he was thrust into power, "while he was still a boy, he began to seek the God of his ancestor David" (34:3). By the time he was twenty he was purging his country of its idolatry, and at twenty-six he began a campaign to repair the temple. It was at this point that they found the lost book of law. When Josiah heard the words of the law, "he tore his clothes" in anguished sorrow (34:19) and began renewing the divine covenant (34:31).

PRAYER: As I see some follow your ways and some reject them, I realize anew that I must choose you for myself. Help me, I pray. Amen.

2 CHRONICLES 35, 36; PSALM 90   *Week 22, Day 3*

*T*his section begins with a wondrous celebration of the passover—"No passover like it had been kept in Israel since the days of the prophet Samuel" (35:18)—but in a very special sense it becomes a transition to a new day when there is an emphasis in God's use of gentiles for his purposes.

The first instance is King Neco of Egypt, against whom Josiah went to battle. Neco didn't intend to fight Josiah, but insisted that his mission was at God's command. Other pagan kings had said such things, but in Neco's case it was so (35:22); unfortunately, Josiah failed to recognize it, and lost his life in a battle against Neco.

121

Then there is Nebuchadnezzar, king of Babylon. For generations the people of Judah had broken their covenant with God, and though God spoke "persistently to them by his messengers, . . . they kept mocking . . . despising his words, and scoffing at his prophets" (36:15, 16). So at last, judgment must come, and for it God employs Nebuchadnezzar ("Therefore [God] brought up against them the king of the Chaldeans" [36:17]).

And when at last the captivity comes to an end, again it is a gentile ruler—this time, King Cyrus of Persia. In the first year of his reign, "in the fulfillment of the word of the LORD . . . the LORD stirred up the spirit of King Cyrus" (36:22). With the voice of an evangelist, he calls God's people to return to their homeland. A new day has come.

PRAYER: Thank you, Father, for using such varieties of people for your purposes. Help me, in time and place, to be willing. Amen.

EZRA 1, 2, 3   Week 22, Day 4

$\mathcal{K}$ ing Cyrus, confident that God has ordained him to build a temple in Jerusalem, issues an invitation to the people of Judah and Benjamin, and "everyone whose spirit God had stirred" (1:5) accepted the call. Cyrus shows remarkable commitment to his mission by being certain the vessels of the old temple, still available after two generations, are sent back for this new house of God.

Again we are given a long list of names. They are important because this is the rebirth of the nation and a record must be kept. We're also given a report of their resources, as measured primarily in livestock; and with all of that, a report of their "freewill offerings for the house of God" (2:68). At best they had to be a subsistence people as they set out to rebuild a country that had been relatively undeveloped for so long, but their generosity was great.

Their first act was to build an altar. We can easily forget it, but all of worship is built around the point where we make our commitments and our sacrifices to God. The foundations of the temple itself were not laid until months later. The completed foundation was reason for celebration, with trumpets and cymbals and the resounding singing of the "steadfast love [which] endures forever" (3:11). The new generation simply shouted for joy, but those who remembered the old temple "wept with a loud voice" as they saw the beginning of a new house (3:12, 13).

PRAYER: Thank you, Lord, for new starts in life! Whatever they may be, I want to build them around your altar; in Jesus' name. Amen.

EZRA 4, 5, 6   *Week 22, Day 5*

*O*nly rarely does a good cause proceed long without opposition. In this case the opposition came from some other inhabitants of the area who at first feigned sympathy but who, when their plan was rejected by Zerubbabel and his council, undermined them in the court of the king of Persia. They convinced King Artaxerxes to stop the building program. But in time the prophets Haggai and Zechariah stirred the people to action once again so that they once more began building, even without permission.

Now a showdown came. The Jews asked King Darius to search the records so he might see that they had been empowered long before by King Cyrus. When the records were found, Darius ordered that the work should go forward without hindrance: "Let the work on this house of God alone; . . . I, Darius, make a decree; let it be done with all diligence" (6:7, 12). So the people completed the work on the house of God, "by command of the God of Israel" and by decree of the kings of Persia (6:14).

This is a remarkable development, a miracle in its own right. Why would the chief of state of what was then the world's greatest power show such respect for the God of Israel? They were a downtrodden people who hadn't held a major place in political history for a number of generations. Why did the king feel that the God of a recently captive people could be a God of power, whose wishes were significant?

PRAYER: I'm very grateful, O Lord, that you work in the hearts and minds of some who might not seem naturally sympathetic; in Christ. Amen.

$\mathcal{A}$ great many years—probably as many as sixty—elapsed between the events at the beginning of this book and the appearance of Ezra, the man whose name it bears and who is traditionally felt to be the author. During those intervening years, deterioration had set in. The original fire of commitment had died, and the people were accommodating themselves to the pagan cultures around them.

Ezra was a different breed. He had "set his heart to study the law of the LORD and to do it, and to teach the statutes and ordinances in Israel" (7:10). One marvels that he possessed such an earnest commitment. The people had been isolated from their spiritual and theological roots for generations; why would he conclude that the law of the Lord was important enough that he should dedicate his whole being to studying and teaching it? When you answer this question for Ezra, you probably have an insight to explain all the other renewals of biblical faith that have occurred over the centuries, including such persons as Francis of Assisi, Martin Luther, and John and Charles Wesley. In repeated instances remarkable people have arisen on the spiritual landscape at times when one might conclude that the cause is lost. Such was Ezra.

The king believed in him, and he believed in God. When he wavered at the hazards of a dangerous journey, he confessed that he "was ashamed to ask the king for a band of soldiers" when he had told the king God would take care of him. So he fasted and moved with courage! (8:22, 23).

PRAYER: Thank you for sending light in the midst of dark times. Amen.

EZRA 9, 10; PSALM 93   *Week 22, Day 7*

$\mathcal{A}$ modern reader is inclined to see Ezra as a bigot in this report of his handling of the mixed marriages into which the people had entered. He is unbending, no doubt about it, and he offers no compromise. But let's see if we can understand him from something other than our own vantage point.

We should note, at the outset, that the issue was a spiritual, not a racial or ethnic one; he was committed, in the tradition of Israel, to religious purity. We should also remember that restrictions against mixed marriages were common in many cultures at that time.

I'm also impressed by the intensity of Ezra's suffering over the issue; "I tore my garment and my mantle, and pulled hair from my head and beard, and sat appalled" (9:4). Probably one element that bothered him most is that a number of the offenders were major persons: "in this faithlessness the officials and leaders have led the way" (9:2). Of the 113 men with foreign wives, 17 were priests and 10 were Levites. It is as if they judged themselves to be above the law of the common masses.

We should also see the matter in the context of their history. Israel had been called to be a separate, holy people, with practices that were dramatically different from those of the nations around them. Instead they had failed repeatedly. Now God had restored them for another chance, but instead of responding with high commitment, they were sinning just as their ancestors had. A severe remedy was needed, and Ezra gave it.

PRAYER: Help me, O God, to follow you with passionate devotion. Amen.

NEHEMIAH 1, 2, 3   *Week 23, Day 1*

*E*zra is usually identified as the spiritual leader in the restoration of Jerusalem, and Nehemiah as the political administrator, but no book or work is so constantly marked by prayer as Nehemiah's. His work and his decisions are punctuated by a running commentary of conversations with God.

His story begins in the courts of King Artaxerxes, to whom Nehemiah is the cupbearer. There is ordinarily great stability in his person, for the king had never seen him sad (2:1). But the bad news Nehemiah had received about Jerusalem—that her walls had been broken down and her gates destroyed—was more than he could hide. When the king asked the reason for his distress, he confessed his concern and the king benevolently offered help. Once again we see a gentile ruler cooperating with the purposes of God for the Jews.

So Nehemiah returns to Jerusalem. The work begins with enthusiasm as the people "committed themselves to the common good" (2:18). Nehemiah gives us a list of the workers and their assignments, providing more details than we're likely to want. But these names reflect his joy in the dedication of the people. And of course it is right that such credit should be given. If any names are to be recorded in our human history, let us be sure they include the people, small and large, who work for the common good and who gladly give themselves to a high purpose.

PRAYER: Thank you for people like Nehemiah, who care about their heritage and who will work for its restoration; in Christ. Amen.

NEHEMIAH 4, 5, 6   *Week 23, Day 2*

*T*he course of a great cause never runs smooth. As surely as a work is worthy, it will have opposition; perhaps there is no better proof that there is a devil. Nehemiah's first opposition came from people in the area who had a stake in Jerusalem's remaining weak. At first they mocked the Jews: "any fox going up on [the wall] would break it down!" (4:3). This is one of those times when Nehemiah interjects a prayer: "Hear, O our God, for we are despised" (4:4).

But Nehemiah did more than pray. He organized his workers and reminded them that they were fighting for their kin and their homes and that God was with them (4:14). From that time on, they were ready to fight even as they worked: "each of the builders had his sword strapped at his side while he built" (4:18). Nehemiah and his closest associates weren't even able to change clothes during these difficult days.

A problem that was perhaps even worse, because it struck at the morale of the people, came from within their own ranks. Some of the more prosperous Jews were exploiting the poor within the community. Nehemiah was fearless in bringing charges gainst the nobles and the officials. He called them to a public assembly and demanded that they restore what they had taken unfairly from their fellow Jews.

In spite of problems, the wall was completed; Josephus says it took two years and four months. Nehemiah said that the neighboring nations knew it had been accomplished with the help of God (6:16).

PRAYER: Keep me steadfast, O Lord, in the face of my opposition. Amen.

NEHEMIAH 7, 8; PSALMS 94, 95   *Week 23, Day 3*

*O*n the first day of the seventh month—Rosh Hashanah, the Jewish New Year—the people gathered to hear Ezra read the law of Moses and to listen while a group of Levites explained it. Both men and women were there and anyone else "who could hear with understanding" (8:2), and the people were attentive. It was a remarkable occasion, marked at first by great mourning and then by celebration.

Which raises the question, what should the law of God do for us? To begin with, it should get our attention. All the people stood as Ezra began reading the law (8:5); this was no casual, picnic atmosphere. No doubt one of the reasons the scriptures are not more effective in our lives is not only because we do not read them enough, but that when we do, it is too often on the run, with limited concentration.

But then (and perhaps this will surprise you), God's law is a matter for rejoicing, for feasting and thanksgiving. "This day is holy to the LORD your God," Nehemiah and the others explained; "do not mourn or weep" (8:9). There is a time for mourning and a time for rejoicing. If we have sinned we should repent, but we shouldn't wallow in our sorrow. Having found the way, we have the best reason in life for rejoicing.

Nehemiah put it memorably: "the joy of the LORD is your strength" (8:10). There is no joy to compare with that of the forgiven heart that has now found the way. In such a state, we can live with strength.

PRAYER: Help me find such riches in your word, O Lord, that my life shall possess a strong and constant joy; in Jesus' name. Amen.

*H*aving written yesterday about joy, I may seem inconsistent when my theme today includes fasting, sackcloth (the garment of sorrow), and earth on the head (9:1). But the point, of course, is simple. The spiritual life must, like the physical life, have its ebb and flow, its inhaling and its exhaling. There is a time for feasting, but there is a time also for fasting.

I expect we are guilty of two lapses. We fast hardly at all, of course; this is one of the forgotten disciplines of the spiritual life in our time. But on the other hand, we don't really know how to feast. We know how to overeat mind you, but not how to feast. That is, we don't celebrate the joy of the Lord in a meal. We eat for sustenance, which is necessary, and we eat for friendship, which is refreshing; but we almost never eat a festive meal in a real sense of gladness of faith and thanksgiving to God. And we are the poorer for it.

But back to the fasting. In that setting of personal restraint, the leaders of the people recalled their national history. We know by now what a mixed story it was, and this recital is altogether candid in its acknowledgment of inconsistency and unfaithfulness. They feel that they are now paying the price: "Here we are, slaves to this day—slaves in the land that you gave to our ancestors" (9:36). In such a mood, they sign a covenant of new commitment to God.

PRAYER: Teach me to fast and to feast—to repent when I have sinned and to rejoice in your great goodness; in Jesus' name. Amen.

NEHEMIAH 11, 12, 13   *Week 23, Day 5*

*A*nyone who has ever lived with the imperfections of the church has to feel some comfort in the story of Nehemiah. On the one hand, there are those high moments when all the people "rejoice with great joy," so that "the joy of Jerusalem was heard far away" (12:43). But then, after Nehemiah has been gone for a time, he finds all sorts of lapses on his return. Tobiah has been given lodging in the courts of the house of God, and Nehemiah promptly throws out his furniture and orders the area reconsecrated. Then he discovers that the Levites have forsaken their posts in the house of God in order to take care of their farms. The sabbath is being desecrated, too, with work and commerce carried on shamelessly. Nehemiah again takes command, and with little patience.

He worries, too, about the issue that had so upset Ezra, intermarriage with pagan cultures. He reminds the people that even King Solomon was destroyed by such unions, so how can they hope to survive them? Nehemiah fights tirelessly for what he believes to be right, and with it all prays, "Remember me, O my God, for good" (13:31).

Good came, no doubt about it. It was during this period that some patterns of Jewish worship and of prayer liturgy were established which exist in the synagogues to the present time, and it was also during this period that certain books were added to the Hebrew canon. The times were difficult, but people like Ezra and Nehemiah made the most of them.

PRAYER: Make my faith adequate, O Lord, for all occasions. Amen.

ESTHER 1, 2, 3; PSALM 97   *Week 23, Day 6*

Great events are sometimes born in less than auspicious circumstances. When Ahasuerus (some would say Xerxes I) was king of Persia, he had a monstrous celebration of his power. The events concluded in what must have been a drunken party until the king, "merry with wine" (1:10), ordered that the queen be brought in so he could "show the peoples and the officials her beauty" (1:11). It wasn't a nice scene, and we honor the queen for refusing.

But that was the beginning of a series of fortuitous events. The king's associates were distressed, fearing that if word got out of Queen Vashti's refusal, the whole social order would break down! They therefore recommended that the king begin search for a new queen. The choice fell upon a Jewish girl, Esther (Hadassah), an orphan who had been raised by her cousin Mordecai. She quickly became a favorite, but she did not reveal her Jewish heritage.

Meanwhile her cousin Mordecai took a spot daily at the king's gate. There one day he overheard a plot on the life of the king, and passed the word to Esther. His action saved the king's life, and the matter was recorded in the annals of the king.

Then there was Haman, a self-important man who had risen so high in the king's employ that everyone bowed to him, except Mordecai. Haman was so upset he arranged to massacre the Jews in order to get Mordecai.

PRAYER: Teach me, O Lord, to know that you are always at work. Amen.

ESTHER 4, 5, 6   *Week 23, Day 7*

Mordecai was the kind of person who caused trouble, not because he wanted to be a troublemaker, but because he was a person of strong convictions. When he learned of Haman's edict, he sought Esther's help. She explained the perils of her position, but Mordecai put the matter memorably: "Perhaps you have come to royal dignity for just such a time as this" (4:14). Esther answered, with courage comparable to his, that she would take the chance; "and if I perish, I perish" (4:16).

She arranged a banquet at which she could make her case before the king. But meanwhile (a great deal of this book happens "meanwhile," because its whole plot depends on the realization that God is working behind the scenes) the king is suffering from insomnia. He asks that they read from his annals to relieve his sleeplessness, and they read, of all things, the story of the plot against him which was thwarted by Mordecai. Learning that no recognition has ever been paid to his benefactor, he asks Haman (who just happens to be around) what should be done for someone the king wants to honor.

Haman, being the kind of person he is, thinks the king has him in mind, so he outlines an impressive event—only to discover it is for his despised "enemy," Mordecai. And worse, he must implement all these honors! Haman, who had anticipated destroying this man, must now robe him and lead him through the city in a proud processional. So the plot develops, but the end is not yet.

PRAYER: Help me remember, O Lord, that you are always standing in the shadows, keeping watch over your own; in Jesus' name. Amen.

130

*A*t last it is time for Esther to speak. Her petition, she says, is that her life be given to her; and her request, that the lives of her people be saved. Now she identifies Haman as not only the enemy of her people, but as the enemy of the king's best purposes. Haman's flustered conduct makes his situation still worse; "so they hanged Haman on the gallows that he had prepared for Mordecai" (7:10).

But now steps must quickly be taken to subvert the scheduled destruction of the Jews. So by the king's command the day that was to have been a day of disaster became instead a day "when the Jews would gain power over their foes" (9:1). It is a bloody end to the story, but one that saw their sorrow turned into gladness (9:22).

This story explains the origin of the Jewish celebration of Purim, which continues to the present time. The book of Esther is read during the celebration, and each time Haman's name is mentioned, it is customary to drown it out with noisemakers, symbolizing that his name has been blotted out from memory.

The name of God is never mentioned in this book, nor is there any reference to prayer or worship. It is a portrayal of God at work behind the scenes—so hidden that the unsuspecting will not even be conscious of his existence, but so active that those with faith will see the divine hand in every circumstance and coincidence.

PRAYER: Give me the faith, I pray, to see how you are at work in so many of the apparently inconsequential events of my life; in Christ. Amen.

*T*homas Carlyle, the nineteenth-century essayist, said that there is nothing written in the Bible, or out of it, of equal literary merit with Job. One can hardly read it without being moved. It is the living story of one human being in mortal turmoil, and it has become a symbol for intense human suffering as well as the embodiment of our questions about the significance of suffering.

As the story opens, Job has everything going his way. He is "blameless and upright" (1:1), "the greatest of all the people of the east" (1:3), so earnest in both parenting and religious commitment that he rises early in the morning to make sacrifices for each of his children, just in case they may have sinned, or cursed God in their hearts.

Then one day his life begins to fall apart. Satan ("the accuser") is allowed to invade his perfect world. He loses his wealth and then his seven sons and three daughters. But he says, from his pit of grief, "blessed be the name of the LORD" (1:21).

Then he is afflicted with a distasteful, extremely painful disease. His wife (herself a sufferer in all that has thus far happened) advises him to curse God and die. He answers that he has received good at the hand of God, so why should he not receive bad (2:10). Now friends come to comfort him, and at last Job lets out his first cry of despair as he curses the day of his birth. And yet, he sins not.

PRAYER: As I read this book, loving Savior, give me a heart for those in pain, and faith for my own days of trial; in Jesus' name. Amen.

JOB 4, 5, 6

Now we begin the continuing dialogue between Job and his friends. We can see, almost from the outset, why Job will eventually say, "miserable comforts are you all" (16:2). Perhaps their greatest fault is that they can never get far enough past their own preconceptions to really hear what Job is saying or to enter into his pain.

Eliphaz makes his major point early:

> "Consider now: Who, being innocent, has ever perished?
> Where were the upright ever destroyed?" (4:7 NIV)

This was the basic theological posture of the times, that the righteous prosper and the wicked suffer, on this earth, for their sins. As Job's friends see the devastation that has hit him, they can draw only one conclusion—that he must be a sinner and probably, in light of the extent of the devastation, a very serious sinner.

[Marginal handwritten notes:]
Allowed /owed/ legally permitted & maybe on a leash.

why is he even back in heaven?

If YHWH hides face from sin?

Even hereditary sin, perhaps, or original sin?

Eliphaz admits that life is difficult, because we are "born to trouble as surely as sparks fly upward" (5:7 NIV). But were he in Job's shoes, he would lay his cause before God (5:8). Meanwhile, Job should be thankful for the correction he is receiving (5:17).

Job begins his reply with a cry of anguish, insisting that they have no idea of the extent of his pain (6:2-4). Then he appeals to his friends not to bargain him away, because his very integrity is at stake (6:27, 29). He should not be brushed aside lightly.

PRAYER: Dear Lord, I pray that you will give me a heart for those in pain, so I will enter into their sorrow; in Christ. Amen.

JOB 7, 8, 9   *Week 24, Day 4*

I know of few places in life or in literature where a person's ultimate anguish is more eloquently expressed than in these chapters. Job confesses that God's attention to him is burdensome, even terrifying:

"What are human beings, that you make so much of them,
    that you set your mind on them?" (7:17)

Job wishes God would give him relief for even a moment: "let me alone until I swallow my spittle" (7:19).

His friend Bildad stands in defense of God. "Does God pervert justice?" he asks (8:3). He means well, and in the close of his address promises Job that God "will yet fill your mouth with laughter, / and your lips with shouts of joy" because "God will not reject a blameless person" (8:21, 20).

Job gladly acknowledges that this is so, "but how can a mortal be just before God?" (9:2). He has a feeling that even his best efforts are doomed:

"If I wash myself with soap
    and cleanse my hands with lye,
yet you will plunge me into filth,
    and my own clothes will abhor me." (9:30, 31)

So Job makes his desperate plea for an "umpire . . . who might lay his hand on us both" (9:33). We call that umpire, that mediator, Jesus Christ.

133

PRAYER: When I think, dear Lord, that my cause is lost, remind me that I have an umpire pleading for me, even Christ my Lord. Amen.

JOB 10, 11, 12   *Week 24, Day 5*

*J*ob has two problems in addition to his great pain—God and his friends. So he pleads with God while expressing outrage and sarcasm to his friends. He reminds God that heaven has a stake in him:

> "Your hands fashioned and made me;
> and now you turn and destroy me." (10:8)

Zophar is less patient than his two predecessors. He condemns Job for his "babble" and for protesting his innocence. As a matter of fact, Zophar says, you should "know then that God exacts of you less than your guilt deserves" (11:6). Nevertheless, he holds out the hope that if Job will put away his iniquity and will lift up his face without blemish, his life "will be brighter than the noonday" (11:17).

By this time Job has had about all he can take. "No doubt you are the people, / and wisdom will die with you" (12:2). Even in his utterly miserable state, he hasn't lost his spunk: "I am not inferior to you" (12:3). Then he reminds his friends of a fact all of us ought to remember when we look at people in trouble: "Those at ease have contempt for misfortune" (12:5). But misfortune looks different from the inside.

So Job reminds himself and his friends that wisdom is not with the aged, it is with God. Ultimate power is in God's hands; and even the counselors, kings, and priests of earth are hopeless before him.

PRAYER: I'm very grateful, O Lord, that although all wisdom resides in you, you are willing to reason with the likes of me; in Christ. Amen.

JOB 13, 14, 15; PSALM 98   *Week 24, Day 6*

*B*oth Job and his accusers are right, of course. It's just that they aren't working on the same issues. Job is asking for help in the despair of his life, while his friends are try-ing to defend God. They mean well. They intend to be God's advocates. But that's a dangerous role, since it implies that we fully understand the mind of the Eternal. We will discover later in the story that they weren't as fully possessed of the facts as they thought.

Meanwhile, Job decides he'd rather argue his case directly with God than deal with his friends who "whitewash with lies," who are all "worthless physicians" (13:3, 4). But as for God, "Though he slay me, yet I will hope in him" (13:15 NIV). At this point, Job's faith is so sure that even if he loses in his controversy with the Almighty, he will still believe.

But Eliphaz is afraid Job will do away with the fear of God (15:4). He reminds him, with fine scorn, that other people, wiser people, disagree with Job; "the gray-haired and the aged are on our side" (15:10). Job, however, has raised a huge ques-tion: "If mortals die, will they live again?" (14:14). At the time of the writing of this book, immortality was not commonly believed. In the midst of the hopelessness of his present earthly state, Job hopes that there may be more than this life, and though he has no assurance at the moment, he dares to hope.

PRAYER: Dear Lord, when I visit with someone in distress, give me the grace to listen compassionately, and to hear; in Jesus' name. Amen.

JOB 16, 17, 18   Week 24, Day 7

*J*ob pauses in his eternal dialogue long enough to speak some common sense to his friends:

> "I also could talk as you do
>   if you were in my place;
> I could join words together against you,
>   and shake my head at you." (16:4)

But his deeper grievance is against God. "I was at ease, and he broke me in two; / he seized me by the neck and dashed me to pieces" (16:12). Now Job's spirit is weak and he sees no relief. His plans are broken, the desires of his heart gone (17:11), and all he can look forward to is death itself.

"If I say to the Pit, 'You are my father,'
   and to the worm, 'My mother,' or 'My sister,'
where then is my hope?" (17:14, 15)

At this moment, Job feels little but despair. His friends offer no hope, and God appears to be his enemy, so where can he go?

And his friends now seem spiritually destitute. Perhaps they are exhausted with the dialogue. In any event, Bildad can only accuse Job of too much talking (18:2), and remind him of what he and his friends have already said so often, that the wicked suffer and are forgotten—and the unspoken assumption is that Job is included in their number.

PRAYER: Help me, O Lord, to remember that even when heaven seems to be silent, you are there, and you love me; in Jesus' name. Amen.

JOB 19, 20, 21   *Week 25, Day 1*

*J*ob's greatest declaration of faith—perhaps as great a declaration as can be found anywhere—comes after he has made the most graphic statement of his despair. He says that God has "set darkness" upon his paths (19:8), and has isolated his family from him so that his "serving girls count me as a stranger" and "my breath is repulsive to my wife" (19:15, 17). Though once the most esteemed man in the area, now "even young children despise me" and "intimate friends abhor me" (19:18, 19). No wonder, because "my bones cling to my skin and to my flesh" (19:20).

But with all that being the case, suddenly Job rises up from his bed of pain to call for a way to inscribe his words in a book—or better, "engraved on a rock forever" (19:24). And here's why:

"For I know that my Redeemer lives,
   and that at the last he will stand upon the earth;
and after my skin has been thus destroyed,
   then in my flesh I shall see God." (19:25, 26)

It is no wonder that these words have become one of the most beloved pieces of Easter music, because Job's declaration sounds like a preview of the Easter hope.

136

In a sense, the book of Job ought to end here or at least move quickly to its conclusion. Instead, it continues through still more dialogue including further gropings of pain by Job. But this, in truth, is the way life is. The majestic testimony is rarely the end of the story.

PRAYER: Thank you for a glimpse of Easter in Job! Hallelujah! Amen.

JOB 22, 23, 24   *Week 25, Day 2*

*E*liphaz's accusations against Job in 22:5-11 come as a shock in light of all we have heretofore known about him. Is it true that Job has stolen from the poor, refused to help the hungry, and crushed the arms of orphans? I doubt it. But if you have ever seen a person of esteem come into a vulnerable place (or have experienced it yourself), you know that surprising things are said about a person when he or she is down. Here were some more "boils" for Job's suffering.

The psalmist (Psalm 139) testified that he couldn't flee from God; no matter where he went, God was already there seeking him. Job testifies to the very opposite experience; try as he will, he cannot find God.

> "Oh, that I knew where I might find him,
> that I might come even to his dwelling!" (23:3)
> "If I go forward, he is not there;
> or backward, I cannot perceive him." (23:8)

Both persons are describing true human experiences. The difference, I'm sure, is not in God, but in our perception of him. But what we perceive is, from our personal point of view, what is true; and for Job just now, the experience is that of God's absence. Yet he refuses to be shaken. This is why this book is a monumental expression of faith. So Job declares, "But he knows the way that I take; / when he has tested me, I shall come out like gold" (23:10).

PRAYER: Dear God, I want the kind of faith that believes in you as much in your perceived absence as in your presence; in Christ. Amen.

*B*ildad's short statement is strongly stated and of course is true; a mortal creature cannot hope to be righteous before God (25:4) because we fall so far short of divine holiness. But one has the feeling that Job's friends are running out of arguments; they can do no more than restate, in emphatic language, what they've said before.

I'm amused by the sarcasm with which Job responds: "How you have assisted the arm that has no strength!" (26:2). And I'm inspired by the unbending way he holds to his integrity: "until I die I will not put away my integrity from me" (27:5). As William Ernest Henley would have said, his head was bloody but unbowed. With all that life had done to him in recent months and with all that had been said by his friends (and apparently by others) to discredit him, Job is still saying, "I hold fast my righteousness, and will not let it go" (27:6).

And I listen thoughtfully while he compares, in chapter 28, our human success in searching out earth's jewels and minerals and our failure in finding wisdom, the greatest treasure. Our problem, Job knows, is that we do "not comprehend its worth" (28:13 NIV), and for that reason we do not pursue wisdom with the same passion that we spend in seeking gold or silver. Nor do we really know where wisdom comes from (28:20). But Job knows; he puts it in the same language as Proverbs:

> "Truly, the fear of the Lord, that is wisdom,
>   and to depart from evil is understanding." (28:28)

PRAYER: May my passion for wisdom be greater than for wealth. Amen.

*N*ow Job is ready to make his closing summation. He tries, as a human being can, to examine his heart and to see to what degree he may be at fault. It seems to him that he did justly:

"I was eyes to the blind,
    and feet to the lame.
I was a father to the needy,
    and I championed the cause of the stranger." (29:15, 16)

But he cannot help wishing for the good old days when he "sat as chief, and . . . lived like a king" (29:25), because now people mock him in song and make him a byword (30:9); in fact, "they do not hesitate to spit at the sight of me" (30:10).

He wonders, too, if he might have done better. He speaks not only of his conduct, but of his inner person, approaching the standards of the Sermon on the Mount as he wonders if "my heart has followed my eyes" (31:7). Or has he been inhumane in any way in his treatment of those working for him? Even as he raises the question, he expresses shame that a person could do so, for "did not he who made me in the womb make them?" (31:15). And with all that he had, did he ever make gold his trust, or rejoice in the greatness of his wealth (31:24, 25)? Or did he sometimes take pleasure in the misfortunes of his enemies (31:29)? *Jehovah fond of this seemingly*

Here is a person who is searching the deep places of his soul to see if he has fallen short of God's glory; and, frustrated in the search, he pleads, "Oh, that I had the indictment written by my adversary!" (31:35). He doesn't know that his adversary simply charged him with having a very good thing and with serving God for ulterior reasons (1:9-11). *Did his wife ever learn? kids?*

PRAYER: Savior, help me be honest with my own soul; in Christ. Amen.

JOB 32, 33, 34   *Week 25, Day 5*

*N*ow a new personality appears, Elihu. He is a younger man and has been quiet until now because he felt that age deserved a full hearing. But he is "angry at Job because he justified himself rather than God" and at the three friends "because they had found no answer" yet continued to attack Job (32:2, 3).

Elihu gives a long speech, longer than any of the three older men. His major contribution to the discussion is his insistence that God does indeed speak to us human beings, and though he doesn't specifically say so, it seems he may be answering Job's complaint that he is cut off from God. To the contrary, Elihu suggests, the suffering itself may be the voice of God. "For God speaks in one way, / and in two, though people do not perceive it" (33:14). He lists the ways: a dream, a vision of the night (33:15), and also when they are "chastened with pain upon their beds" (33:19), even to the point where "their souls draw near the Pit" (33:22). Sometimes, too, there is a mediator, "one of a thousand," who will plead for the person (33:23).

> "God indeed does all these things,
>   twice, three times, with mortals,
> to bring back their souls from the Pit,
>   so that they may see the light of life." (33:29, 30)

And if God is so gracious in pursuing us, "far be it from God that he should do wickedness" (34:10). If it were not for his mercy, God would take back his spirit and "all flesh would perish together" (34:14, 15).

PRAYER: Heavenly Father, help me to hear your voice and see your purposes in the common, sometimes painful, events of my life. Amen.

JOB 35, 36, 37; PSALM 99   Week 25, Day 6

*E*lihu, like the three older friends, is intent on defending the purposes and the holiness of God, but he has a better sense of where he is going—perhaps partly because he can benefit by the mistakes the others have made. He reminds Job that any wickedness he does will affect others and that, in turn, his righteousness will bless others (35:8). So Job's experiences fit into a greater purpose, a purpose in which God is at work in so many ways, including this way which Job has not considered, even though it is happening in his own life:

> "He delivers the afflicted by their affliction,
>   and opens their ear by adversity." (36:15)

In the portion that follows, Elihu seems almost to be preparing the way for God's confrontation with Job. He points to the majesty and power of God in nature: "Can anyone understand the spreading of the clouds?" (36:29). And, "Listen, listen to the thunder of his voice" (37:2). Still more awesome, "From its chamber comes the whirlwind," and "by the breath of God ice is given" (37:9, 10). No wonder, then, that "around God is awesome majesty" (37:22).

But this power of nature is more than just display. Elihu feels that "whether for correction, or for his land, / or for love, he causes it to happen" (37:13). There is a word for us in the steady stream of natural phenomena, large and small, if only we will hear it.

PRAYER: When I look at your grand creation, O Lord, help me to see your message, whether of correction or of simple love; in Christ. Amen. vs Numbers 21:6?

JOB 38, 39, 40, 41   *Week 25, Day 7*

*J*ob has wanted for so long to have an audience with God. Now he gets it. God pays him the sublime compliment with a summons:

"Gird up your loins like a man,
    I will question you, and you shall declare to me." (38:3)

God leads Job on a grand excursion of the wonders of nature, but it is no pleasure trip. Instead, each new marvel is a basis for confrontation: "Where were you when I did this? Have you ever been here before? Do you know who's behind all this? Can you explain even the simplest procedures of the animal kingdom? That horse you ride: did you give it its might or clothe its neck with mane?"

When God pauses for a moment, Job answers cautiously, "See, I am of small account; / what shall I answer you?" (40:4). And immediately God picks up the theme again, overwhelming Job with the creatures of earth and sea and the wonders of their natures. It isn't carefully reasoned logic, no syllogism at the end of which Job is compelled to say, "You've made your point." At times God's manner with Job seems almost unmerciful, because it's clear Job is completely out-matched. But in truth, it is the ultimate honor to be con-fronted by God, and Job knows it. And in this momentous display of God's power, Job is reassured of God's existence, to the point where he can conclude that he can have faith in God even if he doesn't fully understand God's ways. It is enough.

PRAYER: Lord of my life, give me the faith to trust you even when I cannot fully understand all that is happening; in Jesus' name. Amen.

JOB 42; PSALMS 100, 101   *Week 26, Day 1*

*A*ll is at last made right. First, Job is made right, for contrary to our usual conceits, our world—large or small—will not come right until we are right. Even if everything around us were perfect, we would not accept or enjoy its perfection as long as our own souls are out of joint. So we must begin with Job, as he confesses a new level of faith:

> "I had heard of you by the hearing of the ear,
>   but now my eye sees you."

And with that seeing comes repentance (42:5, 6).

Job's friends are made right, too. Probably much to their embarrassment they learn that Job has loved God all along, and that they will need his prayers if they are to be restored. (It's interesting that Elihu is not reprimanded with the others.) Then Job's siblings come around and a host of other friends; one wonders where they've been all this time! At any rate, they show him sympathy and bring him gifts.

And then Job's wealth is restored as a kind of symbol of heaven. Everything has been made right; and whatever the sufferings along the way, all is now well. One thing we know for sure: though he wavered (and with reason!), Job kept the faith. He came out as well as God has predicted he would.

PRAYER: I don't want Job's troubles, but give me a measure of his faith; in Jesus' name. Amen.

ECCLESIASTES 1, 2, 3   *Week 26, Day 2*

*E*cclesiastes can easily be seen as the work of someone who has had too much. He's spoiled. In that respect, he may be a good object lesson for much of the middle and upper-middle class of our Western world. But he is also experiencing the kind of struggle any human being can encounter when a person begins to wonder about the purpose and meaning of life. The writer has done us a favor in recording his sometimes gloomy thinking, but as we read each day we need to remember that we're following a soul through his groping and we should wait for the conclusion.

His theme is like an orchestral motif that emerges repeatedly: all of life is a vanity, a waste. He tells us what he has tried, beginning with that cherished goal, wisdom. But it didn't satisfy; it was a "chasing after wind" (1:14). Then, pleasure, including wine and folly, perhaps in the style of people whom we describe today as "living in the fast lane." Then he concentrated on the affluent life: houses, gardens, pools, slaves, gold, culture (singers), and sexual indulgence. He had more than all who were before him in Jerusalem, but it was "vanity."

So he struggles with some preliminary conclusions. Wisdom, he decides, is better than folly, yet no one will remember the wise or the foolish. And if one accumulates riches, it will go to those who haven't worked, so perhaps a person should just live for today (2:24). Then he takes the pragmatic position, which is perhaps the best known portion of this book: "for everything there is a season," good and bad (3:1-8).

PRAYER: Keep me sensitive to the fullness of life in you. Amen.

ECCLESIASTES 4, 5, 6   *Week 26, Day 3*

*A*mong other things, Ecclesiastes shows how important is the hope of life beyond the grave. This writer had no such hope, and therefore he was particularly despairing at some of the disillusionments of life as he observed and experienced it. In many ways, from his vantage point, he was right. He is grieved that "solitary individuals" toil and have no one with whom to share their gains (4:8), and he sees that people who love money and wealth won't be satisfied when they get what they seek (5:10). He is especially troubled for those who work hard yet do not enjoy life's good things, for "do not all go to one place?" (6:6).

So he keeps identifying short-term objectives. "Two are better than one . . . for if they fall, one will lift up the other" (4:9, 10). A three-fold cord (what sociologists would call a triad) is even better, if you can make it work (4:12). And there's hope for "a poor but wise youth," because he may someday replace a foolish king (4:13).

And he has advice for us, too, mostly of a pragmatic kind. Approach the house of God cautiously, minding your tongue (5:1, 2); and if you make a vow, be sure by all means to fulfill it, otherwise it would be better if you hadn't made it (5:4, 5). He is cynical about the oppression of the poor. He acknowledges that it is a bad thing, but he doesn't think much will be done about it—largely because of an ineffective and indifferent bureaucracy (5:8, 9). Sound familiar?

PRAYER: Yes, Lord, I see many reasons to be cynical about life. But I still hope in you, and I still believe in goodness; in Christ. Amen.

ECCLESIASTES 7, 8, 9   Week 26, Day 4

This is a cynical, disillusioned man, no doubt about it. So much so that he feels the day of death is better than the day of birth, and that it is better to go to the house of mourning than to the house of feasting, and that sorrow is better than laughter (7:1-3).

He has come to these conclusions because he has seen so many of life's inequities. He is troubled (as are most of us) that he has seen "righteous people who perish in their righteousness and . . . wicked people who prolong their life in their evil-doing" (7:15). He recalls a "poor wise man" who "by his wisdom delivered the city," yet no one remembered him; his wisdom was despised (9:15, 16). Because of such instances he concludes that "the same fate comes to all, to the righteous and the wicked, to the good and the evil" (9:2). He doesn't think very well of the human race; "the hearts of all are full of evil" (9:3).

Yet he keeps grasping for some verities that will give meaning to life, rather than vanity, and occasionally he finds

some. With all his disappointment in the mistreatment of
the wise, he still praises wisdom; it "makes one's face shine"
(8:1). And he believes that God notices the difference, and
that eventually "it will be well with those who fear God" and
that it "will not be well with the wicked" (8:12, 13). So he
keeps searching. Honor this often unhappy and cynical man
for this, that he keeps searching. In the seeking, there is
hope.

PRAYER: Hardly a day goes by, O Lord, without my seeing
some injustice; help me, nevertheless, to believe in what is
right; in Christ. Amen.

ECCLESIASTES 10, 11, 12   *Week 26, Day 5*

*A*fter all of his struggle and confusion, this cynical man
comes at last to an appeal for faith. But it isn't easy.
A person with his kind of inquiring, speculative mind is
likely to travel a circuitous route before coming to faith.
During that journey he leaves us with a variety of good
counsel. We agree when he warns that "a little folly out-
weighs wisdom and honor" (10:1), for we've seen it happen.
He's right, too, in warning that the curse we entertain even
in our thoughts or the privacy of our bedroom will somehow reach the wrong person (10:20). And we gladly concur
that bread sent out upon the waters will be returned after
many days (11:1).

But especially, we're glad to see him conclude, "Remember
your creator in the days of your youth, before the days of trouble come" (12:1). Does this counsel reflect something that
was missing in his own life, so that he traveled long and far
before finding what he most needed? Perhaps. One feels a
return of his sense of despair as he speaks of old age and the
sorrow of learning the lesson too late (12:2-8).

So the end of the matter, he says, is to "fear God, and keep
his commandments; for that is the whole duty of everyone"
(12:13). And although he doesn't have an eternal view of life,
he nevertheless believes deeply in the justice of God; "God
will bring every deed into judgment, including every secret
thing" (12:14). Better, then, do right!

PRAYER: Thank you, Father, for giving me an early start in

the pathway of faith. Help me influence someone else who is young. Amen.

SONG OF SOLOMON 1, 2, 3; PSALM 102   *Week 26, Day 6*

*T*his is a love song, or perhaps a collection of love songs. Pious Jews read it allegorically as an expression of the love between God and Israel, and generations of Christian scholars saw it as the love between Christ and the Church.

But its basic plot, some say, is the story of a shepherd girl who loves a shepherd of the same village. Her brothers disapprove and move her to a vineyard to keep her from meeting with her shepherd. The king happens upon her there and, struck by her beauty, seeks her love. At his court, the ladies mock her for her love for the shepherd, but the girl dreams only of him. At last the king, impressed by her loyalty to her true love, dismisses her and she rejoins her shepherd. The repeating of "song," in the phrase, "The Song of Songs, which is Solomon's," is a biblical way of saying that this is the greatest of the songs Solomon wrote.

The language of love in this poem is extravagant. It uses imagery that would have meant more to a person in the ancient Middle East than to someone in the modern western world, but with a little empathy we can find ourselves caught up in its beauty. It's easy to see why mystics have used its verses to express their love for God, because the language is so enrapturing. Use it as you see best, but recognize that it is, at the least, a biblical tribute to the beauty of physical, married love.

PRAYER: Thank you, dear Lord, for giving us human beings the capacity for friendship and love. Help us to use it well; in Christ. Amen.

SONG OF SOLOMON 4, 5, 6   *Week 26, Day 7*

*W*hen I go to a symphony I can listen with a program guide that will explain the movement of the music and its significance, or I can simply sit back and enjoy the sensation without trying overly hard to intellectualize it. I recom-

146

mend something of a middle ground in reading this book. Many modern Bibles have broken down the passages to indicate who is speaking at a given moment; these aids can be helpful, but they don't all agree, and they don't necessarily increase our enjoyment or perception. The material is best read slowly and thoughtfully, but not too analytically. There are times when we should turn off our critical sensibilities, and this may be one of them.

Every culture has its own language of love because we have to find our figures of speech in the images that are significant to our time and place. Here was a people who found beauty in the world of nature in ways rather beyond us. We may be amused when the man says that the hair of his beloved is "like a flock of goats, moving down the slopes of Gilead" (4:1), but it was a vivid, lovely scene to him; and we stumble still more when he describes her neck as "like the tower of David, / built in courses" (4:4). But we understand what he means when he says,

> "You are altogether beautiful, my love;
> there is no flaw in you." (4:7)

That spells love in any language, any time. And that's how he felt.

PRAYER: Help me, I pray, to see the beauty in other cultures and other times, that my life may be deeper and wider; in Jesus' name. Amen.

SONG OF SOLOMON 7, 8; PSALM 103   *Week 27, Day 1*

The Song of Solomon is one of the most ancient recorded expressions of love, and it has blessed many thousands over the centuries, both those who have seen it as an allegorical expression of the divine-human relationship and those who have read it as a purely human love song. Many modern Jews have two phrases from this book carved into the wedding band or embossed on marriage contracts: "My beloved is mine and I am his" (2:16), and "I am my beloved's, and his desire is for me" (7:10).

The language of love reaches something of a peak as the writer says:

"Many waters cannot quench love,
    neither can floods drown it.
If one offered for love
    all the wealth of his house,
    it would be utterly scorned." (8:7)

Anything so precious comes, of course, at a high price. We can't really experience love without giving it, and we can't give it without making ourselves vulnerable. One religious philosophy says that happiness exists in learning not to love, for as surely as one loves—even if the love be only for a pet—one will experience pain in its loss. But Christianity and Judaism contend that love is worth the pain, and the Christian gospel gives God's measure of it in saying that he so loved the world that he gave his only begotten Son. Such love, indeed, cannot be quenched.

PRAYER: Teach me, I pray, to love ever more fully; in Christ. Amen.

ISAIAH 1, 2, 3   *Week 27, Day 2*

*W*e met Isaiah quite some time ago, in his influence on King Hezekiah. Jewish tradition places him second only to Moses in greatness. He began to prophesy in the last year of King Uzziah (740 B.C.) and continued through the reigns of Jotham, Ahaz, and Hezekiah. One tradition says he was put to death by King Manasseh.

This book is an intermittent mix of wrath and hope. The prophet opens with the burden of God's pain, that "the ox knows its owner, / and the donkey its master's crib; / but Israel does not know, / my people do not understand" (1:3). Isaiah then attacks the very base of their religious practices. God says, "I have had enough of burnt offerings. . . . Your new moons and your appointed festivals / my soul hates" (1:11, 14). That's hard language for religious people; how would we respond if Isaiah said to us, "God hates your stewardship pledges, your church conferences, your hymns and anthems and liturgies"?

But Isaiah wants, in the name of God, to bring the people back to honest, heart-deep faith, and he promises:

"Come now, let us argue it out, says the LORD:
though your sins are like scarlet, they shall be like snow;
though they be red like crimson, they shall become like wool."
(1:18)

God offers hope for those who want more than superficial religiosity; he gives the prospect of vital spiritual communion.

PRAYER: Save me, O Lord, from religion that simply goes through the motions; take lodging deep in my heart and conduct; in Jesus' name. Amen.

ISAIAH 4, 5, 6; PSALM 104   *Week 27, Day 3*

*E*very great effect has to have an adequate cause. When one sees a ministry as profound as Isaiah's, one wonders what made it happen. Isaiah gives the answer when he describes his experience in the temple "in the year that King Uzziah died" (6:1). It was a crisis time for the people. They had had the same ruler for over fifty years, and while he had not always done right, on the whole he had been a good and effective king. Now that he has gone, what would happen?

When Isaiah experiences the shattering holiness of God, he is struck first of all that he is "a man of unclean lips" who lives "among a people of unclean lips" (6:5). Any time we think words are incidental, we need only ponder that Isaiah's revelation of the glory of God caused him, first of all, to be distressed at what was passing through his lips.

Isaiah accepts his call and learns immediately that it will be a heartbreaking assignment, because he must minister until "cities lie waste . . . and the land is utterly desolate" (6:11).

He is working with a people who have repeatedly rejected and disappointed God. The history of their relationship is summarized in the love-song for the vineyard. God had invested heavily in this vineyard, Judah, and when it was time for a return on the divine investment there were not grapes but "wild grapes" (5:1-4). So now judgment will have to come, and it is Isaiah's job to declare it.

PRAYER: When next I go to your house, O Lord, give me a revelation of yourself that will change my speech and conduct; in Christ. Amen.

*T*hese chapters contain two passages that have been cherished by Christians since the earliest days of the faith. Both have been seen traditionally as prophecies concerning Christ. The first (7:14) promises, "Look, the young woman [Greek Septuagint, "virgin"] is with child and shall bear a son, and shall name him Immanuel." The Gospel of Matthew quotes this verse in one of the many instances where it declares that Jesus is the fulfillment of prophecy (Matt. 1:22, 23).

The other passage (9:2-7) is a favorite of the Christmas season; part of it constitutes one of the most dramatic portions of Handel's *Messiah*: "For unto us a child is born, unto us a son is given: and the government shall be upon his shoulder" (9:6 KJV).

It seems clear that Isaiah has in mind something relatively close to his own times, yet there is also the feeling of a farther view, as if he were getting a kind of double exposure of a near shot and a distant one. How does one dare to say when a Hebrew prophet is speaking of some distant event or simply of an occasion in his own lifetime, or nearly so? One easily imagines what bizarre ideas might be introduced (and are!) if passages are applied and adapted indiscriminately. Do we have any guide? It seems to me that we have a basic and safe rule of thumb in this: that we interpret a passage as being beyond the prophet's rather immediate time only when the New Testament does so.

PRAYER: Help me, I pray, to find all that is in your Book, but save me from reading into it things that are not there; in Christ. Amen.

*I*saiah, like all the Hebrew prophets, is convinced that tyranny, arrogance, and unrighteousness will cause a nation to fall. The judgment of God is written into such situations. And this is true whether the nation be a pagan people or Israel or Judah.

The act of judgment usually comes through human instrumentality. In this instance, Assyria is "the rod of my anger" (10:5). But Assyria doesn't recognize that she is being used of God, feeling that she is powerful in her own right (10:8-11), so in time God "will punish the arrogant boasting of the king of Assyria" (10:12). And eventually the "remnant of Israel" will return to God, and the country will be restored (10:20-27).

Isaiah 11 is one of those passages which Christians have for many centuries seen as prophecy fulfilled in Jesus Christ. The message must have been especially heartening in Isaiah's day, as they saw their national enemies growing stronger and wondered if ever there would be a better day. In warm and moving language, Isaiah assures them that such a time is coming, when

> The wolf shall live with the lamb,
>   the leopard shall lie down with the kid,
> the calf and the lion and the fatling together,
>   and a little child shall lead them. (11:6)

That dream, that hope, impels us still.

PRAYER: Make me, O Lord, an instrument of your purposes. Amen.

ISAIAH 13, 14, 15, 16   *Week 27, Day 6*

*J*saiah's prophecies run the course of Judah and her neighbors, in this instance with messages to Babylon, Assyria, Philistia, and Moab. They are warned of the judgment of God, and are begged to desert their patterns of pride and arrogance.

A passage in chapter 14 tells of the "fall from heaven" of one called the "Day Star, son of Dawn" (14:12). The Latin Vulgate and the King James Version used the term *Lucifer* for this person. Early Bible students saw this as a reference to the devil and understood it to be the story of the first rebellion against God and thus as the beginning of the conflict of right and wrong. John Milton followed this idea in his classic, *Paradise Lost*. These early interpreters (and some to this day) understood the passage that way because the subject is guilty of ultimate presumption against God, saying:

> "I will ascend to heaven;
> I will raise my throne
>   above the stars of God; . . .
> I will make myself like the Most High." (14:13, 14)

We bother ourselves a good deal about the beginnings of evil, and of course it is a fascinating philosophical and theological question. But from a pragmatic point of view, it isn't the most important one. That is, the issue is not who first rebelled against God or brought evil into the world, but how do I, in my life, deal with it.

PRAYER: Help me, I pray, to win in my personal struggle with evil. Amen.

ISAIAH 17, 18, 19   *Week 27, Day 7*

The prophet Isaiah continues to direct his prophecies to a variety of ancient nations; here we have Damascus, Ethiopia (Cush), and Egypt. The final word for each of these countries is that they will acknowledge God. So the day will come, Isaiah says, when the people of Damascus "will regard their Maker, and their eyes will look to the Holy One of Israel" (17:7). So, too, with Ethiopia. In time "gifts will be brought to the LORD of hosts from a people tall and smooth" (18:7).

And in Egypt, there will come a time when "there will be five cities . . . that speak the language of Canaan [that is, accept Israel's way] and swear allegiance to the LORD of hosts." There will even be "an altar to the LORD in the center of the land of Egypt, and a pillar to the LORD at its border" (19:18, 19).

I don't think Isaiah's prophecy has ever been literally fulfilled. Perhaps its fulfillment is still to come. Isaiah understood, with his enlightened insight, that any significant peace would have a spiritual quality. He saw a time when Egpyt, Assyria, and Israel would be "a blessing in the midst of the earth" so that God will say of them, "Blessed be Egypt my people, and Assyria the work of my hands, and Israel my heritage" (19:24). That kind of peaceful alliance would look wondrous even in this late twentieth century.

PRAYER: As I read the news of the world in the daily press, I ask that you will bring peace among the nations of the earth; in Christ. Amen.

ISAIAH 20, 21, 22, 23   *Week 28, Day 1*

*J*saiah becomes an object-lesson preacher in chapter 20. This is often the case with the prophets; Hosea's home life is a full-scale object lesson, and Jonah's wandering itinerary, too. The dramatic presentation was calculated to make the message stay with the hearer/viewers.

As we read Isaiah's oracles for Babylon, Edom, Arabia, and Tyre, as well as Jerusalem, we are reminded again that the man or woman of God carries a great load because he or she accepts burdens and concerns far beyond the self. To love God is to live with a large globe. This is a heavy task, as Isaiah, I'm sure, came to know.

But it also means a far bigger world. It is quite inconceivable to be a Christian and live a small, narrow life. To have God's view means to extend one's boundaries wonderfully. This was a lesson for the Jews, in the era of the prophets, because in the process of seeing themselves as God's special witnesses (as indeed they were), they easily slipped over into thinking that they were the only ones that mattered. Christians sometimes get the same outlook. We forget that our uniqueness is for the purpose of blessing others, not for the purpose of isolating and exalting ourselves.

There's a wonderful side benefit in the enlarging of our world: we get ourselves off our hands a bit. If our borders are too small, we're likely to become miserably self-centered. Seeing the world through God's eyes will save us from that.

PRAYER: Make my heart in your image, O Lord, loving your world. Amen.

ISAIAH 24, 25, 26   *Week 28, Day 2*

*J*t is often difficult for us to see the logical order in Isaiah's prophecies; they seem to skip from one subject to another without any apparent order. Perhaps they constitute a collection of prophetic works over an extended period, with no attempt at order; or perhaps, on the other hand, they have an order that we don't easily discern, since we come from a different culture and a different style of learning.

We have sad songs in chapter 24, as the prophet describes the desolation that is coming on the earth. It will reach all classes of people equally (24:2). And if one wonders why there is such utter destruction, Isaiah makes it clear: "transgression lies heavy upon it" (24:20).

But then, a song of thanksgiving. The language makes us think of similar words in Revelation:

> Then the Lord GOD will wipe away the tears from all faces,
>   and the disgrace of his people he will take away from all the
>   earth. . . .
> It will be said on that day,
>   Lo, this is our God; we have waited for him, so that he might
>   save us. (25:8, 9)

The prophet continues in a similar vein as he rejoices in victory. Generations of believers have loved 26:3 as it reads in the King James Version: "Thou wilt keep him in perfect peace, whose mind is stayed on thee: because he trusteth in thee." It was good for Isaiah and good for us.

PRAYER: Help me, indeed, to keep my mind on you; in Christ. Amen.

ISAIAH 27, 28, 29   *Week 28, Day 3*

When Isaiah says, on God's behalf, that "this is a people without understanding; / therefore he that made them will not have compassion on them" (27:11), it sounds very harsh. Why would people be rejected for their failure to understand? Yet Jesus expresses something of the same idea in the parable of the sower, when he says of the seed which fell on the roadway that it represents anyone who "hears the word of the kingdom and does not understand it" (Matt. 13:19). It is a failure not of intellectual apprehension, but of moral response. To understand, from a biblical point of view, is to accept, to make it one's own.

154

The same issue is stated another way when the prophet complains:

> Because these people draw near with their mouths
> and honor me with their lips,
> while their hearts are far from me,
> and their worship of me is a human commandment
> learned by rote . . . (29:13)

As Jesus said to the woman of Samaria, God looks for a people who will worship in spirit and in truth (John 4:24).

For those who do, life has a strong foundation (28:16). Those who trust "will not panic," because "justice [is] the line, / and righteousness the plummet" (28:17). Cultural norms and mores flow with the headlines in our times, but righteousness and justice change not.

PRAYER: Help me, I pray, to build my life and my thinking on the sure foundation of your truth and righteousness; in Jesus' name. Amen.

ISAIAH 30, 31, 32   *Week 28, Day 4*

One of the signs of the latter days is that people will have "itching ears" so that they will "accumulate for themselves teachers to suit their own desires" (2 Tim. 4:3). Isaiah faced the same problem in his day. The people were telling the seers not to see, and were saying to the prophets, "Do not prophesy to us what is right; / speak to us smooth things, prophesy illusions" (30:10). We want to hear words that will make us feel good, even if the feeling is only temporary. That's why the prophets' job was so often a lonely one; not because they always spoke of doom but because they insisted that we must do right before we can expect blessing. It's the insistence on doing right that is so troublesome to most of us.

For Judah, at this point, doing right meant not calling on Egypt for help. Isaiah warned that "the Egyptians are human, and not God; their horses are flesh, and not spirit" (31:3)— and as we read his words, we can almost imagine someone in his ancient audience saying, cynically, "That's what I want in battle—horses that are flesh. Spirit will do for a tranquil day." That's our mood much of the time. We think of God and

155

faith as a last resort, but "practical people" depend on practical solutions. Of course the scriptures never suggested that we should leave it all to God; we're supposed to do what is in our power. But relying on the Egpytians was to trust in their pagan faith, and that was a denial of the Lord God.

PRAYER: Help me to do what I can, and to trust you for the rest. Amen.

ISAIAH 33, 34, 35 Week 28, Day 5

*B*oth the secular optimist and the secular pessimist will be disappointed in the Bible. It is too realistic for either one. The secular optimist wants only good news, without facing the hard work (including repenting), without which real good news is impossible. The confirmed pessimist is equally disappointed because even in the times of greatest distress there is unrelenting hope in the scriptures.

In chapters 33 and 34 we have a promise of deliverance, but it is set in the midst of judgment. The details of the judgment are particularly severe and graphic:

> Their land shall be soaked with blood,
>   and their soil made rich with fat. (34:7)

But suddenly, in the midst of what seems like increasing gloom, we come upon one of the loveliest pictures of hope to be found anywhere:

> The wilderness and the dry land shall be glad,
>   the desert shall rejoice and blossom. (35:1)

In the light of such hope, the weary pilgrims are encouraged to "strengthen the weak hands, and make firm the feeble knees" (35:3). The writer of the New Testament letter to the Hebrews uses this same language to encourage his generation of believers who are tempted to give up (Heb. 12:12). "Joy and gladness" are coming, and "sorrow and sighing shall flee away" (35:10). Hold on, hold on; good days are coming!

PRAYER: Help me to remain strong, O Lord, in times of struggle. Amen.

156

*I*saiah now interrupts his prophecy to give us some history. Biblical prophecy is always set in history, and biblical history speaks with the accents of prophecy. Which is to say that the scriptures see God at work on the human scene. The writers of Judges, Kings, and Chronicles are never content to offer nothing but dates and events; they put their historical data in a moral context. On the other hand, the prophets never speak in a vacuum; their preachments are set in the cauldron of historic events.

The historical material in this section has already come to our attention in 2 Kings and 2 Chronicles. King Hezekiah is himself a godly person, but in his time of crisis, he seeks help from Isaiah. We need one another; life wasn't meant to be a solitary business. Fortunately, Isaiah has something to offer. He not only brings an encouraging word ("Do not be afraid"), he tells Hezekiah how help will come.

I am always impressed with Hezekiah's handling of King Sennacherib's letter. He went to the right place—"the house of the LORD"—and did the right thing—he spread the letter before God (37:14). With such a procedure, he got a different perspective. In this instance, Hezekiah was saved by a miraculous intervention. In most cases, the new perspective gives us the opportunity to use our own gifts to their full potential. And that's a miracle in its own right.

PRAYER: Help me, dear Lord, to see you at work in my life. Amen.

*W*e human beings are a mixed bag, and Hezekiah, one of the best of Judah's kings, shows it. In an illness that brings him to the point of death, Hezekiah seeks God with great earnestness. He doesn't want to die just yet; most of us can understand that. He had had a good life and he wanted more of it. He probably felt that his nation needed him, and with good reason.

God granted his request and extended his life. But during

those extra years he entertained a delegation from the king of Babylon and he did a foolish thing, born—as so many foolish deeds are—of pride. He showed off his possessions. It was a naive, childish act, almost as if he were asking for trouble, and God warned him that the trouble would come.

But it would come in his children's lifetime, not his. Here again we see something of the underside of Hezekiah's character. It's good, he thought, because "there will be peace and security in my days" (39:8). Hezekiah was not the first person to buy some benefit for which his descendants would have to pay, nor would he be the last. A nation that goes madly into debt or that squanders earth's natural resources is in the same category. But no one would consider this an honorable attitude, and we're disappointed that Hezekiah could be at peace with it.

PRAYER: Help me to have a good conscience, dear Lord, not only for my own time but for the generation that will follow; in your name. Amen.

ISAIAH 40, 41, 42   *Week 29, Day 1*

A wise man said that preaching ought to comfort the afflicted and afflict the comfortable. In truth, that is the prophetic pattern. At this point the prophet (some feel it is a different one from the author of the earlier chapters) calls for comfort for God's people. Perhaps no passage more effectively fulfills that assignment.

Each of the four Gospels quotes a portion of 40:3-5 by way of introducing the ministry of John the Baptist as the forerunner of Christ. Verse 11 is often seen as a description of Jesus Christ as the Shepherd; this verse has a memorable place in Handel's *Messiah*.

Isaiah probably strikes out more vigorously against idols than any other prophet. This is consistent with his emphasis on the glory and power of God. Here, between two moving statements about God's majesty, he interjects with a touch of scorn, "To whom then will you liken God . . . ? [to] wood that will . . . rot[?]" (40:18, 20).

But the glory of Isaiah's God is not only his great might, but that this might is used to bless and empower the helpless and the needy. God gives such power to the faint and the powerless that though "even youths will faint and be weary, . . . those who wait for the LORD shall renew their strength, / they shall mount up with wings like eagles, / they shall run and not be weary, / they shall walk and not faint" (40:30, 31).

PRAYER: I am grateful that you use your power, O Lord, not only in the glory of creation but also in sustaining the weary; in Christ. Amen.

ISAIAH 43, 44, 45   *Week 29, Day 2*

*T*he prophet continues his case against idols. Once again he points out their absurdity, between his descriptions of the goodness and power of God. He reminds us, too, of God's caring love:

> When you pass through the waters, I will be with you;
>   and through the rivers, they shall not overwhelm you. (43:2)

But not only does God care for us, he provides forgiveness:

> I, I am He who blots out your transgressions for my own sake,
>   and I will not remember your sins. (43:25)

By contrast, the idols are something an ironsmith fashions, then bows down to what his own hands have made; or a cedar that one has planted and watched grow, but now cuts and divides so that part becomes wood that he burns to warm himself and the rest a god to which he bows down, saying, "Save me, for you are my god!" (44:14-17).

But again, see the power of God. The Lord will take a foreign king, Cyrus, and will say, "He is my shepherd, / and he shall carry out all my purpose" (44:28). Cyrus doesn't know the Lord, but the Lord will use him nevertheless (45:4, 5). So Isaiah wonders why, with such a God as this, anyone would "carry about their wooden idols, / and keep on praying to a god that cannot save" (45:20).

Our generation, which has a love affair with the wonders of its own creating, ought to listen well. We have our idols, too.

PRAYER: Help me, I pray, never to confuse the works of my hands and mind with your everlasting glory; in Jesus' name. Amen.

159

typical

$\mathcal{I}$ saiah's anger with idol worship may seem strange to our culture, where we know nothing about idols as a visible form of worship. In our time he would attack materialism. The apostle Paul says as much when he equates greed with idolatry (Col. 3:5).

The prophet's wrath is especially poignant because he sees that idols are dead, helpless, and impersonal, while his own experience with God has been so vital. He reminds the people that they have to "stoop [and] bow down" to carry their idols, while we have been "carried from the womb" by the Lord; "even when you turn gray I will carry you," God promises (46:1-4). And Isaiah wonders how anyone could possibly compare God with such as these "as though [they] were alike" (46:5).

How personal is God's care? The prophet uses the most vivid image imaginable:

Can a woman forget her nursing child,
or show no compassion for the child of her womb? (49:15)

Very unlikely, he says, but even that could happen before God will forget you. Because, you see, "I have inscribed you on the palms of my hands" (49:16). Charles Wesley applied Isaiah's figure of speech to the crucifixion wounds of Christ and said, in one of his greatest hymns, "My name is written on His hands." We cannot be forgotten by such love.

PRAYER: I am grateful, dear Lord, that in our often impersonal world, I am not unknown to you; you have inscribed me on your hands. Amen.

$\mathcal{Q}$ uite often the prophet seems to go rather quickly from speaking in a personal vein, then in the national/historic. This would not be as great a leap for the original hearers and readers, because Jews saw themselves as part of the corporate body of God's people, yet retaining their individual identity. We don't have the same sense of corporate unity, not even in the church—though certainly the New Testament would encourage us to do so.

But even when the passages in Isaiah are concerned with the nation, one is moved at a personal level. Through the centuries, Christians have seen prophetic significance in Isaiah's words,

> I gave my back to those who struck me,
>> and my cheeks to those who pulled out the beard;
> I did not hide my face from insult and spitting (50:6)

because they seem so descriptive of Jesus' suffering at the time of trial and crucifixion.

The prophet's words, "Look to the rock from which you were hewn," a passage identified with the Jews and their tie to Abraham and Sarah (51:1, 2), are also descriptive of our own faith heritage. And our hearts respond when Isaiah promises, "So the ransomed of the LORD shall return . . . and sorrow and sighing shall flee away" (51:11) because we have experienced God's faithfulness in some personal time of sorrow or distress.

PRAYER: Thank you for the good words which, by faith, are mine. Amen.

ISAIAH 52, 53, 54   *Week 29, Day 5*

Since New Testament times Christians have looked upon Isaiah 52:13–53:12 as a description of the suffering Messiah. These verses are often read as part of Holy Week observances and in the celebration of holy communion. Some contemporary scholars see the section, however, as referring to an unnamed "suffering servant" of God—perhaps the nation of Israel itself.

We can never finally know what was the intention of the ancient prophet in this passage, nor the purpose of the Holy Spirit. But the devout feel a sense of adoration as they study this picture of One who chooses to suffer for others:

> But he was wounded for our transgressions,
>> crushed for our iniquities;
> upon him was the punishment that made us whole,
>> and by his bruises we are healed. (53:5)

And the penitent see themselves in the words:

> All we like sheep have gone astray;
>   we have all turned to our own way,
> and the LORD has laid on him the iniquity of us all. (53:6)

Several hundred years ago an anonymous poet asked, "What language shall I borrow, to thank thee, dearest friend?" Sometimes the devout look not so much for the language of understanding as for a medium of adoration. Isaiah provides that. We can borrow his language.

PRAYER: I do so worship thee, dearest Friend. Amen.

ISAIAH 55, 56, 57; PSALM 109   *Week 29, Day 6*

*H*enry David Thoreau said that the mass of people live lives of quiet desperation. For many it may be even more a matter of bland routine in which there are few moments of exalting purpose or joy. Isaiah turns street corner evangelist in making a startling offer that should appeal to both:

> Ho, everyone who thirsts, come to the waters;
>   and you that have no money, come, buy and eat!
> Come, buy wine and milk
>   without money and without price. (55:1)

Unfortunately, many choose instead to content themselves with "that which does not satisfy" (55:2). Why would we do such a thing? Why miss the life exuberant to have instead a life tedious? Quite simply (so simply that some resent it) because we will not "return to the LORD, that he may have mercy" on us (55:7). Of course, returning to the Lord has a price. It requires that we "maintain justice, and do what is right" (56:1). But again, why would we want to live any other way? Especially when one ponders the amazing grace of One who dwells "in the high and holy place," yet is ready also to meet "with those who are contrite and humble in spirit" (57:15). Because of our spiritual myopia, we don't realize that when we are humble and contrite, we take on the quality of the truly high and holy.

PRAYER: Forgive me, Lord, for being sometimes content in the lowlands of life. Lead me on, please, to higher ground; in Christ. Amen.

*L*ike so many other Hebrew prophets, Isaiah pleaded for consistent religion of the heart. He rebuked the people for their surface piety, for going through the motions of fasting and humility, but only for their own interests (58:2-4). God is looking for something better. Here is the fast, Isaiah says, that God has chosen:

> to loose the bonds of injustice,
> to undo the thongs of the yoke,
> to let the oppressed go free . . .
> . . . to share your bread with the hungry,
> and bring the homeless poor into your house. (58:6, 7)

The message could hardly be more appropriate to our own times. Nor could it be more upsetting, if we are guilty of superficial religion.

But neither would Isaiah be satisfied with simple social service. He reminds the people of their ritual obligations, especially in relationship to the sabbath. They had been using the holy day for pursuing their own interests and going their own ways (58:13, 14)—perhaps the ancient equivalent of Sundays spent at shopping malls or sporting events. God, meanwhile, is waiting to meet us; "the LORD's hand is not too short to save, nor his ear too dull to hear./Rather, your iniquities have been barriers between you and your God" (59:1, 2).

PRAYER: Give me, I pray, a religion that respects my relationship with you and cares about the world around me; in Jesus' name. Amen.

*W*hen Jesus returned to his home town, Nazareth, to teach for the first time, he chose as his text Isaiah 61:1. When he had finished reading the passage, he announced, "Today this scripture has been fulfilled in your hearing" (Luke 4:21). The words from Isaiah are so full of grace that we're not surprised the people received the word with gladness— until it occurred to them that Jesus was making strong claims for just a hometown boy.

So many of the verses in this section are gracious words of hope. Not only are the people promised that they will receive "the oil of gladness instead of mourning,/ the mantle of praise instead of a faint spirit" (61:3), but they are told that whereas once they were a people named "Forsaken" living in a land "termed Desolate," now they would be called "My Delight Is in Her" (62:4).

But Isaiah knows how perilous their position is, because he realizes:

> We have long been like those whom you do not rule,
> like those not called by your name. (63:19)

We become so conditioned by an alien culture that we seem almost to lose our identity as part of the family of God. Worse, we become so absorbed in the alien culture that we don't realize that our godly identity has been lost; we don't realize how far we have strayed.

PRAYER: Help me to love this world in which I live, but to keep unbroken my ties to you and your will; in Christ. Amen.

ISAIAH 64, 65, 66   *Week 30, Day 2*

*I*saiah's prophecies end with a mixture of blessings and judgments, a pattern we have seen often in this book. Perhaps we wonder if this sometimes uneasy juxtaposition of material is the work of some ancient editor or of the author himself, and why they would be so apparently haphazard. Or is it, perhaps, because life is indeed like this, so if God is to speak to our imperfect world, it will be with a voice that alternates between blessing and warning?

The prophet grieves because even their "righteous deeds are like a filthy cloth" (64:6). He appeals to God, "Do not remember iniquity forever" (64:9). But the problem, God answers, is that he has been ready all along to be found by them, yet

> when I called, you did not answer,
> when I spoke, you did not listen. (65:12)

I expect our dialogue with heaven will always follow some such lines. We think sometimes that we're doing rather well, and we congratulate ourselves on our sensitivity to God and our world. But then comes a moment of enlightenment when we realize just how far we have fallen short of God's expectations and of our own potential. Our faith journey is made up of just such fits and starts. Fortunately, God doesn't give up on us, so we oughtn't to give up on ourselves.

PRAYER: Be with me, dear Savior, in the ebb and flow of my life; and in the end, make me more nearly in your image, in your name. Amen.

JEREMIAH 1, 2, 3; PSALM 110   *Week 30, Day 3*

*P*resident Franklin Roosevelt told Depression-era America that some generations have a "rendezvous with destiny." Jeremiah's generation had a rendezvous with despair. It was not an easy time to be God's prophet. It isn't surprising that Jeremiah wept a lot.

He came from priestly stock and was called to the prophetic ministry when he was still young—so young that he objected that he wasn't really qualified, because "I am only a boy" (1:6). But God answered that he would speak whatever was commanded, without fear, because "I have put my words in your mouth" (1:9).

The message begins plaintively, as God recalls the relationship with Israel in their earliest days. But they so soon and so often forgot God, committing a double evil: "they have forsaken me, / the fountain of living water, / and dug out cisterns for themselves, / cracked cisterns that can hold no water" (2:13). This language of logic is compelling; how on earth could one give up fresh water to eke out existence from a broken cistern of essential emptiness? Now Jeremiah turns to a more emotional image. He reminds the people that they have been God's beloved bride, yet they have responded in shameless unfaithfulness and "have played the whore with many lovers" (3:1). How can God deal with a people who are so indifferent to his love, so scornful of divine caring?

PRAYER: I'm sure, dear Savior, that I am often thoughtless of your caring; forgive me, I pray, and draw me to yourself; in Christ. Amen.

*E*ach person is responsible for his or her own soul, but some people, by virtue of their office, have added responsibility. In Israel and Judah, this was true of three groups—the rulers, the priests, and the prophets. The latter two were especially significant because they were the moral conscience of the people and the voice of God. In the midst of Jeremiah's distress, the failure of these two groups is repeatedly mentioned: "the prophets are nothing but wind" (5:13); "the prophets prophesy falsely, / and the priests rule as the prophets direct" (5:31); "from prophet to priest, / everyone deals falsely" (6:13). And the worst of it all is this, that "my people love to have it so" (5:31). There is hope in even the worst of times if God still has a witness among those who speak for righteousness; but when these voices are corrupted, then how are the people to know the truth? Still worse, if the people sense that these messengers are misleading them, but like it that way—well, then, what hope is there?

And with it all, the people "were not ashamed, / they did not know how to blush" (6:15). This describes, it seems to me, a version of the unpardonable sin—a state of soul in which people have so shut themselves off from correction that they are incapable of response. And to think that this could happen to a people chosen by God!

PRAYER: I know the hardening of the heart is a slow process; stop such action in my soul before it even begins; in Jesus' name. Amen.

*T*he singular burden of Jeremiah's ministry is that it seems so much of the time to be without hope. God instructs him, "Do not pray for this people, do not raise a cry or prayer on their behalf . . . for I will not hear you" (7:16). It seems Jeremiah still has in his heart a longing for the deliverance of his people, because of his love for them and for the purposes of God in their lives, yet even God does not sympathize with his longing. So Jeremiah recognizes that it is too late:

> "The harvest is past, the summer is ended,
>   and we are not saved." (8:20)

No wonder, then, that he cannot find tears enough to carry the weight of his sorrow:

> O that my head were a spring of water,
>   and my eyes a fountain of tears,
> so that I might weep day and night
>   for the slain of my poor people! (9:1)

For the people of God are not that different from the people around them. The pagan nations are uncircumcised, but "the house of Israel is uncircumcised in heart" (9:26). They have the outward sign of their religion, but within they are as pagan as those who have never encountered the Lord God. Religious rituals without heart commitment are meaningless.

PRAYER: Thank you, O God, for those like Jeremiah who continue to be burdened for human failure even when the cause seems hopeless. Amen.

JEREMIAH 10, 11, 12; PSALM 111 *Week 30, Day 6*

*T*here are seasons in the human soul. The warrior of one day can be the frightened child of another. Jeremiah is fearless in his scornful attack on idolatry; he sounds like Isaiah as he mocks the idols that "are like scarecrows in a cucumber field" (10:5). But then he is crushed by the unfaithfulness of the people in breaking the covenant of God; how can they walk "in the stubbornness of an evil will" and turn "back to the iniquities of their ancestors of old" (11:8, 10)?

Then Jeremiah discovers that the people he has loved so much and to whom he has prophesied with such longing are waiting to slay him, "so that his name will no longer be remembered" (11:19). Under such a threat, he tries to reason with God:

> You will be in the right, O LORD,
>   when I lay charges against you;
> but let me put my case to you. (12:1)

What a hearty soul Jeremiah is, knowing he cannot win but insisting on his right to put his case before God!

It seems he gets little sympathy. "If you have raced with foot-runners and they have wearied you, / how will you compete with horses?" (12:5). Yet God encourages him still, by assuring him that one day he will "again have compassion" on Judah (12:15). Hold steady, Jeremiah!

PRAYER: I am very grateful, O God, that you will allow me to argue with you, even when I know you will win. Thank you! Amen.

JEREMIAH 13, 14, 15   *Week 30, Day 7*

*J*eremiah is in the peculiar position (one that Moses occupied on several occasions) of seeming to care more about the people than God does. It is as if God were pushing Jeremiah to see the degree of his commitment to the people, forcing him to recognize the seriousness of their offenses. God reminds the prophet of the abominations, the adulteries, the shameless prostitutions of the people (13:27); how can one expect that a people like this will change?

Then Jeremiah has to cope also with the tragedy of a drought. He confesses that the iniquities of the people are many, but reminds God that "we are called by your name; do not forsake us" (14:9). But Jeremiah has no idea how badly the people have cut themselves off from God. So much so, the Lord says, that even if "Moses and Samuel stood before me, yet my heart would not turn toward this people" (15:1). It was Moses who twice stood to defend Israel before God, and Samuel who said, "God forbid that I should sin against the Lord in ceasing to pray for you." If these two, who pleaded so passionately and effectively for the people, cannot be heard, then what hope is there?

The issue is this, that at some point the people (or an individual) must turn Godward for themselves; no one else's prayers can be ultimately effective without the cooperation of the object of the prayer.

PRAYER: Give me, I pray, something of Jeremiah's unceasing love for people, that I will not lose heart even when they reject you. Amen.

168

*I*f at times Jeremiah is convinced that God has irrevocably given up on Judah, there is always an encouraging word. The day is coming, he is assured, when they will refer not simply to their long-ago deliverance from Egypt, but for deliverance "out of the land of the north" (16:14, 15). Then "they shall know that my name is the LORD" (16:21).

Meanwhile, Jeremiah again has troubles of his own. When the people mock his preaching, he prays, "let them be dismayed, / but do not let me be dismayed" (17:18). Then he hears again that they are plotting against him, recompensing his good with evil, and he asks God:

> Remember how I stood before you,
>   to speak good for them,
>   to turn away your wrath from them. (18:20)

Yet now they have turned against him.

But he is sustained by his communion with God, and by the continuing revelation of the supremacy of God. At the potter's house he gets a dramatic portrayal of the dissimilarity between God and humans. God is the potter, and it is his right to deal with the clay as he wishes. As Paul would say later, drawing upon this scene, it is the potter's privilege to make from the clay "one object for special use and another for ordinary use" (Rom. 9:21). God, after all, is God.

PRAYER: Give me the faith, I pray, to trust you with the clay of my life, knowing that your will for me is always, ultimately, good. Amen.

*J*eremiah tells us more about the circumstances of his preaching and his personal anguish than any other prophet. One of his greatest disappointments comes when, himself a priest, he is humiliated by a fellow priest, Pashur, who strikes him, then puts him in stocks for a night. Jeremiah responds angrily upon his release; but alone with God afterward, he confesses the struggle of his soul. He feels God has betrayed and overpowered him. If he could, he would stop prophesying. But he can't; when he says, "I will not speak any more in his name,"

> then within me there is something like a burning fire
> shut up in my bones;
> I am weary with holding it in, and I cannot. (20:9)

Jeremiah's call to preach and the "fire in his bones" are more than he can contain. Whatever the circumstances—even when he wishes he had never been born—he will speak for the Lord.

His message continues to be a difficult one. King Zedekiah's messengers hope Jeremiah will give some word of reprieve from the Lord, of the kind Israel and Judah have received so often in the past. Not so, Jeremiah answers, because God has set his face "against this city for evil and not for good" (21:10). However much Jeremiah might want to speak a comforting word, he is compelled to speak a harsh one.

PRAYER: Whatever the circumstances of the times in which I live, O Lord, help me to hold fast to your will; in Jesus' name. Amen.

JEREMIAH 22, 23, 24; PSALM 112   *Week 31, Day 3*

As surely as there are prophets of God, there are false prophets. This shouldn't really surprise us. Perhaps there is no better proof of the validity of the prophetic ministry than that there are counterfeits, because counterfeits are developed only to compete with that which is of value. And the greater the value of the real, the more certainly some will try to counterfeit it.

In a time like Jeremiah's, false prophets would seem especially attractive. Jeremiah's message wasn't pleasant for a people who wanted a comforting word. They hoped someone would say, "Peace, peace," even though there was no peace (8:11). Jeremiah's contemporaries were speaking "visions of their own minds, not from the mouth of the LORD" (23:16). God is against such prophets. When they ask, "What is the burden of the LORD," Jeremiah answers, "*You* are the burden" (23:33).

170

But hope remains. In the midst of what sometimes seems to be unmitigated gloom, Jeremiah is told, in the vision of good figs and bad figs, that for those who will allow themselves to be exiles in Babylon, there will be blessings; they will someday return. "I will give them a heart to know that I am the LORD; and they shall be my people and I will be their God, for they shall return to me with their whole heart" (24:7). God always has a people. Then and now.

PRAYER: May I never, dear Lord, lose hope. With you, the end must surely, inevitably, be victorious. Thank you! Amen.

JEREMIAH 25, 26, 27   *Week 31, Day 4*

*P*rophecies in the Hebrew scriptures were hardly ever final; they were open to change if the people changed. Jonah realized this was so and was unhappy about it, because he wanted the Assyrians to be punished. Jeremiah, on the other hand, is glad to know that if the people "will listen . . . and will turn from their evil way," God will change the plans for the trouble that was to come upon them (26:3).

But when he delivers his message, the priests, the other prophets, and the people do not repent; instead, they feel that Jeremiah "deserves the sentence of death" because of his prophecies (26:11). They think of him as a traitor to their nation because his message is negative. Fortunately, the government officials and the people are kinder and more sensible in their attitude toward Jeremiah than are his professional colleagues, the priests and prophets. There's a message in this, and it's not a pleasant one, but it is repeated throughout scripture and church history. Religious professionals are not always as sensitive to God's will as their calling would indicate.

So Jeremiah gives a hard word. God means for Judah and certain other nations to take on themselves the yoke of the King of Babylon. This had to be an almost impossible message to accept, and we can empathize with the people of Judah in wondering if Jeremiah can be right in insisting that it is God's will for them to submit to a pagan nation.

PRAYER: Give me the grace, I pray, to listen well when a

message is contrary to my expectations; in Jesus' name. Amen.

JEREMIAH 28, 29, 30   *Week 31, Day 5*

I doubt that Hananiah and Shemaiah intended to be false prophets. I think they simply wanted to say the pleasing word; and because that's what they wanted to do, it was easy for them to believe a lie. Since Jeremiah's prophecy about Babylon's victory proved to be true, we might think the people would be more open to his next message. But not so. When he told the people in captivity to settle in for a long stay—seventy years!—they were as resentful as ever. They couldn't endure the idea that they should work and pray for the city into which they had been carried in exile, and that "in its welfare you will find your welfare" (29:7). Even Jeremiah's promise that in time God would restore their fortunes and bring them back to their homeland was not enough to persuade them. One reason for their resistance is obvious: to accept Jeremiah's prophecy was to postpone hope until the next generation. Not many of us are willing to wait until then!

I expect they may have reasoned, "If God wants to do a good thing for us, why can't he do it now?" Most of us look at things that way. But there were issues to be worked out before God could "restore the fortunes of . . . Israel and Judah" (30:3). At this point their "guilt is great, because [their] sins are so numerous" (30:14) so there will have to be "fierce anger"; but "in the latter days you will understand this" (30:24). Sight will in time reveal what faith cannot yet grasp.

PRAYER: Make my heart open to your message and your purposes, O God, so that I will not resist your will; in Christ. Amen.

JEREMIAH 31, 32, 33; PSALM 113   *Week 31, Day 6*

T here is a mercy in God's restoration that quite overwhelms us. We have heard the prophets speak repeatedly of the spiritual adulteries and whoredoms that Judah and

Israel committed against their covenant with God. But now Jeremiah addresses them, "O virgin Israel" (31:4, 21). Their restoration will one day be so complete that it will be as if they had never failed God.

Jeremiah is privileged also to announce a "new covenant." It will not be like the covenant that was made when their ancestors were leaving Egypt; for the Lord says, "I will put my law within them, and I will write it on their hearts; and I will be their God, and they shall be my people" (31:33). This covenant surpasses anything the people have had before; Jeremiah, the prophet of tears, is able to speak the most hopeful words of all.

And now he is called to act upon his hope. He has an opportunity, as the nearest of kin, to buy a property at Anathoth. From an economic point of view, such a purchase flew in the face of all logic. Why buy property in a ghost town, where there was no future? But the same faith that compelled Jeremiah to accept the Babylonian invasion now compels him to anticipate a day of renewal. He is so sure of the future that he will buy this property, believing that "houses and fields and vineyards shall again be bought in this land" (32:15).

PRAYER: Give me a faith, I pray, that will believe in you and your purposes, no matter what the circumstances; to your glory. Amen.

JEREMIAH 34, 35, 36   *Week 31, Day 7*

*W*e often show the hardness of our hearts toward God by the bitterness we show to our fellow human beings. The Jews, who had themselves been slaves for generations in Egypt, had been instructed by the law never to make any of their fellow Jews into lifelong slaves; but again and again they violated this commandment. They desecrated both their people and their divine law. And even when they repented of these deeds, they easily slipped back into their shameful conduct. In doing so, the Lord says, "You profaned my name" (34:16). When we belittle or abuse a human being, we violate the God who created us.

Jeremiah keeps hoping. He sends his faithful scribe,

Baruch, to read his prophecy to some officials. They are sympathetic enough with Jeremiah to warn him and Baruch to hide while they present the scroll to King Jehoiakim. As the king hears the message, he methodically and cynically burns each portion after it is read—a book burning, indeed! It is his regal way of saying that nobody is going to frighten him into changing his ways!

From their place of hiding, Jeremiah and Baruch replace the destroyed manuscript. If something is true, it is quite useless to burn it; opponents of the scriptures have proved that point, against their own will, through hundreds of years and in scores of cultures. The truth will rise again, because God has a stake in it.

PRAYER: Thank you, Father, for those courageous persons who have given their very lives to make the scriptures available; in Christ. Amen.

JEREMIAH 37, 38, 39   *Week 32, Day 1*

*J*t's easy to see why people rejected Jeremiah's message. Patriotism makes one want to defend a country, not desert it, and that feeling had to be especially strong with the people of Judah because they thought of their country as God's special possession. Whatever faith they had was no doubt tied to this belief so that they would reason that to deny their country was to deny God. To their eyes, Jeremiah was "discouraging the soldiers . . . and all the people" by his message (38:4).

King Zedekiah swayed with the wind. He believed in Jeremiah enough to try to deliver him from his enemies and to seek his counsel. But he didn't quite have the courage to follow the prophet's advice. Or perhaps we should say that he didn't believe strongly enough in the advice to act upon it. He was simply too afraid of general opinion.

The brightest spot in this section is the Ethiopian Ebedmelech. When the king acquiesced to Jeremiah's enemies ("the king is powerless against you" [38:5]), and allowed Jeremiah to be thrown into a cistern to die, Ebedmelech appealed on the prophet's behalf. Still more, he worked physically for his deliverance, gathering rags from the destitute city in order to pull Jeremiah from the cistern. He is such a remarkable hero; one wonders how he came by the faith to believe in Jeremiah and his prophecies—all the more so since he was not himself a Jew. God finds worthy servants among all peoples at all times.

PRAYER: Thank you for the peripheral people who have blessed my life; I'm grateful that you are never without a witness; in Christ. Amen.

JEREMIAH 40, 41, 42, 43   *Week 32, Day 2*

*A*lthough Jeremiah had urged the people to accept captivity in Babylon, he chose to stay in Judah with "the poorest of the land who had not been taken into exile to Babylon" (40:7). Gedaliah, appointed to govern this remnant, counseled them just as Jeremiah had recommended for so long. But fearful, violent times breed still more violence, and Gedaliah and those around him are brutally killed by Ishmael.

Now a new delegation comes to Jeremiah. It's quite astonishing that with all their discrediting of the prophet, the people kept coming back to him for help. They recognized his integrity and his relationship with God, so they asked him to pray for them, promising "whether it is good or bad, we will obey the voice of the LORD" (42:6).

Jeremiah prayed for ten days. That may be a message for us, when we expect quick answers! His message wasn't what the people wanted to hear. They were hoping to be confirmed in their desire to immigrate to Egypt; perhaps they reasoned that since Jeremiah had previously urged the people to go to Babylon, he would now be sympathetic with an Egyptian alternative. Instead, he insisted they should stay and work the land in Judah. Egypt was much more appealing than this now-deserted land so they rejected Jeremiah's message; "they did not obey the voice of the LORD" (43:7). They knew what they wanted to hear before they came to Jeremiah, and when he gave them something else, they went their own way.

PRAYER: When I say, "Show me your will," help me to mean it, and to live and act accordingly; in Jesus' name. Amen.

*H*ow does one decide what is good religion? The people who argued with Jeremiah had a simple measure: did it pay? They no longer hide their affection for the queen of heaven, but glory in it. They insist that this is part of their religious tradition: "we and our ancestors, our kings and our officials" used to do these things "in the towns of Judah and in the streets of Jerusalem" (44:17). And for them, here's the trump card: it paid off! "We used to have plenty of food, and prospered, and saw no misfortune" (44:17).

One wonders where they got their data, but it doesn't really matter; most of us read our life stories selectively at times, to come to the conclusions that appeal to us. Jeremiah insists that God has been very patient, but that now they can expect judgment in even greater measure. He reads their experiences another way: "It is because you burned offerings, and because you sinned against the LORD and did not obey the voice of the LORD . . . that this disaster has befallen you" (44:23).

I expect people will always interpret the circumstances of their lives, the mixture of successes and failures, pretty much as they want to do, and if this is the basis for their religion—or their life philosophy—they may end up worshiping some version of the queen of heaven. Biblical religion calls us to a faith in which there is moral integrity. If blessings come, fine; but if not, we will still be true.

PRAYER: Yes, Lord, I'd rather live with enough than to live in poverty, but let me never make my well-being my faith; in Jesus' name. Amen.

*I*f there is any single theme that dominates the Hebrew prophets, it is the justice of God at work in the nations of earth. Many of the psalms pick up the same theme, usually at a more personal level, in prayers for God's blessing on the righteous and judgment on the wicked, but in the prophets the theme is enunciated in message after message. If God is fair, there must be justice on the earth. Nations cannot continue indifferent to God, justice, and morality without there someday being a showdown. This is the burden of the prophets, and we will never understand their passion or their occasional tone of wrath unless we realize their commitment to justice on earth.

This is true of all the nations. Jeremiah goes through a series of countries and rulers: Egypt, Philistia, Moab, Ammon, Edom, Damascus, Kedar, Hazor, Elam. Most of these names are little more than footnotes to history now, but they were significant powers from time to time in the ancient world. The English poet Rudyard Kipling warned his generation that their pomp, too, "is one with Nineveh and Tyre." That kind of insight will help us keep our own times in perspective.

But judgment is never simply to set things right. Israel, in particular, learns this. God promises that they will be saved "from far away . . . from the land of their captivity" (46:27), but they will nevertheless be chastised "in just measure" (46:28). Justice demands it.

PRAYER: Help me, O Lord, to know that you are at work in the history of our human race, and to live accordingly; in Christ. Amen.

JEREMIAH 50, 51, 52   *Week 32, Day 5*

*M*ost of the nations whose fate is described in yesterday's chapters were victims of the Babylonian war machine. The prophet understood that God was using Babylon as the instrument of justice and judgment. But they were to show restraint in the exercising of their power; if they failed to do so, judgment would in turn come upon them.

We read of that judgment in these chapters. Babylon became drunk on its power, so now the sword will come upon them:

> for this is the time of the LORD's vengeance;
> he is repaying her what is due. (51:6)

Her fall is commensurate with her previous position of grandeur:

> for the LORD's purposes against Babylon stand,
> to make the land of Babylon a desolation, without inhabitant.
>   (51:29)

The book of Jeremiah ends in a positive word regarding King Jehoiachin of Judah; he is allowed to dine regularly at the king's table after he is released from prison (52:31-34). We're not told what happened to Jeremiah. Post-biblical legends say that he was stoned to death by the refugees who took him with them to Egypt. This is easy to believe. The people had always resisted his message and had threatened any number of times to kill him, so it is more likely than not that eventually they did so. Jeremiah was one of those persons who lived out his mission in a hard and bitter time, but he did so with unfailing integrity.

PRAYER: Our times change, O Lord, with the fortunes of life; help me, please, always to be true to you; in Jesus' name. Amen.

LAMENTATIONS 1, 2; PSALM 115   *Week 32, Day 6*

*H*ere is a song of sorrow, traditionally credited to Jeremiah and usually thought to have been written when Jerusalem was destroyed by the Babylonians. The description of anguish is so vivid that at times we feel we are sitting with the writer as he looks upon the desolation of his beloved city.

But he knows why it has happened:

> Jerusalem sinned grievously,
>   so she has become a mockery. (1:8)

It appears that no one cares: "Is it nothing to you, all you who pass by?" (1:12). Perhaps the writer is reflecting the indifference of neighboring nations that might have risen to Judah's defense, or perhaps even more, the spiritual dullness with which the people had allowed their nation to come to such a time as this.

This book is written as an acrostic poem. Chapters 1, 2, 4,

178

and 5 have 22 verses each, with each verse beginning consecutively with the 22 letters of the Hebrew alphabet. The 66
verses of chapter 3 follow the same pattern, but in consecutive groups of three. One wonders why the writer, at a time of
suffering, would try to put his feelings into such an intricate
structure. A modern reader might reason that he did so as a
form of therapy. Perhaps it was a heroic effort to find and
make beauty in the midst of sorrow—especially, to make
something beautiful for God.

PRAYER: Even in pain, O God, may I seek your beauty; in
Christ. Amen.

LAMENTATIONS 3, 4, 5   *Week 32, Day 7*

The prophet's song moves back and forth between trust
and despair. In this he is true to the human experience
and our response to it. One moment he says that it does him
no good to "call and cry" because God shuts out his prayer
(3:8), but soon he reassures himself with the confidence that
"the Lord will not reject forever" (3:31). Most of us have
known such occasions when the pendulum of our souls has
swung to the same extremes.

There is a moment of high faith, at almost the middle of
the book, when the poet says:

> The steadfast love of the LORD never ceases,
>   his mercies never come to an end;
> they are new every morning;
>   great is your faithfulness. (3:22, 23)

It would be hard to find a stronger statement of faith. Out of
it has come a favorite hymn of our time, "Great Is Thy Faithfulness."

Lamentations concludes with a movement of hope and
despair:

> Restore us to yourself, O LORD, that we may be restored;
>   renew our days as of old—
> unless you have utterly rejected us,
>   and are angry with us beyond measure. (5:21, 22)

We feel his titanic struggle, and we want him to hold on.

179

PRAYER: In my times of despair, O Lord, help me hold firmly to your grace; in Jesus' name. Amen.

EZEKIEL 1, 2, 3   Week 33, Day 1

Like Jeremiah, Ezekiel is both priest and prophet. But where Jeremiah prophesied to a nation that was about to be invaded by the Babylonians, Ezekiel is called to minister to the people after they have been captive for some years in that foreign land. Ezekiel's audience wasn't inclined to be any more receptive than Jeremiah's, however. He is warned at the outset that "they are a rebellious house" (2:7). If he had been sent to "a people of obscure speech and difficult language" (3:5), they would have heard him more readily than will these, his own people.

The prophecies of Ezekiel are characterized by many exotic visions, of the kind we will find in Daniel, Zechariah, and Revelation. The first readers of these books all lived in hazardous times, when they might be killed for any presumed misstep. The strange imagery hid the meaning of the books from enemies; but more than that, it lent the message a kind of transcendent power, reminding the people that even in captivity or in peril, they were associated with One who was far beyond the puny power of their enemies.

Indeed, there is a note of victory even in the matter-of-fact opening words of this book. The prophet is in a foreign land, far from the sacred precincts of Jerusalem, "among the exiles by the river Chebar," but even there heaven can be opened and the vision of God received (1:1).

PRAYER: Remind me, O Lord, that I am never beyond your care. Amen.

EZEKIEL 4, 5, 6   Week 33, Day 2

The Hebrew prophets often used dramatic means to give added impact to their messages and to make them memorable. In a pre-television world—and one in which structured drama was rare—they found ways to capture the atten-

180

tion of people. Ezekiel bakes defiled bread to make a point, and argues God's cause with the shavings from his beard. To us his approach may only seem odd, but a veteran advertising specialist would probably say, "But the people will remember it." And that's the point.

There are many ways that we humans can learn; the most painful is by trouble. But painful as this method is, we seem perversely to choose it. So Ezekiel warns the people that their wicked high places will be broken down, their bones scattered around the pagan altars; their houses will be laid waste, and they will be dispersed among the nations. There will be sword, famine, and pestilence. And again and again, the refrain: and they "shall know that I am the LORD" (6:7, 10, 13, 14). It would be so much better if they would learn without such pain!

Why are we so slow, so obstinate, to learn? Why is it that the stories in meetings of Alcoholics Anonymous seem so often to say, "I had to hit rock bottom before I was willing to get help." The psalmist said, "Before I was humbled I went astray, / but now I keep your word" (Ps. 119:67). Why not take an easier, better way of learning?

PRAYER: Make me a quick and willing student, I pray, so that I will learn by ways other than hard, personal experience; in Christ. Amen.

EZEKIEL 7, 8, 9, 10   Week 33, Day 3

Nearly all theology agrees that omniscience is a characteristic of God; that is, that God knows everything. As surely as one gets such an idea, one is likely to seek, rather foolishly, for ways of evading this penetrating eye. Some of the best of Ezekiel's contemporaries, seventy elders, were engaging in idol worship, each with "his censer in his hand and . . . the incense was ascending" (8:11). They seemed to feel that if they did their abominations in the dark, "each in his room of images" (8:12), the Lord would never know.

They reasoned this way because they believed "the LORD has forsaken the land" (8:12; 9:9). This conclusion may have been based more on wish than on evidence. The presence of God, which is so comforting when we are needy, is a burden when we want to go our own way. So we play mind games. When it is to our convenience, we meditate on God's availability; and when God's presence is troublesome, we argue that God isn't that essential in our daily lives. A percentage of those who are atheists are in truth convenience-atheists; to believe in God would require moral restraint, so they choose not to believe.

Ezekiel's seventy elders were wrong, of course, when they said, "The LORD does not see." And they were the losers. For it is in God's seeing that we have God's help. For God to know is for God to care. Why lose that?

PRAYER: I cherish your knowing me, even when I err, for my true hope is in your knowing me; in Jesus' name. Amen.

EZEKIEL 11, 12, 13   *Week 33, Day 4*

*T*he prophets were God's special instrument for awakening Judah and Israel, and often for warning gentile nations as well. But it was easy to imitate the prophets and to offer a more attractive message. The false prophets avoided the difficult issues and moral decisions, saying, "'Peace,' when there is no peace" (13:10, 16), and gladly polluting the people "for handfuls of barley and for pieces of bread" (13:19).

Meanwhile, Ezekiel has to deal with a rebellious people "who have eyes to see but do not see, who have ears to hear but do not hear" (12:2), people who brush aside his warnings with a reassuring proverb: "The days are prolonged, and every vision faileth" (12:22 KJV).

Nevertheless, Ezekiel is reassured. God promises him that a day is coming when the people will receive a new spirit, when God will "remove the heart of stone from their flesh and give them a heart of flesh" (11:19). When that day comes, the people will walk in God's statutes; "Then they shall be my people, and I will be their God" (11:20).

Martin Luther King, Jr., said, "I have a dream." Prophets and reformers and the courageous souls who follow them always do. Dreams fuel the engine of reform and ignite the fire of flickering vision. Even rebellious, indifferent people and false prophets weren't able to stop Ezekiel. And still today, Ezekiel's spiritual descendants draw upon resources beyond themselves; they follow God's dream.

182

PRAYER: Give me faith, O Lord, to see the glory of your coming even when times are bad; in Jesus' name. Amen.

EZEKIEL 14, 15, 16   *Week 33, Day 5*

*I*t is bad enough that people erect idols all about them, but it is far worse when they "take their idols into their hearts" (14:4). Such was the state of the people. They had wandered so far from God that "even if Noah, Daniel, and Job" were present, they wouldn't be able to save their own children; "they would save only their own lives by their righteousness" (14:20). Israel had always felt that if there were enough righteous people in a community, the community would be spared, but Ezekiel is warned that the wickedness is now so great that even three of the most notable faithful could not make a difference.

The message recorded in chapter 16 is one of the most moving in the Hebrew scriptures, but it is not for the faint of heart. It is set (as are so many of the prophecies) in the imagery of Israel as God's bride. God sought out Israel before her navel cord was cut (16:4), when she was abhorred (16:5). God wanted her when no one else did, and under his care she "grew exceedingly beautiful, fit to be a queen" (16:13).

But with her beauty came temptation; Israel used God's favors for her adulterous relationships with other gods, exemplified by her courting the aid of the Egyptians, the Philistines, the Assyrians, and even the Chaldeans (16:26-29)—all the while forgetting the love shown in "the days of your youth" (16:22). Nevertheless, God will remember the covenant from the days of Israel's youth and will still "establish with you an everlasting covenant" (16:60). God's love still pursues.

PRAYER: Give me a new sense of the reach of your divine love. Amen.

EZEKIEL 17, 18, 19; PSALM 116   *Week 33, Day 6*

*A*ncient peoples had a greater sense of community than we usually do. As a result, they assumed that the sins of the parents would be visited upon the children; as a popular proverb put it, "The parents have eaten sour grapes, and the children's teeth are set on edge" (18:2). But now Ezekiel refutes that idea; "it is only the person who sins that shall die" (18:4).

It's surprising to us, but this change upset the people of Ezekiel's day; they felt God was being unfair in insisting that each person must bear the weight of his or her own conduct. Perhaps it bothered their sense of solidarity; it may even have seemed to them that the new code would undermine the authority of the elders. In any event, Ezekiel had to reason out the matter with them.

The prophet's examples of sinful conduct are interesting. They range from ritual sins (to "eat upon the mountains") to sexual morality ("does not defile his neighbor's wife") to social responsibility ("gives his bread to the hungry and covers the naked with a garment") (18:6, 7). We tend to divide conduct into categories, but Israel was taught that holiness is a seamless garment; all conduct is important before God.

Ezekiel had to disabuse the people of another mistaken idea. They saw God as wrathful. The prophet explained that God's purpose is redemption. "For I have no pleasure in the death of anyone, says the Lord GOD. Turn, then, and live" (18:32).

PRAYER: I thank you, Lord, that your will always is good. Amen.

EZEKIEL 20, 21, 22   Week 33, Day 7

*M*y personal heritage is such that I am inclined to minimize ritual religion; I am more impressed with its dangers than with its values. But the values are there, and Ezekiel makes his appeal for them. As he reviews with the elders the history of their people, reminding them that God had brought them into "a land flowing with milk and honey" (20:6), he gave them "ordinances, by whose observance everyone shall live"; especially "my sabbaths, as a sign between me and them" (20:11, 12). But they profaned the very sabbaths which formed their union with God.

The worst of it was that the profanation was led by the very ones who should have been a strength for righteousness, the

184

priests. The "priests have done violence to my teaching and have profaned my holy things; they have made no distinction between the holy and the common, neither have they taught the difference between the unclean and the clean, and they have disregarded my sabbaths" (22:26).

Rituals and observances can deteriorate into mere formalities, but they provide a structure for the practices of faith, and order for times of uncertainty. As such, they were particularly important to this people in exile. In a foreign land, cut off from the securities of their heritage, some things remained secure: the sabbath, the holy observances, the distinctions between the holy and the common, the clean and the unclean. We need such structures, too, in the secular culture (an exile of a type) in which we must live.

PRAYER: Renew my ties, O Lord, to the structures of faith. Amen.

EZEKIEL 23, 24, 25   *Week 34, Day 1*

*I*n biblical religion, ritual is never an end in itself. The end is a relationship—first, between God and us human beings, and then between persons. Ezekiel returns now to the relationship allegory that is the favorite of both Testaments, the courtship and marriage of God and his people.

In chapter 23, Ezekiel tells it as the story of "two women, the daughters of one mother" (23:2), to trace the particular relationships of the northern kingdom, Israel (Samaria), and the southern, Judah (Jerusalem). The symbolic names, Oholah ("She who has a tent") and Oholibah ("Tent in her") were apparently meant to refer to their sacred tent, the covenant tabernacle, which was for so long the physical evidence of their union with God.

The Middle Eastern language is not delicate, but neither is it salacious. The prophet describes vividly the infidelities of the two sisters with the several pagan nations. Both Israel and Judah were guilty, again and again, of worshiping the power and wealth of their neighbors, then embracing the gods of those nations, in the assumption that they would thus get the same benefits. Instead, Ezekiel says, they have been delivered "into the hands of those whom you hate" (23:28). The nations they pursued eventually became their captors and their destroyers. So it is with any relationship that draws us from God.

PRAYER: I want such a commitment to you, O Lord, that I will be able to resist any voice that might lead me astray; in Christ. Amen.

EZEKIEL 26, 27, 28   *Week 34, Day 2*

*I*t probably seems strange to us that three consecutive chapters are dedicated to Tyre, a city-state that is now only a small entry in an encyclopedia. But perhaps that in itself is a lesson, for Tyre was once a symbol of power and sophistication, like Paris, London, or New York in our time. It was a major seaport and trading center, and famous for its products, especially purple dye and fine glass. You will remember that both David and Solomon looked to Tyre (and its neighbor, Sidon) for sailors and for craftsmen. Later, Tyre had its own malevolent effect on Israel via their princess, Jezebel, who became Ahab's queen and Elijah's most powerful adversary.

But now judgment is to come upon Tyre. At first the prophet seems nothing but glad as he describes her destruction:

> They will plunder your riches and loot your merchandise. . . .
> I will silence the music of your songs. (26:12, 13)

Then, however, he mourns the tragic loss:

> They weep over you in bitterness of soul. . . .
> Who was ever destroyed like Tyre? (27:31, 32)

The source of her trouble was her king. He is described in bigger-than-life terms:

> You were in Eden, the garden of God. . . .
> You were blameless in your ways. (28:13, 15)

His power and potential could only be described in Edenic terms.

PRAYER: Kingdoms come, kingdoms go; you are eternal. Hallelujah! Amen.

*U*nlike Tyre and Moab, Egypt is still an identifiable nation today. But it is hard to imagine the strength and prestige it once enjoyed; we recognize its history now in museum exhibits or in pictures of the pyramids and the Sphinx. One might wonder to what degree the present place is a result of the judgments that Ezekiel describes, and one might wonder even more how much of God's judgment on history's erring nations is written into the very circumstances (the near inevitabilities!) of life. The prophets would say that a nation that becomes utterly materialistic and that is heart-less in her relations to others will surely be destroyed.

It is especially sad in Egypt's case, because once her great-ness was like a lofty cedar:

> So it towered high above all the trees of the field. . . .
> All the birds of the air made their nests in its boughs . . .
> and in its shade all great nations lived. (31:5, 6)

But "now you shall be brought down with the trees of Eden to the world below" (31:18). The fabled glory is gone.

And as with Tyre, special blame is laid on the ruler. "Raise a lamentation over Pharaoh king of Egypt" (32:2). Power, whether it be military (as in the case of political leaders), eco-nomic, intellectual, or artistic, is a divine responsibility and will be judged accordingly.

PRAYER: I don't think of my limited power as being very sig-nificant, but I know you will hold me responsible to use it well; in Christ. Amen.

*T*here seems to be so much judgment in the prophets that we might easily feel that God's very nature is judgment and that he delights in it. Not so! God's will and purpose are deliverance. Ezekiel gets that message in an unforgettable way. He is to be "a sentinel for the house of Israel" (33:7). They must be warned to turn from their wicked ways; told that God has "no pleasure in the death of the wicked" and that he is pleading with them, "why will you die?" (33:11). If only they will turn from their sins and "walk in the statutes of life . . . they shall surely live, they shall not die" (33:15).

But the gracious appeal from God, via the true sentinel, can be lost through the influence of those who claim to be "shepherds of Israel," but "who have been feeding" themselves (34:2). The occasional religious leaders who exploit their office to benefit themselves are not a twentieth-century invention. Ezekiel told the religious leaders of his day, in the name of God, "You eat the fat, you clothe yourselves with the wool, you slaughter the fatlings; but you do not feed the sheep" (34:3). It is a dreadful indictment, because it is a violation of trust; and such shepherds will suffer accordingly. The Lord says, "I am against the shepherds; and I will demand my sheep at their hand" (34:10). More than that, God says, "I myself will be the shepherd. . . . I will seek the lost, and I will bring back the strayed, and I will bind up the injured" (34:15, 16). We will see this picture again, in Jesus, in John 10.

PRAYER: Whatever my flock, O Lord, keep me true to you; in Christ. Amen.

EZEKIEL 35, 36, 37   *Week 34, Day 5*

Sometimes the encourager needs encouraging. This must have been especially true of Ezekiel, who was required so often to give messages of judgment. Now it is his privilege to say to Israel that "they shall soon come home" (36:8). Their population is to be multiplied (36:10), and they will be gathered from the countries to which they have been dispersed (36:24); their towns will be inhabited and their waste places rebuilt (36:33).

Hearing this, Ezekiel might easily have said, "It's a nice idea, but not very likely." Perhaps there was such a thought in his mind, and perhaps his vision of the valley of dry bones was God's persuasive answer. The valley was "full of bones" and "they were very dry" (37:1, 2). Could they live? Ezekiel's mind must have said, "Hardly," but he wisely answered, "O Lord GOD, you know" (37:3).

He learned that his part was to prophesy. Perhaps this gathering of bones was no more intimidating than the people to whom he had been prophesying for so long. In any event, he did as he was told, until sinews, flesh, and skin appeared. Then breath came "from the four winds" (37:9), and Ezekiel found himself with "a vast multitude" (37:10).

So Ezekiel was assured that "the whole house of Israel" would one day return to their homeland—even if graves had to be emptied to make it so (37:13). Spiritually speaking, it would take just such a miracle; and as for Ezekiel, he now had the heart to believe it.

PRAYER: Remind me, O Lord, that no place is too dead for you. Amen.

EZEKIEL 38, 39; PSALMS 118, 119:1-24   *Week 34, Day 6*

*G*og and Magog have fascinated Bible students for centuries, particularly since the New Testament book of Revelation (20:8) makes reference to them. Many explanations have been offered. A modern Jewish scholar has found that by reading Magog backward in the Hebrew and substituting letters in a systematic way, it becomes Babel, or Babylon. Others have proved, from time to time, that the reference is to Alexander the Great or to Antiochus Epiphanes, the persecutor of the Jews.

I would urge only that we not try to fit Gog and Magog to each passing international headline; to do so embarrasses the scriptures and ought to embarrass those who, in every such instance, are eventually proved wrong.

It does seem quite clear that Ezekiel is envisioning a worldwide conflict, out of which comes a new day. The enemies are not from the countries that were Israel's traditional foes; they seem if anything to represent some unknown, massive barbarian force. That isn't surprising; anyone who reads a little history discovers that as surely as the tyrant of one generation is removed, a new one is likely to appear from out of nowhere.

But Ezekiel assures us that in the end the glory of God will be revealed "among the nations," and that "Israel shall know that I am the LORD their God, from that day forward" (39:21, 22). Whatever else one may find in these chapters, don't miss that!

PRAYER: Whatever the headlines, dear God, I trust in you. Amen.

*T*he psalmist said:

> How lovely is your dwelling place, O LORD of hosts!
> My soul longs, indeed it faints
>   for the courts of the LORD. (Ps. 84:1, 2)

Ezekiel says the same thing, but in a very different way, by his detailed description of all its prospects. He seems to savor every cubit. What to us may be boring is to him a dear detail.

Jewish tradition says that Ezekiel had this vision of the house of the Lord in the year 572 B.C. on the Day of Atonement. From the point of view of any faith-reader, it is impressive that the vision came "in the twenty-fifth year of our exile" (40:1). Far from his homeland, with no prospect of return except as faith envisioned it, he was nevertheless more captive to his dreams than to his captors. In this he is like John on the Isle of Patmos (Rev. 1:9), Paul writing his prison epistles, and John Bunyan developing *Pilgrim's Progress*.

The prophet knows that when the people return to their homeland, it will be essential that there be a place of worship. He leaves nothing to chance. His intricate details can hardly help being tedious to us, but for him and for his immediate audience, these details are the natural language of love. If we keep that in mind, we will feel something of the excitement that impels him.

PRAYER: I thank you for all the houses of worship that have blessed my life over the years; in Jesus' name. Amen.

*W*hen King David was dying, his son Adonijah organized a coup to succeed him. Among those who rallied to support Solomon was a priest named Zadok. For his loyalty, he replaced Abiathar, who had joined the coup (1 Kings 1, 2) and he was assured that he and his descendants would always have "the charge of my sanctuary" (44:15). Ezekiel was himself in Zadok's line, so he must have felt especially committed to the cause of the new temple that had been revealed to him.

For the Jews, the emphasis was on their differentness. This was all the more the case as they struggled to survive captivity in a foreign land. The elements of their worship and ritual were crucial to this sense of their being a special people. Priests in other nations sometimes shaved themselves bald or let their hair grow long, but not the priests of Israel (44:20). Their ritual garments must be only linen, and they must not "bind themselves with anything that causes sweat" (44:18). Their standards are different, because "they shall teach my people the difference between the holy and the common" (44:23).

We notice once again that in the midst of these ritualistic details there are reminders of social holiness. They must "put away violence and oppression" and cease evicting their people (45:9), and they must use only honest weights (45:10). For Israel there was always a tie between ritual observance and practical integrity. Religion was never isolated from the routine of life.

PRAYER: Make me different, I pray, by purity of life; in Christ. Amen.

EZEKIEL 46, 47, 48   *Week 35, Day 2*

*W*ater is a symbol of life in every part of the world, but the symbol has more impact in the Middle East, where times and places of scarcity mean literal death. When the prophet saw water flowing from below the threshold of the temple he had envisioned (47:1), it must have struck him much as the vision of the valley of dry bones (chap. 37). The depth of the water increases, steadily and surely, from ankle-deep to knee-deep to waist-high, and then a full river.

The miracle grows: along the banks of the river, "a great many trees on the one side and on the other" (47:7). This is a still greater symbol of life. Now the water rushes into "the sea of stagnant waters" (47:8), the Dead Sea; but instead of becoming stagnant, as all waters do when they reach that body, this river transforms it so that soon there are people standing "fishing beside the sea," with fish "of a great many kinds, like the fish of the Great Sea" (the Mediterranean) (47:10). Such is the prophet's vision of a new day, a day of life so powerful that it brings life wherever it goes, even into the dead places of the earth.

The secret seems to be in the temple itself. As the prophet describes the measure and distribution of the new land, he sees "the sanctuary of the LORD in the middle of it" (48:10). And if there is any doubt about the special quality of this place, remember that "the name of the city from that time on shall be, The LORD is There" (48:35).

PRAYER: Help me, O Lord, to bring fresh water to the dead places of our world; in Jesus' name. Amen.

DANIEL 1, 2, 3; PSALM 119:25-48   *Week 35, Day 3*

*M*illions of Sunday school children have looked upon Daniel as one of their favorite heroes. Scholars feel the book was written to encourage the Jews in a time of captivity and national despair, but people of many other times and cultures have also gotten strength from the Hebrew captive and his three friends, Shadrach, Meshach, and Abednego.

As the book opens, the four young men courageously insist on being true to their religious dietary laws, though to do so could mean death. Instead, at the end of their test "no one was found to compare" with them; they were "ten times better than all the magicians and enchanters" in the kingdom (1:19, 20).

Daniel (like Joseph) has a gift for understanding and interpreting dreams. The Hebrew scriptures see this, not as a kind of magic, but as a divine endowment and as a form of wisdom. Nor does such wisdom stand alone; it is part of the character and integrity of its possessor.

The success of these young men arouses jealousy, especially since they are foreigners, and particularly since they refuse to compromise their religious convictions. King Nebuchadnezzar sees their beliefs as an insult to his authority and commands that they be executed. The young men are confident they will be delivered; but they are even more certain that they will do what is right, deliverance or not; their "but if not" (3:18) is a grand statement of commitment. As it happens, they win, but with their commitment they would win even if losing.

PRAYER: Give me, O God, a "but if not" faith; in Christ. Amen.

DANIEL 4, 5, 6   *Week 35, Day 4*

S o many lessons can be drawn from each of these wonderful stories, but perhaps the theme that runs through them all is this, that kings may come and go, and their kingdoms, too, but the people of God go on forever. Nebuchadnezzar receives a gracious warning and an opportunity to "atone for your sins with righteousness, and your iniquities with mercy to the oppressed," which would have meant a prolonging of his prosperity (4:27), but he follows the course of arrogant pride and comes to praise God only after an experience of dire abasement. A new king, Belshazzar, insists on repeating the lesson learned by his predecessor, but, unlike Nebuchadnezzar, he gets no second chance. He seems to have been so absorbed in the luxuries and excesses of his office that he didn't even know of the wise man Daniel. Each time we hear the phrase, "the handwriting on the wall," we have a reminder of Belshazzar.

And then, Daniel the old man, still faithful to God, still in a position of power, and still resented by the natives of the land—by this time, the Medes and Persians. They confess that the only way to destroy him is "in connection with the law of his God" (6:5) and his faithfulness to that law. They succeed in arranging his execution, but they fail, of course, to destroy him. "My God sent his angel and shut the lions' mouths," Daniel testifies (6:22), and Darius, like the kings before him, acknowledges that the Lord "is the living God, enduring forever" (6:26). No wonder we used to sing, "Dare to be a Daniel!"

PRAYER: Keep me true to you, O Lord, in all times and places. Amen.

*B*roadly speaking, the prophecies of Daniel are interpreted in two ways. Many have seen them as predicting
future events, and in doing so have usually tended to apply
them to the political scene in their own time. I have lived
long enough to have heard several such interpretations, but I
would not, for that reason, want to discredit a futuristic interpretation. I would plead, however, that we should not be so
anxious to fit a passage to our times that we treat it dishonestly
or wishfully. Let the scriptures speak for themselves, without
forcing them into a Procrustean bed of our current headlines.

On the other hand, more recent scholars feel that this portion of Daniel was written after some, or perhaps all, of the
events had already occurred, and that the writer was simply
reporting them in this highly symbolic language to show that,
in the end, God is at work in all times and nations. They give
a later date to the writings on the basis of the language used.
Perhaps they also have a prejudice against the idea of prophecies predicting future events.

And how shall we read it? Don't fence God in; if God so
chooses, I see no reason why scripture cannot be predictive.
But don't be anxious to stake out your own predictive claim.
And in all we read, let us rejoice that God is at work in all
times and places, even though we may not presently see how.

PRAYER: Let me read your Word with awe, amazement, and
love; in Jesus' name. Amen.

*D*aniel gives us the best possible guide for studying his
visions. At the conclusion of one such moving experience he says, "my thoughts greatly terrified me, and my face
turned pale; but I kept the matter in my mind" (7:28). Awe
and remembering: that's a good approach. At another time he
"was dismayed" by his vision, and confessed that he "did not
understand it" (8:27). Humility is good, too!

But above all, he prayed (9:1-19). We will never do justice
to these passages or to any others, except as we read prayer-

fully. God's Word speaks to the will and the emotions as well as to the mind, and these elements are not likely to respond unless we are prayerful readers. In the instance of an especially troublesome vision, Daniel entered also into a fast; "no rich food, no meat or wine . . . for the full three weeks" (10:3).

Then Daniel learns that the answer to his prayers has been delayed by a conflict in another realm (10:12, 13). His experience will give us further insight into some of the ramifications of prayer if we don't let the style of presentation cloud the message. When we pray, we enter into the conflict between good and evil, as surely as when we work physically or intellectually for some cause. It seems that if Daniel had stopped praying too soon, the desired end would not have been won.

Like us, Daniel wants to know how things will turn out (12:8). But he must wait for understanding, assured that his reward will come (12:13).

PRAYER: Forgive me, please, when I stop praying too soon. Amen.

HOSEA 1, 2, 3   *Week 35, Day 7*

*M*any of the prophets dramatized their messages in various ways, but none more so than Hosea. His life—particularly his family life—became his message. The theme, which is enunciated in other prophets but more briefly, is God's marriage to Israel and her subsequent infidelities. Hosea understands the problem by way of his own marriage to Gomer.

Hosea is told from the outset that his marriage will be marked by betrayal and pain (1:2). Their children are given names that symbolize Israel's relationship with God (1:4-9), and it seems that in time Gomer does indeed forsake Hosea; so that at last, in order to re-establish their relationship, Hosea buys Gomer in the slave market, for less than the standard price of a slave (3:2).

In this he portrays God's continuing pursuit of Israel. Although she has gone "after her lovers" and forgotten God (2:13), in time "she shall respond as in the days of her youth . . . when she came out of the land of Egypt" (2:15). When that day comes, it will be a wonderfully different relationship: "I will take you for my wife forever; I will take you for my wife in righteousness and in justice, in steadfast love, and in mercy. . . . And you shall know the LORD" (2:19, 20). And while once the children were named "Not pitied" and "Not my people," now they will receive pity and God will say, "You are my people" (2:23).

PRAYER: Thank you for the divine love revealed through the prophet Hosea; in the name of Jesus, your ultimate expression of love. Amen.

HOSEA 4, 5, 6 *Week 36, Day 1*

*H*osea mourns the evil he sees in the land—swearing, lying, murder, stealing, and adultery (4:2). The impact of this evil is so great that nature itself feels it; "even the fish of the sea are perishing" (4:3). Hosea realizes that sin is so contrary to the intended quality of our universe that it disrupts even the wild creatures. And what is behind such conduct? "My people are destroyed for lack of knowledge" (4:6), and this lack is the fault of the priests, whose responsibility it is to train the people. Such knowledge is more than simply an accumulation of facts or a facile grasp of data; it includes a moral content and responsible conduct.

Hosea pleads for the people to return to God:

"Come, let us return to the LORD;
for it is he who has torn, and he will heal us;
he has struck down, and he will bind us up." (6:1)

But the Lord responds with sorrow: "What shall I do with you, O Ephraim?" (6:4). Their times of spiritual renewal are brief and superficial, "like the dew that goes away early" (6:4). God wants something far beyond religious formality:

"For I desire steadfast love and not sacrifice,
the knowlege of God rather than burnt offerings." (6:6)

It's easy to rephrase that message in words which fit our day and our failings, but it's as hard as ever to respond with a whole heart.

PRAYER: Give me, I pray, the steadfast love that pleases you. Amen.

196

*H*osea has especially graphic ways of describing Israel's spiritual condition. "Ephraim [the name of this major tribal region is often used by the prophets to represent all of Israel] is a cake not turned" (7:8)—that is, she is "half-baked." Her religion is well done on one side (probably her ritual practices), but the cake has never been turned over so the other side of her religion—her moral obligations—is left undone. Then Hosea says, "Gray hairs are sprinkled upon him, / but he does not know it" (7:9). The signs of aging are all about; decrepitude has set in, but the nation is going blithely on its way. And for all the warning signs, "yet they do not return to the LORD their God" (7:10).

In fact, their indifference to God is so great that they seem to flaunt their role:

"They made kings, but not through me;
    they set up princes, but without my knowledge." (8:4)
"Israel has forgotten his Maker and built palaces." (8:14)

There will be a time of reckoning. What we sow, we reap, and of course the crop usually exceeds the sowing. So Hosea warns,

"For they sow the wind,
    and they shall reap the whirlwind." (8:7)

As Charles Reade put it, "Sow an act, and you reap a habit. Sow a habit, and you reap a character. Sow a character, and you reap a destiny." We sow a wind, perhaps only a breeze, and the whirlwind follows.

PRAYER: Remind me, O Lord, that deeds have consequences. Amen.

HOSEA 10, 11, 12   *Week 36, Day 3*

*T*hrough most of his appeals, Hosea pictures God as the rejected Lover of Israel, but now he turns to a different, yet still compelling, analogy, the relationship of parent and child:

"When Israel was a child, I loved him,
    and out of Egypt I called my son." (11:1)

Yet the more God called, the more they wandered, "sacrificing to the Baals,/and offering incense to idols" (11:2).

> "Yet it was I who taught Ephraim to walk,
>   I took them up in my arms;
>   but they did not know that I healed them." (11:3)

With such rejection, God might be expected to abandon Israel. But Hosea hears God uttering a heartbroken cry:

> "How can I give you up, Ephraim?
>   How can I hand you over, O Israel?" (11:8)

Admah and Zeboiim were cities near Sodom and Gomorrah that perished in their destruction. The prophet knows that Israel could easily be wiped out just as those forgotten cities were, except that God longs for Israel's redemption.

The biblical descriptions of God's relationship to our human race are always at personal, relational levels: lovers, friends, parent-child, wife-husband. At the core of our universe, the Scriptures remind us, is not an impersonal computer, but a heart. God's heart of love.

PRAYER: Tune my heart, O God, to sing the praises of your love. Amen.

HOSEA 13, 14; PSALM 119:73-120   *Week 36, Day 4*

*W*hen the prodigal in Jesus' parable decided to return to his father, he began rehearsing the speech he would make when they met (Luke 15:18, 19). Hosea seems to make such a recommendation to Israel:

> Take words with you and return to the LORD;
>   say to him,
>   "Take away all guilt;
>   accept that which is good,
>   and we will offer the fruit of our lips." (14:2)

It's true that words can be "mere words" and that words are best when they are supported by deeds, but words have a power all their own. They convey the business of the heart and mind. When people stop communicating with one another, their relationship is in danger. No wonder Hosea says, "Take words with you." As we speak with God, and in turn listen to him, our relationship grows.

It's interesting that this last chapter of Hosea is recited in synagogues on the first Sabbath of the Jewish New Year, at one of the holiest seasons of the year. Hosea assures us that "the ways of the LORD are right," but he concludes by reminding us that we will determine for ourselves how we use this right path:

> and the upright walk in them,
> but transgressors stumble in them. (14:9)

Good as the way is, we decide to use or to misuse its possibilities.

PRAYER: Dear Lord, give me a heart that so much desires you that I will find words to declare my repentance and my love; in Christ. Amen.

JOEL 1, 2, 3   Week 36, Day 5

*J*oel is the prophet of loss and of restoration. He has a word for those who feel all hope is gone. Joel describes in most vivid terms an invasion of locusts. It isn't always clear whether he is prophesying that such will happen or describing what has taken place and using the tragedy as a means of drawing the people to God; I am inclined to the latter view.

He portrays the locusts as an army. They come "with the rumbling of chariots . . . like a powerful army drawn up for battle" (2:5). Their ranks are so disciplined that "they do not jostle one another" (2:8), and their numbers so great that "the sun and the moon are darkened" (2:10) by their coming. They work utter disaster:

> Before them the land is like the garden of Eden,
> but after them a desolate wilderness,
> and nothing escapes them. (2:3)

Joel pleads with the people to return to God, "with fasting, with weeping, and with mourning; / rend your hearts and not your clothing" (2:12, 13). For God, Joel says, "will repay you for the years / that the swarming locust has eaten, / the hopper, the destroyer, and the cutter" (3:25). All they have lost will be restored, and with it, an outpouring of God's spirit (3:28-32). The apostle Peter used these words as his text on the Day of Pentecost, telling the assembled multitude that Joel's prophecy was being fulfilled before their eyes (Acts 2:16-21).

PRAYER: Thank you, Father, for restoring the years of loss. Amen.

AMOS 1, 2, 3; PSALM 119:121-144   *Week 36, Day 6*

*A*mos is usually considered the first literary prophet—that is, the first prophet whose messages were put in writing. A herdsman by trade, he was "among the shepherds of Tekoa" (1:1) when he was called to prophesy. His influence has been far-reaching, beginning with the prophet Isaiah and continuing to our own day.

When he sends warnings to Damascus, Gaza, Tyre, Edom, Ammon, and Moab, as well as Judah and Israel, one thinks of a line from Shakespeare's *Richard III*: "Thou setter-up and plucker-down of kings." Perhaps Amos wasn't making God directly responsible for the fall of these empires, but surely God was announcing their end (1:5, 15; 2:3).

Judah and Israel may have expected to escape because of their favored status, but Amos tells them that, because of their position, more—not less—is expected of them:

> You only have I known of all the families of the earth;
> therefore I will punish you for all your iniquities. (3:2)

Other nations suffer simply because they have been unjust, but Judah's situation is worse "because they have rejected the law of the LORD" (2:4). When Amos describes Israel's mistreatment of the poor, he portrays it as a direct affront to God:

> they lay themselves down beside every altar
> on garments taken in pledge. (2:8)

Privilege is a fearful responsibility.

PRAYER: Because you have given me much, you have a right to expect much; in Jesus' name. Amen.

*T*he worst fact about Judah and Israel is that they were so oblivious to their condition:

> Alas for those who are at ease in Zion,
>   and for those who feel secure on Mount Samaria. (6:1)

They have received so many warnings. Amos lists one and another, and always with the dreadful summary, "yet you did not return to me, says the LORD" (4:6, 8, 9, 10, 11). But they were sure of themselves, because of their wealth and their religion!

You see, it's hard for people to recognize their peril when they can "lie on beds of ivory" and "eat lambs from the flock, and calves from the stall" (6:4), not needing even to let their animals reach maturity. They have time for idle songs and improvisations (6:5), rich wines and bathing oils (6:6). They are so comfortable they are oblivious to tragedy; they "are not grieved over the ruin of Joseph!" (6:6).

As for religion, they can hardly wait for "the day of the LORD" because they assume it will mean judgment on others (5:18-20); after all, they are a pious, observant people! It has never occurred to them that their ceremonies might be an offense to God. Amos tells them that God hates their festivals, because he is looking for a people who will "let justice roll down like waters, / and righteousness like an everflowing stream" (5:24). Such is the religion that will please the Lord.

PRAYER: Save me, O God, from superficial piety! In Jesus' name. Amen.

*A*s one called from tending sheep, Amos clearly did not belong to the religious establishment. But a member of the establishment, the priest Amaziah, came to resent him and his message. "The land is not able to bear all his words," Amaziah reported to the king, and suggested that Amos return to Judah to prophesy (7:10-12). Amos answered with a classic defense of his calling: "I am no prophet, nor a prophet's son; but I am a herdsman, and a dresser of sycamore trees, and the LORD took me from following the flock, and the LORD said to me, 'Go, prophesy to my people Israel" (7:14, 15).

At last Amos can predict better days. First there will be judgment: "I will turn your feasts into mourning" (8:10), then a scattering of Israel ("I will . . . shake the house of Israel among all the nations / as one shakes with a sieve" [9:9]). But at last, a restoration:

I will restore the fortunes of my people Israel,
    and they shall rebuild the ruined cities and inhabit them. (9:14)

I wonder if the priest Amaziah ever heard that word of hope?

In his short book, Obadiah deals with an enmity that existed between Israel and Edom (the descendants of Esau) from the earliest days. This feeling was so intense that rabbis came to use the name Edom to represent any national enemy. Obadiah cries, "You should not have gloated over your brother / on the day of his misfortune" (vs. 12). Since they did, "your deeds shall return on your own head" (vs. 15).

PRAYER: Make my heart sensitive, O God, to human pain; in Christ. Amen.

JONAH 1, 2, 3, 4   *Week 37, Day 2*

*J*onah is himself the sermon in the book that bears his name. One day he is called to warn Nineveh that "their wickedness has come up before" God (1:2). That was an assignment Jonah didn't want, because like most people in his day he despised Nineveh and the Assyrians, a people infamous at the time for brutality.

So he boarded ship in the opposite direction and was soon caught in a violent storm. He confessed that he was the cause of the trouble, because "he was fleeing from the presence of the LORD" (1:10). Thrown overboard—reluctantly—by the sailors, he was swallowed by a great fish. There he prayed:

202

> "As my life was ebbing away,
> I remembered the LORD." (2:7)

Now he goes to Nineveh to preach. The people of Nineveh (including the king) repent; and God, in turn, "changed his mind about the calamity that he had said he would bring upon them" (3:10). Jonah had feared this possibility all along, because he sensed that he was dealing with "a gracious God and merciful, slow to anger, and abounding in steadfast love, and ready to relent from punishing" (4:2).

As the book ends, God uses still another device to press Jonah toward mercy. "Should I not be concerned about Nineveh?" God pleads (4:11). We never hear Jonah's reply. His book shows that God cares about *all* the human race—even Nineveh!—but it makes us give Jonah's answer.

PRAYER: Help me, O Lord, to love all your human race; in Christ. Amen.

MICAH 1, 2, 3   *Week 37, Day 3*

*J*udah and Israel were under biblical restrictions on the amassing of great wealth. The laws of land tenure, which sought to keep holdings within the ancestral family, and periodic remission of debts, which gave families and individuals a chance to make a new start, meant that there would seldom be great extremes of wealth and poverty.

But human greed was at work:

> They covet fields, and seize them;
> houses, and take them away;
> they oppress householder and house,
> people and their inheritance. (2:2)

Micah, a younger contemporary of Hosea and Isaiah, was of rural stock, and he was shocked by the inequalities he saw. He was especially troubled that those who already had so much were using their influence immorally to get still more:

> Its rulers give judgment for a bribe,
> its priests teach for a price,
> its prophets give oracles for money. (3:11)

Why do people want so much more than they need, and

why do they exploit those who already have less? Micah knew that such evil would destroy not only individuals, but in time, the nation itself. The problem still exists today. We need to hear Micah again.

PRAYER: Help me, O God, to be content with enough, and to have a heart and a hand for those who have less; in Jesus' name. Amen.

MICAH 4, 5, 6   *Week 37, Day 4*

*L*ike Isaiah (2:4), Micah envisioned a day of peace, when

> nation shall not lift up sword against nation,
>   neither shall they learn war any more (4:3)

and a day when everyone would have enough. And he saw the village of Bethlehem (ordinarily an unlikely choice) play-ing a key role in this better age coming:

> But you, O Bethlehem of Ephrathah,
>   who are one of the little clans of Judah,
> from you shall come forth for me
>   one who is to rule in Israel. (5:2)

The New Testament writers saw this verse as a messianic prophecy, fulfilled in Jesus (Matt. 2:6; John 7:42).

Micah is powerful in his impassioned plea for true religion. The Lord, he thunders, will not be pleased with "thousands of rams, / with ten thousand of rivers of oil," nor will he be moved if we give our firstborn for our transgression (6:7). God looks for so much more, and we have no right to plead igno-rance:

> He has told you, O mortal, what is good;
>   and what does the LORD require of you
> but to do justice, and to love kindness,
>   and to walk humbly with your God? (6:8)

True religion translates ritual and offering into justice and compassion.

PRAYER: Let my faith show itself in deeds of mercy; in Christ. Amen.

*W*hen we are not right with God, our human relationships will eventually be corrupted. A modern Czech, looking back on the years when his country operated under a philosophy of political atheism, said, "We lost the ethical norm of God." Micah saw this deterioration in his people, until at last they were doubting even their closest bonds:

> Put no trust in a friend,
> have no confidence in a loved one;
> guard the doors of your mouth
> from her who lies in your embrace. (7:5)

But Micah is confident that, in the end, God's mercy will triumph. "Who is a God like you," he cries, "pardoning iniquity / and passing over the transgression / of the remnant of your possession?" (7:18). In one of those instances where the Hebrew scriptures foreshadow the New Testament concept of grace, Micah says:

> You will cast all our sins
> into the depths of the sea. (7:19)

Orthodox Jews have made this verse the basis for their *Tashlich* ceremony, in which they journey to a body of water on the Jewish New Year and, while reciting verses from Micah, cast their sins into the watery depths. Sometimes such a physical, ritual act brings a spiritual reality more nearly into our grasp.

PRAYER: I bring to you this day, O God, the burden of my sins; bury them, please, in the ocean of your grace; in Christ. Amen.

*P*erhaps no ancient nation was more despised than Assyria (Nineveh). Their military conquests were marked by brutal ravishing of the peoples they conquered. No wonder Nahum says, regarding her downfall:

> All who hear the news about you
> clap their hands over you.
> For who has ever escaped
> your endless cruelty? (3:19)

Nahum's prophecy is a passionate song of retribution. When he promises that "the LORD is slow to anger but great in power" (1:3), he is reminding us that the people of Nineveh have had their opportunities to repent; consider Jonah. But mercy does not mean divine indifference; "the LORD will by no means clear the guilty" (1:3). If a nation (or an individual) refuses to change its ways, there will come a day of reckoning.

People sometimes have difficulty with the idea of divine judgment. But judgment is itself a mercy. Nahum is right in saying, at one moment, "The LORD is good. . . . He protects those who take refuge in him" (1:7), but continuing in the next breath, "He will make a full end of his adversaries" (1:8). God cannot be good to those who trust him except as he sends judgment on those who oppress them.

PRAYER: Thank you, dear Lord, for the acts of judgment through which your mercy is revealed. Give me the faith to understand; in Christ. Amen.

HABAKKUK 1, 2, 3   *Week 37, Day 7*

The prophet Habakkuk, about whom we know almost nothing, struggled with a special issue of faith. He realized that God must, in justice, bring judgment on those who have sinned, and he understood that this applied as well to his own people. But he couldn't see how the judgment could come through a people like the Chaldeans, "that fierce and impetuous nation" (1:6). How could God be silent "when the wicked swallow / those more righteous than they" (1:13)?

God tells the prophet that "the righteous live by their faith" (2:4), and that a day is coming when

> the earth will be filled
> > with the knowledge of the glory of the LORD,
> > as the waters cover the sea. (2:14)

It isn't easy to keep hoping and trusting in the face of the ugly and the incongruous. But this almost unknown soul holds on. "I wait quietly," he says (3:16); then he breaks into as strong a declaration of faith as we are likely ever to find:

206

Though the fig tree does not blossom,
and no fruit is on the vines;
though the produce of the olive fails
and the fields yield no food . . .
yet I will rejoice in the LORD. (3:17, 18)

Listen to that *yet*. It is the essence of faith.

PRAYER: I will *yet* believe and praise you, O Lord; in Christ. Amen.

ZEPHANIAH 1, 2, 3   *Week 38, Day 1*

The list of Zephaniah's family line suggests that he came from distinguished stock. It is very possible he helped influence young King Josiah in the days when he led the nation in spiritual renewal.

But Zephaniah had to cope with a problem that has frustrated many a spiritual leader: "those who say in their hearts, / 'The LORD will not do good, / nor will he do harm'" (1:12). For those who found it convenient to think that God was indifferent, the prophet warns:

The great day of the LORD is near,
near and hastening fast. (1:14)

When that day comes, "neither their silver nor their gold / will be able to save them" (1:18), but "righteousness and humility" (2:3)—such an ancient remedy!—will.

The Hebrew prophets found many ways to describe the beauty of God's new day. Zephaniah pictures it as a time when God "will change the speech of the peoples / to a pure speech, / that all of them may call on the name of the LORD" (3:9). Here is a profound reversal of the Tower of Babel. The confusion of speech at Babel was a result of rebellion against God (Gen. 11:1-9); Zephaniah envisions a time when all humanity will have a "pure speech"—that is, a language dedicated to calling on the Lord and glorifying him. It is a goal to which we, too, can dedicate ourselves.

PRAYER: Touch my lips, O Lord, so that I will speak more surely and more consistently of your purpose and glory; in Christ. Amen.

*R*eturning from the Babylonian and Persian captivity was a great victory for the Jews, but the hardest work was yet to come. The people rebuilt their houses and farms but postponed work on the temple. Enter the prophet Haggai! "These people say the time has not yet come to rebuild the LORD's house," he said. "Is it time for you yourselves to live in your paneled houses, while this house lies in ruins?" (1:2, 4). Haggai reminded the people that with all their efforts they were not getting anywhere: "you . . . earn wages to put them into a bag with holes" (1:6). The remedy: build the house of the Lord.

So they set to work, while Haggai assured them that the Lord was with them. Again, it was not easy. Haggai continued to encourage the people, with God's promise that the temple would one day be filled "with splendor" (2:7), and that they would again enjoy prosperity (2:9). I venture that the succinct messages contained in this book probably represent excerpts from frequent words of rebuke and encouragement. According to tradition, Haggai lived to see the dedication of the temple some four years later.

Haggai's warning to people who live in "paneled houses" may have a painful ring for us. People seem often to be more concerned about God's house when they are poor than when they are comfortable. Comfort easily dulls our sensitivity to God and to human need. It may well be the most dangerous of all intoxicants.

PRAYER: Disturb my comfort, O Lord, with your loving reproof. Amen.

ZECHARIAH 1, 2, 3; PSALM 123   *Week 38, Day 3*

*Z*echariah was a contemporary of Haggai, but a younger man. He was another of those persons who was a priest as well as a prophet, which is encouraging evidence that a person can be part of an institution yet not be silenced by it. His prophecies are often expressed in exotic visions, sometimes in poetry but more often in prose.

He is privileged to have a message of encouragement. At a time when the people were still struggling to rebuild the land following two generations of captivity, Zechariah promised, "Jerusalem shall be inhabited like villages without walls," with the Lord serving as "a wall of fire all around it" (2:4, 5). Those who have plundered Zion will suffer, because "one who touches you touches the apple of my eye" (2:8).

Zechariah also gives us one of those Old Testament pictures of grace. When Joshua, the high priest, stands before God, his position is challenged by Satan, who is there "to accuse him" (3:1). This is consistent with the other appearances of the adversary: in Eden, when the serpent accused God to Eve, and in Job, when he attacked Job's integrity. It seems Joshua was contaminated in some serious way, for he was "dressed with filthy clothes" (3:3). But an angel commanded that the filthy clothes be removed and that he be clothed "with festal apparel," because "I have taken your guilt away from you" (3:4). The cleansing is a gift, as is the new garment of purity. They always are gifts. That's what we mean by grace.

PRAYER: Thank you, dear Savior, for undeserved kindness. Amen.

ZECHARIAH 4, 5, 6   *Week 38, Day 4*

God speaks to us according to our need, and according to the circumstances of a given time. An illustration that brings great comfort to one person may seem almost inane to another; but just as surely, a message that might bless the second person would be incomprehensible to the first. Zechariah receives the word of the Lord in visions that are appropriate to his time and need. For his circumstances, symbolism was more powerful than a straightforward declaration. So we have a lampstand, flying scrolls, a woman in a basket, and chariots.

And perhaps each one underlines the message that was to be given to Zerubbabel: "Not by might, nor by power, but by my spirit, says the LORD of hosts" (4:6). The Jews had seen a great deal of might and power over recent generations, especially in the Babylonian and Persian war machines; Zechariah insists that such cannot ultimately win. At last the victory will be by the spirit of the Lord.

Rudyard Kipling gave a similar warning in his *Recessional*:

> If, drunk with sight of power, we loose
> Wild tongues that have not Thee in awe—

And the message fits our own times. Not only in the use of armaments; that issue is too obvious, even if we are slow still to ponder it. But most of us are far more likely to be drunk with the power we see in the latest survey, the newest fashion, the most recent gimmick. And with it all, not heeding Zechariah, we neglect God's spirit.

PRAYER: Let your spirit rest on me, O God; to your glory. Amen.

ZECHARIAH 7, 8, 9, 10   *Week 38, Day 5*

The Hebrew prophets maintained a fierce commitment to justice, especially in relationship to those unable to protect themselves. So Zechariah, after symbolic messages, becomes stunningly clear: "do not oppress the widow, the orphan, the alien, or the poor; and do not devise evil in your hearts against one another" (7:10). He picks up another favorite prophetic theme, the vision of a perfect day, but he has his own wonderfully practical way of describing it. He sees a time and a place so peaceful that "old men and old women shall again sit in the streets of Jerusalem, each with staff in hand because of their great age. And the streets of the city shall be full of boys and girls playing in its streets" (8:4, 5). How better could we describe civic security than a city where the two most vulnerable elements of society, the very old and the very young, are perfectly secure? These verses would make a good campaign theme for a late twentieth-century political aspirant!

We read the prophet Zechariah each Palm Sunday:

> Rejoice greatly, O daughter Zion!
>   Shout aloud, O daughter Jerusalem!
> Lo, your king comes to you;
>   triumphant and victorious is he,
> humble and riding on a donkey,
>   on a colt, the foal of a donkey. (9:9)

210

As Matthew (21:5) and John (12:14, 15) see it, Zechariah got a vision far beyond his immediate day; he saw the Lord.

PRAYER: Keep me always open, O God, to high expectations. Amen.

ZECHARIAH 11, 12, 13, 14   *Week 38, Day 6*

*T*he New Testament writers quote Zechariah several times in applying some of his words to Jesus Christ. When Zechariah describes his encounter with the sheep merchants, in which they value him at thirty shekels of silver (11:12, 13) Matthew sees this passage as referring to the betrayal price that Judas received (Matt. 27:9, 10). Zechariah speaks of an anonymous one who suffers for the house of David and says that they will "look on the one whom they have pierced" (12:10). John's Gospel quotes these words as part of the significance of Jesus' death at Calvary (John 19:37).

At first reading, we may not see in these passages what the New Testament writers saw; it may even seem that they stretch a point in finding messianic significance where they do. But two things should be said: first, that the New Testament writers were generally following the ancient rabbinical style of interpretation and application; and second, that they were reflecting the common understanding of the early church, the body of believers closest to the events that were being interpreted.

I choose, therefore, to accept their understanding. I trust their judgment as to the leading of God's spirit, and I trust their rules for interpreting the meaning of passages in the Hebrew scriptures. I feel that their understanding is closer in both time and spirit than mine, and I'm satisfied that they reflect the mind of the spirit.

PRAYER: Keep my faith both simple and inquiring, I pray; in Christ. Amen.

MALACHI 1, 2, 3, 4   *Week 38, Day 7*

*M*alachi does a fascinating job of catechetical teaching, constantly raising questions ("But you say . . . "), then answering them. This became a standard rabbinical method, and of course became also the pattern for books of Christian catechism. Whether Malachi was the first to use it, we don't know. Certainly it was an effective method for him, especially in light of the dismal times in which he was prophesying. The people were disheartened and probably more than a little rebellious, so when Malachi said, "But you say," he was very likely quoting the complaints he was hearing from the person on the street. In some cases he may have given words to questions that were only in their minds but that they were afraid to venture. In any event, he challenged the people to make their case before God.

In return, Malachi made God's case, especially in reminding them that they had forsaken the tithe. Stop robbing God, he said, and see if God "will not open the windows of heaven for you and pour down for you an overflowing blessing" (3:10).

Most modern scholars would not think of Malachi as the last of the Hebrew prophets, but the book is surely well placed, in light of 4:5—"Lo, I will send you the prophet Elijah before the great and terrible day of the LORD comes." The Jews believed Elijah would return in preparation for the coming of the Messiah. In quoting this verse, Matthew identifies John the Baptist as Elijah (Matt. 11:14).

PRAYER: Prepare me each day, O Lord, for your visitation. Amen.

MATTHEW 1, 2; PSALM 124   Week 39, Day 1

*I*f I were going to write a biography of Jesus, I wouldn't begin with a list of forty-two names. But Matthew wanted especially to reach a Jewish audience, and he knew that for them, Jesus' family history—the fact that he was descended from Abraham, Judah, and David—would carry great weight. Until that point was established, his miracles, teachings, and personal charisma were of little significance.

With this audience in mind, this Gospel repeatedly reminds us (five times in these two chapters alone) that the events in Jesus' life were fulfillments of prophecy. Verses that might seem obscure to us are part of the mosaic of expectation for Jews who had waited for the messiah for so many generations. Matthew wants to be sure that every element of Jesus' story demonstrates that he was, beyond doubt, the awaited one.

At the same time, however, this Gospel brings gentiles into the story from the very beginning. The wise men from the east are outsiders, so to speak, yet they come seeking the one "born king of the Jews." And it is to a gentile nation, Egypt, that the holy family flees in order to survive. It's as if Matthew were telling his primary Jewish audience that it is through this One that they will now fulfill their mission to all the nations.

PRAYER: I want, O Child of Bethlehem, to embrace you as both messiah and king; in your name. Amen.

MATTHEW 3, 4; PSALM 125   *Week 39, Day 2*

*J*ohn the Baptist looks like a Hebrew prophet of the old order, especially Elijah. He is unconventional, unbending, and fearless, like his courageous predecessors. But he is the prophet of the new order, preparing the way for God's messiah. When the crowds flocked to him, he explained that he was not the one for whom they were waiting; he was not fit even to carry that one's sandals (3:11). Yet he was privileged to baptize Jesus, which meant, in a sense, that he ordained him.

Jesus' baptism in water was followed by a baptism of trial. For forty days and nights he waited on God in the wilderness, then encountered the adversary, and was victorious. Then, on to Galilee, and specifically to Capernaum. We tend to miss the importance of Capernaum in Jesus' life, though we're told "he made his home" there (4:13). At first his message was like John's—"Repent, for the kingdom of heaven has come near" (4:17). It was both a command and an invitation. A new day had come, and it was to be entered by way of repentance.

Now Jesus brought together a team. They were an unlikely lot: fishermen, small businessmen, young, probably naive and parochial. They remind us that God can work with the most rudimentary material—indeed, that with such material God can produce saints and geniuses! This motley group walked closest to the Lord of glory.

PRAYER: Help me, dear Savior, never to settle for anything less than my best potential in you; in Christ. Amen.

MATTHEW 5, 6, 7   *Week 39, Day 3*

*A*nother sign that Matthew wanted especially to reach a Jewish audience is his emphasis on Jesus' role as teacher. These chapters, usually called the Sermon on the Mount, are the first of five large teaching segments in Matthew. They describe a mountain-peak kind of life. No wonder that when Jesus finished, "the crowds were astounded at his teaching" (7:28), for he spoke not only "as one having authority" but also as one who dared to command a new way of life.

In the Beatitudes (5:3-12) Jesus redefined the blessed life. He explained that he had come to fulfill the law and the prophets, then showed how he would do so, by extending the meaning of the commandments of murder and adultery to the inner life (5:21-30). He confronted the pragmatic eye-for-an-eye rule with a command based on love, then insisted that such love is the kind of perfection God expects of us (5:38-48).

His teachings regarding the spiritual life left no room for religious poseurs (6:1-18). He called for a life where worry is absurd (6:25-34). He warned that the life he was teaching would not be easy (7:13, 14), but that it is the only foundation upon which one can possibly build for the future (7:24-27).

Are these teachings beyond our present living? Of course! Shall we then stop pursuing them? Never! As Browning said, a person's "reach should exceed his grasp, or what's a heaven for?"

PRAYER: Save me, O Lord, from the lowlands of life; set my eyes and my feet toward higher ground! In Jesus' name. Amen.

MATTHEW 8, 9; PSALM 126   *Week 39, Day 4*

*W*hen Jesus taught, the crowds recognized his authority (7:29); now his actions add an exclamation point to his teachings. These two chapters are a very panorama of gracious power. It's as if Matthew intends to give us a full sampling of divinity at work: healing of leprosy, paralysis, fever, demon possession, blindness and muteness, and raising from the dead. He heals from a distance, by simply speaking the word (8:5-13), and without even a word or an act when a timid woman reaches out to touch him (9:20-22).

Jesus' power extends even to impersonal nature, so that he quiets a storm; "even the winds and the sea obey him" (8:27). And at a very different level, but ultimately as impressive, he draws Matthew from career and wealth to follow him.

But with all of this, he can nevertheless be rejected by those whose hearts are set against him. The Pharisees see a transformed tax collector and are provoked to criticism (9:9-11), or observe miracles of life and healing and credit them to the devil (9:34). All of which reminds us that no miracle is so awesome, no argument so cogent, as to convince those who have closed their minds. The Pharisees, and those associated with them, had too much at stake in keeping things as they were. To acknowledge Jesus for who he was called for a higher price than they were willing to pay.

PRAYER: Save me, dear Lord, from the darkness of heart that will not acknowledge your mercy and power; in Jesus' name. Amen.

MATTHEW 10, 11, 12   Week 39, Day 5

*T*here is a kind of cascading urgency in these chapters. Jesus had said that the harvest was great and the laborers few (9:36-38); now we enter a run of breakneck activity, which is as if Jesus were trying to bring in the harvest immediately. He enlists his twelve, including Judas Iscariot, the betrayer, then tells them how they must go about their work. And see the urgency: "The kingdom of heaven has come near" (10:7). It's a no-nonsense approach, as befits a program in a hurry: "If anyone will not welcome you or listen to your words, shake off the dust from your feet" (10:14).

Jesus warns that they will meet opposition, but he tells his little cadre to go without fear. Even as he speaks, we see that nothing is to stand in the way: not the heartbreaking ambivalence of John the Baptist in his imprisonment (11:2, 3), not the hallowed sabbath (12:1-14), not Beelzebul and those who unwittingly side with him (12:22-32), and not even Jesus' own family (12:46-50). There is work to be done, and nothing will be allowed to stay it.

This is no tea party, no pleasant club. Our Lord was calling disciples for a ministry so powerful that it would dare to offer rest to all "that are weary and are carrying heavy burdens" (11:28). A ministry of such reach and power is possible only at the price of a profound commitment. Half-hearted disciples (an oxymoron indeed) will not do.

PRAYER: Your work demands our best, dear Lord; help me, please, to give nothing less; in Jesus' name. Amen.

MATTHEW 13, 14; PSALM 127   *Week 39, Day 6*

*T*hose who were drawn to Jesus felt he was the king for whom they had waited so long. But what kind of kingdom would he bring? Jesus answers with a series of parables. But when it comes to a parable, as Leander Keck has said, "either you get it, or you don't." Jesus seems to suggest that his parables are intentionally difficult ("You will indeed listen, but never understand" [13:14]), not because he wants to shut persons out, but because there must be an utter commitment to enter in. To understand a parable—*really* understand it, beyond the surface data—is to enter the kingdom, to become a disciple.

We get a sense of the price as we see Jesus rejected by the people of Nazareth, his home town (13:54-58), and still more as we receive the report of the death of John the Baptist. When Jesus, in the wake of this news, seeks "a deserted place by himself" (14:13), the crowds will not let him go. In "compassion for them," he cures their sick; and when the disciples would send them away, he insists, "you give them something to eat" (14:16). He feeds the five thousand on the little that is brought to him, then shows himself master of the storm. The disciples hail him: "Truly you are the Son of God" (14:33), but Jesus doesn't acknowledge their declaration as he will later when Peter makes it under other circumstances (16:16). Awe at a miracle is good, but it is not necessarily a foundation for lasting discipleship.

PRAYER: Still today, dear Lord, you call me to your kingdom. I declare you again to be the Lord of my life; in Christ. Amen.

MATTHEW 15, 16, 17   *Week 39, Day 7*

*A*s we read these chapters, we sense the tension building. The Pharisees continue to challenge Jesus, hoping to prove that he violates the traditions of the elders (15:1-9), or asking for a sign that will prove his role (16:1-4). In each such instance, Jesus turns the challenge around; his anger has about it the quality of the Hebrew prophets who so often were in controversy with the religious leaders of their day.

To add to the problem, the disciples seem often to be slow to understand what Jesus is about. Sometimes they seem almost obtuse, as when they miss his point about the yeast of the Pharisees and Sadducees (16:6). But then there is a moment of pure illumination, when Jesus asks what the people are saying, and presses them to examine their own thinking: "But who do you say that I am?" (16:15). Peter rises to the occasion with the confession that is the very foundation of the church (16:16-18). In a time such as ours, when so many good but secondary matters so often absorb us, we need to remind ourselves that the issue, in the end, is always the person of Jesus Christ.

But while Peter recognizes the Lordship of Jesus, he is not ready to see the place of the cross. It is at the cross that we make Christ's Lordship effective; no wonder it is a hard step! Peter, James, and John have an easier time with the glory revealed at the transfiguration (17:1-8), but I doubt that they linked it with the cross.

PRAYER: Dear Lord, give me a faith that accepts your cross as gladly as your glory; in your name I pray. Amen.

MATTHEW 18, 19, 20   *Week 40, Day 1*

*O*ur lives are such a mixture of the grand and the trivial. Keeping the two in balance is one of the marks of true saintliness. Jesus knows that he is headed toward the final hour, but meanwhile there is work to be done and there are lessons to be taught. So he tells of the search for one wandering sheep, and perhaps applies it to a member of the faith who has offended another (18:10-17). He teaches his disciples (including you and me, of course) that we should be ready to forgive "seventy-seven times" (18:21-35)—that is, unendingly!—and makes the point by a story that shows how great our debt to God is by comparison with the debts others owe us. He calls for a high ethic of marriage, so high that his disciples wonder if "it is better not to marry" (19:10). And he stops to bless children, somewhat to the discomfort of his disciples, who apparently feel he has bigger things to do (19:13-15).

Those "bigger things," for the disciples, seem to be matters of position and gain. They wonder who will be greatest in the kingdom of heaven (18:1-5), and miss the point of Jesus' answer, because the mother of James and John still seeks their preferment (20:20-28). We're not surprised that they are "greatly astounded" when Jesus says that it will be very difficult for the rich to enter the kingdom (19:16-26) because they still see these human standards as paramount. They don't seem really to hear Jesus when he says, "Whoever wishes to be first among you must be your slave" (20:27). And neither do we.

PRAYER: Help me, O God, really to follow you; in Christ. Amen.

MATTHEW 21, 22, 23   Week 40, Day 2

Anyone who holds to a childhood picture of "gentle Jesus, meek and mild" will be undone by these chapters. In them, our Lord confronts his opponents at every turn. The cursing of the fig tree is often called an acted-out parable, because Jesus was thus demonstrating the failure of Israel to bear fruit. In a sense, the cleansing of the temple is also such a parable-in-action, as Jesus chooses a specific shortcoming of Judaism to symbolize a larger failing and pours his wrath upon it.

The parable of the two sons advances the same theme, as

does the parable of the wicked tenants. In each story, Jesus sharply identifies the failure of Israel to fulfill its mission. "The chief priests and the Pharisees . . . realized that he was speaking about them" and wanted to be rid of him, but didn't dare (21:45, 46). The parable of the wedding banquet is equally severe: "The wedding is ready, but those invited were not worthy. . . . Many are called, but few are chosen" (Matt. 22:8, 14).

These were hard words, but the strongest were yet to come. After telling his disciples to obey the teachings of the scribes and Pharisees but not to emulate their lives, he enters upon a series of denunciations against their practices, each beginning with "woe to you, scribes and Pharisees, hypocrites!" But bitter as the denunciation is, it concludes with an impassioned expression of sorrow for Jerusalem's coming fate.

PRAYER: Help me, dear Lord, to be true to you when my contemporary society is indifferent to your claims; in Jesus' name. Amen.

MATTHEW 24, 25; PSALMS 128, 129   *Week 40, Day 3*

*T*he disciples asked Jesus a three-part question (though they may not have intended it as such): tell us when the temple will be destroyed, the sign of your coming and of the end of the age (24:1-3). In the passages that follow, it is difficult to know when Jesus is answering one question or the other. Some portions seem to have been fulfilled at the destruction of Jerusalem in A.D. 70, but for the rest perhaps the most important counsel is this, "But about that day and hour no one knows, neither the angels of heaven, nor the Son, but only the Father" (24:36). Jesus makes the point still more emphatic when he says that it will be "as the days of Noah were," when everything seemed utterly normal—people were "eating and drinking, marrying and giving in marriage," with no idea of how near disaster was (24:37-39).

The parables that follow are really all we need. The bridesmaids remind us that we must "keep awake," since we "know neither the day nor the hour" (25:13). The story of the talents tells us that we must be faithful in our responsibilities in the time when our Lord is absent, so that we can meet him

without fear on his return. And the story of the judgment of
the nations spells out some of the specifics of our manner of
life: we must feed the hungry, welcome the stranger, clothe
the naked, and care for those who are sick and in prison. Our
task is not really to watch the skies, but to be faithfully about
God's business.

PRAYER: It's easy for me to get fascinated with tomorrow;
help me instead, O Lord, to be a faithful steward of today; in
Christ. Amen.

MATTHEW 26, 27, 28   *Week 40, Day 4*

These chapters should be read in the mood of the spiritual
"Were You There?" They are to be entered into, not simply as history or drama (though both are present) but as
events in which we share. Paul said, "I have been crucified
with Christ" (Gal. 2:19); such is our sense of involvement.
We listen with the disciples as Jesus warns that he will soon
"be handed over to be crucified" (26:2). We wonder with
them as Jesus describes the ointment anointing as preparation
for burial, and we gather at the table of the Passover, ponder-
ing that our rather orderly communion ritual began here. We
sense that we are weak, along with Peter, James, and John, as
Jesus prays in Gethsemane.

We feel the fear that caught up Peter and the others during
Jesus' trial, and we understand how quickly the brave words of
one hour can turn into retreat a little later. We hurt for Judas
as he looks for a way to make amends, but looks in the wrong
direction. And we imagine ourselves in the crowd as the people choose Barabbas over Jesus.

And then we stand somewhere not far from the cross, close
enough to hear some mock but also to hear a hardened centurion acknowledge, "Truly this man was God's Son!" (27:54).
We watch with the two Marys as Joseph of Arimathea asks for
the body of Jesus.

Best of all, we are there as the exultant days of resurrection
begin—days that continue to this very moment.

PRAYER: Keep me always near your cross, O Lord, and
always filled with the glory of your resurrection; in your name
I pray. Amen.

220

*T*he Gospel of Mark is said to have been written espe-cially for a Roman audience and to have been influ-enced greatly by the apostle Peter. When one recalls that the Romans were the premier administrators of their day, people of action and accomplishment, it's easy to believe that this Gospel is aimed at them. It begins, not with a birth story, as in Matthew and Luke, or a theological case, as in John, but with Jesus ready to enter his ministry at age thirty. This is a Gospel of action, and its favorite word is *immediately*.

When Mark says, "The beginning of the good news of Jesus Christ, the Son of God" (1:1), he has let us know that his purpose is to show us who Jesus is. Mark embarks quickly on a series of short vignettes—calling disciples, performing heal-ings, preaching in Galilee, cleansing a leper, healing a para-lytic, and answering questions from his opponents. When Mark lists the twelve disciples, he identifies James and John with the use of an Aramaic word (Boanerges). This is one of seven times in this Gospel where Mark bothers to preserve the Aramaic phrases that were actually used by our Lord. It is a particular characteristic of this Gospel, and it gives it a kind of immediacy and intimacy that is unique.

When Jesus heals the paralytic, the crowds are amazed and say, "We have never seen anything like this!" (2:12). That's the mood Mark intends to leave with us all through his short book.

Prayer: Thank you, dear Lord, for the wonderful works done through your Son, our Savior—continuing to this very day; in Christ. Amen.

*B*ecause of his emphasis on action, Mark gives less time to the teachings of Jesus than do any of the other Gospels. Perhaps that suggests that those parables and teach-ings which he includes are all the more significant. The para-ble of the sower is of course a landmark instance, because it shows the followers of Jesus what they are up against, both in their own lives and in the fields where they labor; it isn't easy, because so little of life's soil is truly productive. On the other hand, there is encouragement in the parables of the lamp, the growing seed, and the mustard seed, because each one demonstrates how a relatively small, silent force can eventually be signficant out of all proportion to its size. The disciples are part of something very great, much greater than they are able to realize.

How great? They are linked now with One who can still a storm, and who seems almost bewildered by their lack of faith (4:40). He enters the realm of powers that are mysterious and therefore particularly frightening, and sets the beleaguered free (5:1-13). And when he confronts the ancient, invincible enemy, death, he treats its victim as if she were only taking an afternoon nap (5:41). So, too, he feeds a multitude, in a manner that seems effortless. What makes him most different, in all of this, is that where we marvel at his wondrous works, "he was amazed at their unbelief" (6:6). Knowing what he did, he could not imagine approaching life with doubt or fear.

PRAYER: Give me, I pray, a faith that conquers daily; in Christ. Amen.

MARK 7, 8, 9   *Week 40, Day 7*

*I*t's interesting to compare the stories that appear consecutively in chapter 7. The Pharisees, who ought by virtue of their commitments to have been the first to accept Jesus, were dedicated instead to challenging and discrediting him. But a Syrophoenician woman—an outsider—believed in him so intensely that she refused to be postponed or rebuffed. So the first are last, and the last, first.

What did the Pharisees really want when they came to Jesus seeking "a sign from heaven" (8:11)? Not a sign, because such evidences were available to them every day, wherever Jesus went. They wanted some device by which they could diminish his hold upon the common people.

Clearly enough, the masses of people weren't sure what to think of Jesus; he might be John the Baptist returned to life, or Elijah, or some other prophet (8:28). They knew he was extraordinary, both as teacher or as miracle worker, but it was the disciples—and particularly, Peter—who would recognize Jesus as the Messiah.

But their image of the messiah was one of acclaim and position, so when Jesus spoke of being rejected and killed, they couldn't grasp it; and in the process, they missed entirely his promise of rising again "after three days" (8:31). Nor did they receive it when he told them again, not much later, that after being killed, he would rise again. It's very hard to get past our own preconceptions so that we can effectively hear what God is saying to us.

PRAYER: Open my eyes, my ears, O God, to your truth; in Christ. Amen.

MARK 10, 11, 12   *Week 41, Day 1*

*J*esus upsets our usual measure of values; we have become so used to a tamed version of our Lord that we don't always realize it. When the disciples tried to push aside the children who crowded to Jesus, "he was indignant" (10:14), and I expect the disciples were bewildered; they had their own ideas about who should be given the most attention. The disciples reasoned that it would be easier for those who were wealthy to enter God's kingdom; after all, their wealth must itself be a sign of God's blessing, and besides, they were the ones to whom society paid the most attention. When Jesus said the rich were handicapped, the disciples asked themselves, "Then who can be saved?" (10:26). And when a blind beggar sought healing, the crowds "sternly ordered him to be quiet" (10:48), but Jesus stopped the parade to answer the beggar's request.

I wonder, too, exactly how the disciples responded to the triumphal entry into Jerusalem? Perhaps they saw little future in the kind of people who spread coats and palm branches in his path; the folks who did so surely didn't belong to the power structure! But on the other hand, those who changed money and sold in the temple had the right connections, as did the people against whom Jesus directed his parable of the wicked tenants (12:1-12). And when he hailed the giving of a widow whose total assets were a penny, they must surely have wondered. If we took Jesus more seriously, we would wonder more often, too.

PRAYER: Help me, O Lord, to see things as you do; in your name. Amen.

MARK 13, 14; PSALMS 130, 131 *Week 41, Day 2*

*I*f the prophecies about the end times were more specific, probably even the most devout would relax until the signs were clearly fulfilled. As it is, the prophecies are shadowed enough that one message stands out: "Therefore, keep awake—for you do not know when the master of the house will come" (13:35).

Some people still are uneasy with Jesus' handling of the incident involving the woman who anointed him with costly ointment. They tend to stumble over the phrase "you always have the poor with you," rather than concentrating on what follows: "you can show kindness to them whenever you wish" (14:7). Probably the people of Jesus' day, like many of us today, wrung their hands over the poor more than they ministered to them, and probably they found it easier to criticize someone else's use of money than to give to the poor themselves. In any event, Jesus tells us that there is a time for everything. At this particular time, the issue was a loving preparation of Jesus for burial.

A good word ought to be said for Peter. It is true that he was unduly self-confident when he said that he would die with Jesus rather than betray him, but "all of them said the same" (14:31). And although it is easy to condemn Peter for following Jesus "at a distance," as far as we know, he was the only person (with the possible exception of John) who dared to follow into the danger area—and he did so "right into the courtyard" (14:54). He meant well. And so do we.

PRAYER: Give me the courage to admit that I am yours. Amen.

MARK 15, 16; PSALMS 132, 133 *Week 41, Day 3*

*D*ay by day we show courage and cowardice in surprising ways. When Jesus stood on trial before Pilate, Pilate understood that "it was out of jealousy that the chief priests had handed him over" (15:10), but eventually he gave in to their pressure. Why? Because he "wish[ed] to satisfy the crowd" (15:15). Pilate was not an elected official. There was no reason for him to be so solicitous of the crowd, especially since he saw the issues so clearly. But he gave in.

On the other hand, a centurion, with far fewer advantages than Pilate, spoke his witness for Christ loudly enough that he was heard and the words were remembered. And then there was Joseph of Arimathea. He was "a respected member of the council," someone who had much to lose by affiliating himself in any way with Jesus. Yet he "went boldly to Pilate and asked for the body of Jesus" (15:43). Perhaps no one looks more noble in the dark Friday of Calvary than this man Joseph.

And finally, Mary Magdalene and Mary the mother of Jesus. Apparently they stayed nearer the cross than any of the disciples (15:40). When Joseph took the body away, they followed to see where it would be laid (15:47). So they were first at the tomb on the day we now call Easter—and as a result, they were the first to encounter the new fact of the resurrection. That isn't surprising. It is always the people who dare to believe and to follow closely who are present at the wondrous hours.

PRAYER: Dear Lord, help me recognize the occasions when courage is needed, and give me the strength to act accordingly; in Christ. Amen.

LUKE 1, 2, 3   Week 41, Day 4

*I*t is generally believed that Luke the physician was a gentile—probably the only one among the New Testament writers. His Gospel is directed especially to non-Jews. His picture of Jesus is uniquely appealing in its emphasis on women, the poor, the sick, and the rejected. Several of the most beloved parables appear exclusively in Luke's Gospel, and it is here that we have several hymns.

He begins his story, not with Jesus but with the peculiar circumstances surrounding the birth of John the Baptist. The story concentrates also on two women: Elizabeth, the mother of John, and Mary, the mother of Jesus. Their relationship of mutual support is beautiful, as is the character of Zechariah, John's father.

We enjoy four Advent and Christmas songs in these opening chapters, beginning with Mary's *Magnificat*, then Zechariah's prophecy, the song of the heavenly host (which appears on millions of cards each Christmas season), and at last Simeon's *nunc dimittis*. In all of this, Luke makes us very rich; we're grateful for what he has preserved for us.

And of course, one more special gift. Luke tells us the one New Testament story from the boyhood of Jesus, the incident in his twelfth year when he went with his parents to the Passover and remained behind in the temple (2:41-52). This is our only story from the nearly thirty years from his birth until his ministry began, and it is a very lovely one.

PRAYER: Thank you, heavenly Father, for a faith that has inspired ten thousands of songs through the ages, beginning with Luke. Amen.

LUKE 4, 5, 6   *Week 41, Day 5*

*W*hen we think of Jesus and temptation, we usually think of three questions in the wilderness. But "for forty days he was tempted by the devil" (4:2); the three recorded questions were the peak of the process. Further, when Jesus met those questions successfully, the devil "departed from him until an opportune time" (4:13). The struggle would go on.

Very likely the next test was in Nazareth, where his lifetime friends could only say, "Is this not Joseph's son?" (4:22). Mary Lyon said, "Nine-tenths of our suffering is caused by others not thinking so much of us as we think they ought." Did Jesus have such feelings at Nazareth?

If so, they didn't deter him long. He healed demoniacs, fevers, lepers, and paralytics, preached in the synagogue, and began bringing together his mixed crew of disciples—some fishermen first, then a tax collector. Then he rounded out the group after a night in prayer with God (6:12).

Luke gives us only a portion of the teachings that in Matthew we call the Sermon on the Mount. There are fewer beatitudes, and they seem more earthly; where Matthew's record speaks of the "poor in spirit," Luke simply calls them the poor (6:20), and his whole emphasis seems to be on the promise of blessing to those who suffer on this earth. I don't think of the two versions as contradictions; they probably record the ways Jesus taught on different occasions, and in truth, we need both messages.

PRAYER: Give me strength, dear Lord, for my days of testing. Amen.

LUKE 7, 8; PSALMS 134, 135   Week 41, Day 6

S ince Luke was a physician, we're not surprised that he makes more of the healing stories, often giving more details and of course using specifically medical terms where the other Gospels may use more general terms. And while the compassion of Jesus is emphasized in all of the Gospels, Luke seems by an extra word here and there to give it an even larger place. When he says, in the story of the raising of the young man at Nain, "He was his mother's only son, and she was a widow" (7:12), we have a whole scenario of pain and sorrow. Luke's Gospel is the only one to record this story.

Luke's feeling for the forgotten and rejected elements of society is underscored in the incident at the home of Simon the Pharisee. Most of us have seen enough to realize the truth of Jesus' teaching that we love in measure of the forgiveness we have experienced (7:47). But of course all of us have sinned, and our private thoughts indicate our frightening capacity for still more sin. The greatest saints, it seems to me, have always seen themselves as great sinners. Charles Wesley, whose personal life was extraordinarily exemplary, nevertheless describes himself in his hymns as among the worst of sinners; he had come close enough to the holiness of God to have a clearer estimate of his own failings. Perhaps the advantage of a certain type of sinner—such as the woman who came to Simon's house—is that their sins are obvious enough to be easily recognized. Most of our sins are not so clearly seen.

PRAYER: Give me the grace, O Lord, to see myself as I am. Amen.

*H*aving said so much about the quality of compassion that is emphasized in this Gospel, we should note that Luke does not ignore the hard demands of the faith. With Matthew and Mark, he reports Jesus' words that those who want to be disciples must "deny themselves and take up their cross daily" (9:23). Like Matthew, he tells of those who wanted to follow Jesus tentatively, and how our Lord rejected them. And when a woman spoke to him in highly sentimental terms, Jesus seemed almost to rebuke her by replying, "Blessed rather are those who hear the word of God and obey it!" (11:28). Luke records Jesus' vigorous denouncing of the Pharisees; and when a lawyer in the group said, "Teacher, when you say these things, you insult us, too" (11:45), Jesus as much as answered, "Right you are!" and proceeded to say, "Woe also to you lawyers!"

Luke alone gives us the magnificent story of the good Samaritan. We have it because a lawyer wanted to test Jesus, asking, "What must I do to inherit eternal life?" The lawyer, "wanting to justify himself" (10:29), asked a follow-up question: "And who is my neighbor?" Jesus' story turned the question around so that it said, "To whom will you be a neighbor?" The term "good Samaritan" has become part of our common speech, so that people who never read the Bible use it. But most of us will confess that while we know the story and honor the term, we don't often live up to its standard.

PRAYER: Help me to see, dear Lord, that your compassion calls me to tough and dedicated living. Help me to take your cross; in Christ. Amen.

LUKE 12, 13, 14   *Week 42, Day 1*

*T*here is a face-the-facts quality in Luke's Gospel. He alone tells us Jesus' parable of the rich fool, a warning against greed. The man had so much that his major concern was how to keep what he had. He said to himself, "Soul, you have ample goods laid up for many years," but God said to him, "You fool! This very night your life is being demanded of you" (12:19, 20). In a sense, this legendary rich man had the same problem as Simon the Pharisee (7:36-50), in that he hadn't taken a really complete audit of his resources.

And that's the point of the parable that Luke includes in Jesus' call to discipleship. It is not a casual thing to follow Jesus, and we ought not to set out on such a venture without seeing whether we are prepared to follow through. "For which of you, intending to build a tower, does not first sit down and estimate the cost, to see whether he has enough to complete it?" (14:28). We human beings are inclined to superficial thinking when it comes to matters of the soul.

Jesus gives some very down-to-earth advice for disciples, and Luke includes it. In a world where so much attention is paid to being with the right people and fulfilling social obligations tastefully, Jesus gave a very different rule: "when you give a banquet, invite the poor, the crippled, the lame, and the blind" (14:13)—that is, the very persons who were rejected in the first-century world. How would we translate that to fit the late twentieth century?

PRAYER: Help me, I pray, to count the cost, and then follow! Amen.

LUKE 15, 16; PSALM 136   Week 42, Day 2

*I*n my youth I heard an evangelist describe Luke 15 as "God's Lost and Found Department." I can't improve on that title. There are three parables with a single theme, and only the first of the three appears in another Gospel. The concluding story, of the father and his two sons (both of them prodigals, but in different ways), has been described as the most beautiful short story ever written.

The three parables were Jesus' response to scribes and Pharisees who were grumbling, "This fellow welcomes sinners and eats with them" (15:2). Their desire was not to see sinners redeemed, but to be isolated from them, so they were bewildered that Jesus would choose to associate with such persons. Jesus redefined the terms. A sinner, he said through these stories, is someone who is lost. So what does one do for that which is lost? Despise it? No; find it! Three times over, Jesus said that heaven rejoices because the lost has been found.

229

The series concludes with an unfinished segment, the response of the elder brother. Jesus' questioners were themselves, of course, the elder brothers, so it was up to them to provide a conclusion for the story. Just as it is up to us today.

Luke challenges wealth once again in recording Jesus' story of the rich man and Lazarus. If you think a miracle will convince an unbeliever, the answer is no. If people won't listen to the witness of scripture, they won't be convinced by someone rising from the dead (16:31).

PRAYER: Give me your outlook, dear Savior, for the lost; in Christ. Amen.

LUKE 17, 18, 19; PSALM 137   *Week 42, Day 3*

These chapters contain four events or teachings not found in the other Gospels, and each is a little jewel. The story of Jesus healing ten lepers, with only one returning to give thanks, is a painful insight into human nature at its more insensitive levels (17:11-19). But we're glad for even one, and we hope our spirit is kin to his.

The parable of the woman who persisted in her appeal to a judge "who neither feared God nor had respect for people" (18:2), but who finally acceded to the woman's request because she was about to wear him out by her continual coming is a significant insight into the place of perseverance in prayer. Luke brought up this theme earlier in Jesus' story of a friend who will give bread at midnight, not for friendship's sake but because of persistence (11:5-8). The point of each story is not the character of God but the importance, at times, of perseverance in prayer.

All of us love the story of the self-righteous Pharisee and the repentant tax collector, though perhaps we don't easily recognize how close we may be to the spirit of the Pharisee. That's a problem for us good folks! And it was "good folks," of course, who grumbled when Jesus said he was going to the home of the tax collector Zacchaeus for a visit. The people resented the fact that Jesus associated with "one who is a sinner," simply not understanding that he had come to earth "to seek out and to save the lost" (19:10). This verse could easily be the theme of Luke's Gospel.

PRAYER: Come dine at my house, O Lord, for I am a sinner. Amen.

LUKE 20, 21; PSALM 138   *Week 42, Day 4*

*A*ll the incidents and teachings in these chapters appear also in either Matthew or Mark, and most of them in both. It seems that the events just prior to Jesus' trial and crucifixion were understood by the Gospel writers to be part of the sacred mosaic of those dramatic hours and therefore essential to the story. At other points they might omit or add according to the emphasis they were inspired to make, but there is some measure of near unanimity here.

Two elements stand out. There is, first, the rising tide of opposition as the enemies of Jesus seek to catch him in an incriminating statement. They question his authority, and he chooses simply to deflect their question with one of his own. Any other answer was quite unnecessary, since he had already declared himself any number of times, in one way or another. They sought then to catch him on an issue that might cause the Roman authorities to arrest him, the matter of taxes (20:20-26), but Jesus handled the issue so deftly that "they became silent." The Sadducees then picked up their favorite theme, the resurrection; and some of the scribes, to their credit, said, "Teacher, you have spoken well" (20:39). Jesus then challenged the group with a question of his own, regarding the relationship between David and the Messiah.

The other recurring element is the issue of prophecy. Jesus talks about the destruction of the temple, signs of the times, and his return, and always with the warning: watch and be ready.

PRAYER: Prepare my heart, O God, for whatever is in store; in Christ. Amen.

LUKE 22, 23, 24   *Week 42, Day 5*

*T*he Gospel of John rarely covers the same material as the Synoptic Gospels (Matthew, Mark, Luke), but all four Gospels cover essentially the same ground, though with their

231

own quality of emphasis, in the events we now identify as Maundy Thursday, Good Friday, and Easter.

But Luke, true to his feelings for the least and the lost, includes the story of the conversion of a dying thief. Matthew tells of the time, early in the crucifixion hours, when both thieves were mocking Jesus, but Luke gives us a sequel. One criminal has somehow, by this time, seen something in Jesus that the centurion would see but that the scribes and Pharisees did not. He asked, "Jesus, remember me when you come into your kingdom" (23:42). It was a request of extraordinary faith, for if ever there was a time when Jesus did not look like an heir to a kingdom, it was at this hour. But faith always sees more than is evident to the naked eye.

Luke also gives us the priceless story of the two believers en route to Emmaus, lost in the bewilderment of the crucifixion and the events just preceding it. Jesus joined them (perhaps the first fulfillment of "where two or three are gathered in my name, I am there among them" [Matt. 18:20]) and began explaining the scriptures to them, "beginning with Moses and all the prophets" (24:27). It was not until they began breaking bread together that the two men realized with whom they had walked and talked. Their hearts had burned with the reality, but they didn't realize. We human beings are a slow lot at times, especially when we are heavy with grief.

PRAYER: Help me more often to see you as we walk together. Amen.

JOHN 1, 2, 3; PSALM 139   Week 12, Day 6

Where Mark begins his story with John the Baptist; Matthew with Joseph, Mary, and a flight to Egypt; and Luke with Elizabeth, Zechariah, and shepherds on a hillside, John begins, "In the beginning" (1:1). And he means *the* beginning. Without a doubt he intends to draw our minds back to the Genesis story, because he wants us to understand that the story of Jesus Christ begins not simply at Bethlehem or Nazareth, but in the far reaches of divine history. "In the beginning was the Word, and the Word was with God, and the Word was God" (1:1).

232

It is this One who comes into the world, which "came into being through him," yet is unrecognized when he arrives (1:10, 11). But those who receive him are given "power to become children of God" (1:12).

There are no parables in John's Gospel, but he treats so many of the events of Jesus' life in parabolic fashion, making them into teaching tools. A village wedding at Cana becomes a time of divine illumination, as Jesus turns the routine of life (water) into excitement (wine) (2:1-11). And when the esteemed Nicodemus visits, he too is shaken from his routine. He knows there should be more to life than he has found, even with all of his goodness and his scholarship. Jesus holds out the eternal hope of all those who wish they might start again: "You must be born from above" (3:7). And what Jesus offered to Nicodemus, he offers to all: "for God so loved the world that he gave his only Son, so that everyone who believes in him may not perish but may have eternal life" (3:16). It is a new day!

PRAYER: Let me walk, O Lord, in daily newness of life; in Christ. Amen.

JOHN 4, 5; PSALM 140   Week 42, Day 7

Once there was a woman who drank anxiously from all the wells of life that were in her reach, and always to her ultimate disappointment. So when she met Jesus and he offered "living water," she cried, "Sir, give me this water, so that I may never be thirsty or have to keep coming here to draw water" (4:15). Different as she was from Nicodemus in all outward matters, she was like him in this, that she thought there should be more to life than she had thus far found. Nicodemus was a cautious convert; we will have to wait for the development of his story. But she leaps into faith much as she has earlier leaped into trouble. She is such an enthusiastic convert that many from her city "believed in him because of the woman's testimony" (4:39).

We meet her emotional counterpart in chapter 5. A man has waited for "a long time" (5:6) at Bethzatha because, he explains, "I have no one to put me into the pool when the water is stirred up" (5:7). Jesus takes command of the man's life (something he obviously has needed) and restores him to health.

But he does so on the sabbath day, and when the man is confronted by the religious authorities, he violates Jesus' confidence. Jesus uses the occasion to tell his opponents who he is. John's Gospel makes clear from the beginning, and in numerous confrontations, that Jesus sees himself as "equal to God" (5:18). The burden of decision is then with his opponents—and, of course, with us.

PRAYER: I want, dear Savior, to name you as my Lord. Amen.

JOHN 6, 7; PSALM 141   *Week 43, Day 1*

*J*ohn's Gospel portrays Jesus as being very direct in declaring his person and his role. One of its distinctive characteristics is the series of "I am" statements, as in 6:35 when Jesus says, "I am the bread of life." His challengers had asked for a sign, like Moses and manna in the wilderness. Jesus countered that their ancestors had eaten manna and in time had died, but "I am the living bread that came down from heaven. Whoever eats of this bread will live forever" (6:51). It is not surprising that his enemies said, "This teaching is difficult; who can accept it?" (6:60). Jesus—especially as portrayed in John's Gospel—does not give us the option of seeing himself as an earnest, admirable teacher; we accept him on his own divine, demanding terms, or not at all.

In the same manner, Jesus takes the occasion of the most popular Jewish festival, Tabernacles (Booths), to make a startling statement about himself. The ceremony commemorated the years when their ancestors had traveled from Egypt to the promised land, living in temporary shelters. At its peak a priest took a golden pitcher of water from the Pool of Siloam and poured it out before the people, while they shouted and waved their palm branches. It was an act of thanksgiving for the gift of water and a memory of the water that sprang from the rock at Moses' word. It was at this high moment in the ceremony that Jesus said, "Let anyone who is thirsty come to me" (7:37). It was a daring, magnificent invitation, and he makes it still.

234

PRAYER: Meet my thirst, O Lord, with your living water; in Christ. Amen.

JOHN 8, 9; PSALM 142   *Week 43, Day 2*

*J*ohn's Gospel introduces us to some of the most fascinating characters in the New Testament, including Nicodemus, the woman of Samaria, and the lame man at the pool. Now we meet two more. The woman taken in adultery evokes our sympathy because she is so clearly being victimized; they make her "stand before all of them" (8:3), while the man who was equally involved is nowhere to be seen. Jesus doesn't justify her conduct, but he puts her sin and those of her accusers in perspective, then sends her on her way forgiven and exhorted to a new life: "Go your way, and from now on do not sin again" (8:11).

The blind man in chapter 9 is a wonderful contrast to the lame man we met earlier. He has no reluctance to witness to his healing or to identify himself with Jesus. When his accusers try to discredit Jesus, he answers sharply, "I do not know whether he is a sinner. One thing I do know, that though I was blind, now I see" (9:25). And though he is only a beggar and his opponents are men of position and power, he is not intimidated. "You do not know where he comes from, and yet he opened my eyes" (9:30). Years of survival against odds had made him tough-minded in his understanding of human nature. He wasn't fooled by pomp or position, but he knew reality when he found it. And as Roy L. Smith (editor of the old *Christian Advocate* magazine) said so long ago, the person who has an experience with God has something beyond the reach of any argument. So it was with this man.

PRAYER: Thank you, Lord, for forgiveness of sins and for the privilege of personal religious experience; in Jesus' name. Amen.

JOHN 10, 11; PSALM 143   *Week 43, Day 3*

*J*esus identifies himself with three more "I am" statements: the door (10:9), the good shepherd (10:11), and the resurrection (11:25). By each statement he implicitly challenges his opponents because the claims are so large. And beneficent, too. Jesus' promise, "I came that they may have life, and have it abundantly" (10:10), is one of the greatest declarations of the redeemed life, perhaps even greater than the invitation, "Come to me, all you that are weary" (Matt. 11:28). So, too, the picture of divine love in the good shepherd who lays down his life for his sheep (10:15) is one of the most beautiful to be found anywhere in scripture.

But Jesus' opponents recognized the challenge in his words. Their anger reached a point where they wanted to stone him (10:32), but meanwhile, "many believed" (10:42). In such a quality of tension, the raising of Lazarus proved a tinder point. Two remarkable statements punctuate this story. The first comes from Martha, who for all her absorption with daily tasks obviously has a profound faith, because when Jesus asks her to declare her belief, she replies in the language of the foundational confession of the church (Matt. 16:18): "I believe that you are the Messiah, the Son of God" (11:27). The second comes from an enemy, Caiaphas, who reasons that it is to their political advantage that Jesus die rather than "to have the whole nation destroyed" (11:50). John explains that Caiaphas said more than he knew; he prophesied that Jesus would die "not for the nation only, but to gather into one the dispersed children of God" (11:52).

PRAYER: I hail you, dear Jesus, as Lord of life! Amen.

JOHN 12, 13; PSALM 144   Week 43, Day 4

We noted earlier that John's Gospel is very sensitive to the issue of *time* in Jesus' life. Now, as the time that we call Holy Week begins, Jesus says, "The hour has come for the Son of Man to be glorified" (12:23). Yet he acknowledges the struggle, asking if he should pray, "Father, save me from this hour," then declaring, "No, it is for this reason that I have come to this hour" (12:27). By recording this inner conflict, John helps us to see the enormousness of what Jesus was about to do.

The sense of time (*kairos*) also marks the last pre-crucifixion meeting with the disciples; Jesus recognizes "that his hour had come" (13:1). Judas is a crucial figure in this development. John gives us insight into his character which is not revealed in the other Gospels, telling us that he was defrauding the disciples' treasury (12:6). But Jesus washed Judas' feet along with the rest. He had the magnificent inner strength not only to be a servant, but even to serve one who was betraying him.

No wonder, then, that Jesus at this point makes a "new commandment, that you love one another" (13:34), and that he tells all who follow him that it is by this that "everyone will know that you are my disciples, if you have love for one another" (13:35). The difficulty of this witness of love is that it is so daily. If we could fulfill it in one grand deed or gift, it would be more easily attained. But first-century servants washed feet every day. That's the quality of Christian love. *Every day.*

PRAYER: Cautiously I pray: help me to be your servant; in your name. Amen.

JOHN 14, 15, 16, 17   Week 43, Day 5

*H*ere we have our Lord's Great Valedictory to his disciples as he sends them to the task for which for three years he has been preparing them. Just outside the upper room, peril is mounting, though even the most fearful could not have imagined in what proportions. So Jesus speaks to them of heaven (14), as if to assure them that when the task is done, they will be welcomed home; and when they wonder how they will find such a place, Jesus promises, "I am the way" (14:6). No matter how unknown the destination, there is no doubt about the way.

Then he explains a secret. It is very simple, yet strangely difficult: he is the vine and we are branches, and we will be sustained if only we remain in this relationship (15:5). It is the Father's wish that we be fruitful (15:5), so essentially everything is available to us if only we will remain in his love (15:10). And to make us still more secure, he is sending the abiding presence of the Holy Spirit. This presence is so effective that it is better for the disciples that he go away so the

Spirit can come (16:7). They must have found that hard to believe.

And then, our Lord prays for the eleven. Whatever uncertainties may have remained after the statements about heaven, their union with him through the Vine, and the coming empowerment of the Holy Spirit, must surely have been assuaged in this, that their Lord prays for them. And what he said to them, he says still to us.

PRAYER: May I never forget, O Lord, in any dark hour, that you are on my side, pleading my cause; in your dear name. Amen.

JOHN 18, 19; PSALMS 145, 146   *Week 43, Day 6*

See the uses of power in these dramatic scenes. Pilate has more political power than anyone in the region, but he's afraid to use it. Only after Jesus is crucified does he make a show of bravado in a petty way. When the chief priests challenge the sign he has put over the cross, he answers, "What I have written I have written" (19:22). This show of independence would have been more impressive if he had used it when it would have mattered. Now it is mere strutting.

Nicodemus and Joseph of Arimathea also have power, at least within the Jewish religious and political community. We learn that Joseph is a secret disciple (19:38), and it appears that Nicodemus was, too (19:39). We wonder what an impact they might have made if they had been willing to use their strategic influence earlier. And yet we honor them for endangering their positions by affiliating themselves with Jesus in his death. What happened to them later, I wonder?

And then there is the power we see in Jesus. When impetuous Peter raises a sword in his behalf, Jesus reminds him that he must drink this cup the Father has given him (18:11). When Pilate asks him to identify his kingdom, he declares that he has come into the world "to testify to the truth" (18:37). And as he dies, he is able to say, "It is finished" (19:30). His is the power of absolute commitment to God's will. Such a commitment makes all other power seem trivial.

PRAYER: The world around me finds such glory in what it

thinks to be power. Help me keep my sights set on your will; in Christ. Amen.

JOHN 20, 21; PSALM 147   *Week 43, Day 7*

*J*ohn's Gospel gives us several special insights into the Easter story. Thomas, the natural skeptic among the disciples, misses a resurrection visit, and is not impressed by the experience of his colleagues. He thinks they are easily duped, seeing what they want to see, and he insists that he will believe only on the basis of hard evidence. Eight days later he receives such evidence. When he bows in adoration, Jesus speaks a word for all succeeding generations: "Blessed are those who have not seen and yet have come to believe" (20:29).

At the Sea of Tiberias, seven of the disciples had fished all night and caught nothing. They followed Jesus' counsel, to cast their net on the other side of the boat, and "were not able to haul it in because there were so many fish" (21:6). I remember a preacher from my boyhood who, looking at this story, said to the disheartened and defeated, "How far is it to hope and salvation? Well—how wide is a boat?"

Peter, in the hour following, found his love challenged, yet even then worried himself unduly about a fellow disciple and what benefits he might receive. We find it so hard simply to do our task and to leave God's other workers to God's own discretion.

The author of this book knows why he has written it: that all who read it might "come to believe that Jesus is the Messiah, the Son of God," and so believing, might have life in his name (20:31). Some of us will testify that his purpose has been fulfilled.

PRAYER: Dear Lord, count me among those who believe! In Christ. Amen.

ACTS 1, 2, 3   *Week 44, Day 1*

*T*he four Gospels tell us the story of Jesus' life and ministry through his resurrection. Now, in the Book of Acts, Luke continues the story as it unfolds through Jesus' followers

239

(1:1, 2). Our Lord's final instruction before his ascension is that they should wait in Jerusalem for the baptism of the Holy Spirit (1:5). About 120 do so, carrying on such church business as selecting Judas' successor, and praying. (The church has no bigger business than praying.)

On the Day of Pentecost the group is visited by a series of phenomena—a wind that fills their meeting place, tongues of fire, and each one speaking of the glory of God in a language other than their own. Because it was a festival time, people were visiting Jerusalem "from every nation under heaven" (2:5); they marveled at hearing God praised in their native tongues. Here was dramatic evidence that the new faith was intended for the whole human race—every tongue!—and that the Spirit of God was empowering Jesus' followers to spread the word.

Peter, who a fortnight before had denied Christ before single accusers, now rises to plead his cause before the assembled crowds, until at least three thousand are converted (2:41). And this is only the beginning. Some days later Peter and John bring healing to a lame beggar, just as Jesus had so often healed in their presence. When a curious crowd surrounds them, Peter courageously declares that the miracle has been accomplished in the name of Jesus, the very one they had killed (3:15, 16).

PRAYER: Give me your power, O Lord, for my time and place. Amen.

ACTS 1, 5; PSALM 148   *Week 44, Day 2*

J. B. Phillips said in the introduction to his translation of Acts that "This surely is the Church as it was meant to be." There is an excitement in these chapters that is at times breathtaking. The phrase that stands out is "in the name of Jesus." In one form or another, that phrase appears eight times in these two chapters. The disciples knew to whom they belonged, and so did their opponents.

There is great saintliness in this early church. It is best exemplified in Joseph of Cyprus, whom the apostles named Barnabas ("son of encouragement") because of the quality of his character. He was one of the leaders in the generosity that marked the little body, so that "there was not a needy person among them" (4:34). But there was hypocrisy, too, because as surely as there is reality there will be some who will try to counterfeit it. In this case it was a couple, Ananias and Sapphira (5:1). One wonders how anyone could be part of such a magnificent movement and do what they did, but on reflection most of us realize how open we are to such inconsistency, such irrational living.

But such fearlessness, too! When Peter and the apostles are brought before the high priest, they are clearly overmatched, yet when they are commanded never to speak "in this name," they answer, "We must obey God rather than any human authority" (5:29). Peter follows with a sharply phrased sermon, and when they are flogged and again ordered to silence, they rejoice that they can suffer "for the sake of the name" (5:41)!

PRAYER: Give me, I pray, some measure of their faith! Amen.

ACTS 6, 7; PSALM 149   Week 44, Day 3

*T*he early Christians were so wonderfully human. At first their numbers were made up of Jews who could identify themselves as Hebrews, because they held to their ancient language, and Hellenists, those Jews who preferred Greek or who followed Greek customs. The Hellenists may also have included gentile converts to Judaism. In any event, before long there was controversy between the two groups. The Hellenists felt that their widows were being discriminated against.

The apostles, wisely, selected "seven men of good standing, full of the Spirit and of wisdom" (6:3) to be responsible for the distribution of food, to be sure everything was done fairly.

But almost immediately one of these seven, Stephen, moved into a more visible role. He was "full of grace and power" (6:8), so that people "could not withstand the wisdom of the Spirit with which he spoke" (6:10). When they brought him to trial, "his face was like the face of an angel" (6:15). The presentation he then made to the high priest and the council constitutes the longest sermon in the book of Acts. It is a careful recitation of the spiritual history of the

Israelites, concluding with the kind of language Moses used, but applied now to the new era: "You stiff-necked people, uncircumcised in heart and ears, you are forever opposing the Holy Spirit" (7:51). Not surprisingly, they stoned him to death. But he died praying for them; and it seems likely that, even as he died, he was making a convert.

PRAYER: Give me the commitment, I pray, of your servant Stephen. Amen.

ACTS 8, 9, 10   *Week 44, Day 4*

S ee how the church grows! The death of Stephen seems at first to give more energy to a young persecutor, Saul, who attacks the believers so fiercely that the people "were scattered throughout the countryside of Judea and Samaria" (8:1), where they probably ought to have been in the first place. Saul, unwittingly, is spreading the gospel.

Meanwhile, Philip, another of the seven deacons, begins preaching in Samaria where he has been driven, and great miracles accompany his work. But while he is in the midst of such effective work, he is suddenly told to go to the road between Jerusalem and Gaza. There he encounters an Ethiopian official, a seeker after God who had come to Jerusalem to worship. Providentially, the Ethiopian is reading Isaiah 53. As Philip explains the passage, the man believes and is baptized. Tradition says that he became the founder of the Christian faith in Ethiopia.

Then, Saul! "Breathing threats and murder against the disciples of the Lord" (9:1), he finds himself apprehended by the very One he is opposing (9:5). His conversion is dramatic, but the best of his story is yet to come, in succeeding chapters of Acts, as the great persecutor becomes instead the most vigorous representative of the faith.

And Cornelius! A good but uncircumcised Gentile, his coming to the faith is by way of Peter, himself, coming to a new understanding of the faith. In a sense, it is a double conversion. So the faith spreads: to Samaria, then to an Ethiopian, to Saul the persecutor, and to Cornelius!

PRAYER: And let it continue, O Lord, through me! In Christ. Amen.

242

*W*e expect the believers to be thrilled by the extension of the gospel to the Gentiles. Not so! Like a tiny church that is beginning to grow, they say, "What are all these strangers doing here?" Peter makes an effective defense of the work of the Holy Spirit as he has experienced it: "who was I that I could hinder God?" (11:17). The church leaders, in turn, praised God for giving "even to the Gentiles the repentance that leads to life" (11:18). They had discovered that grace is, indeed, amazing!

We don't fully know what happened to Saul after the first burst of activity following his conversion, but it appears that he dropped from the scene. Now there is a special need in Antioch, and when they ask Barnabas—that "good man, full of the Holy Spirit and of faith" (11:24)—to go there, he eventually seeks out Saul to help in the enterprise, and the two of them minister there for a full year.

But the persecution has not ended; King Herod now leads the way. James becomes a martyr to the faith. Peter, too, is thrown in prison, but his prison stay is marvelously interrupted. It's such a marvel, in fact, that Peter himself "thought he was seeing a vision" (12:9), and when a maid named Rhoda reported that Peter was standing at the gate, the believers who were praying for him advised her that she was out of her mind! I wonder how often we pray that way, so shut in by our troubles that we wouldn't accept a miracle, or even a modest answer, if it came!

PRAYER: I thank you that your work goes on, sometimes through us and sometimes in spite of us. I want to cooperate with you! Amen.

ACTS 13, 14, 15; PROVERBS 1   *Week 44, Day 6*

*W*hen the church sends out Barnabas and Saul, a new era begins. Peter and the other leaders now become peripheral, and the focus is on Saul. When we're told that his other name is Paul (13:9), his Greco-Roman name, it's a signal that we're also moving more surely into the larger world.

243

For Paul and Barnabas (note how quickly the junior partner becomes the leader), it's a tempestuous journey. They preach fearlessly to the Jews, winning both converts and opposition; and when the opposition grows very strong, they vow to concentrate on the gentiles (13:46). Here, too, the path is uneven. In Lycaonia they are at first (after a notable healing) hailed as gods (14:11), but not much later Paul is stoned and left for dead (14:19). If one isn't too taken by adulation, it will be easier to survive the stonings!

Back at Antioch, they find themselves the center of controversy. Earnest traditionalists feel gentile believers can come into the faith only via Judaism (15:1). The matter is referred to the apostles and elders in Jerusalem. Peter argues that Jews and gentiles alike are "saved through the grace of the Lord Jesus" (15:11). A compromise is reached.

But with that controversy settled, Paul and Barnabas have an issue of their own, the role of young John Mark. "The disagreement became so sharp that they parted company" (15:39). Even saints are human. Fortunately the Holy Spirit is ready to work in and through our humanness.

PRAYER: I'm so honored, dear Savior, to be part of a heritage of faith, even when the heritage is embarrassingly human; in Christ. Amen.

ACTS 16, 17, 18   *Week 44, Day 7*

Now we follow Paul and his co-workers through a series of places that are significant to us because later Paul will write letters to them: Philippi, Thessalonica, Corinth. These cities also stand out because they symbolize the spread of the gospel into Europe (16:9, 10). Berea has given its name to several modern communities and to unnumbered study groups because the Bereans "welcomed the message very eagerly and examined the scriptures every day" (17:11).

When Paul preached to a Jewish audience in Antioch of Pisidia, he began, "The God of this people Israel chose our ancestors" (13:17), and based his sermon on the Hebrew scriptures. For the Greek intellectuals at the Areopagus, he quoted "some of your own poets" (17:28). By his approach Paul proved his astuteness not only at meeting people on their own ground, but also of recognizing that the hunger for God is to be found among all peoples, at all times, in all places.

Almost everywhere Paul preaches, there is opposition, often with beatings, public trials, and imprisonments. But there are also wondrous conversions: Lydia the business-woman, the Philippian jailer and his household, "a great many of the devout Greeks and not a few of the leading women" (17:4) in Thessalonica; and in Athens, Dionysius and Damaris (17:34). And even in Corinth, the very symbol of evil in its day, "many . . . became believers and were bap-tized" (18:8). And the work goes on!

PRAYER: I pray that you will find new believers this day, among people as different as those Paul reached so long ago; in Jesus' name. Amen.

ACTS 19, 20, 21   Week 45, Day 1

*P*aul, we might say, is an equal opportunity victim. He is persecuted by both Jews and gentiles, by people of dif-fering faiths and no faith; and he is an object of controversy not only among unbelievers but even within the Christian community. But however great his own discomfort, Paul seems always to be encouraging others (16:40; 20:1, 2). The tiny Christian fellowships were always passing through hard places and were often in danger of their very lives, and Paul didn't want them to lose heart.

By now Paul has a team traveling with him (20:4). They are not only from several communities, but also from two continents. The gospel has gone international! As Paul leaves Ephesus, he glories in the fact that he has paid his own way (20:34); he boasts of this fact also in several of his epistles. Although he believes that "those who proclaim the gospel should get their living by the gospel" (1 Cor. 9:14), he himself follows the ancient rabbinical practice of supporting himself by a trade—in his case, tentmaking.

Paul is certain he must go to Jerusalem, even though he knows that imprisonment and persecution await him there.

When a Christian prophet, Agabus, declares dramatically that bonds await him, Paul answers, "I am ready not only to be bound but even to die in Jerusalem for the name of the Lord Jesus" (21:13). Whatever his limitations may be, Paul is a remarkably committed disciple of his Lord.

PRAYER: Forgive me, I pray, that I settle often for easy discipleship; give me a new commitment to your highest purpose; in Christ. Amen.

ACTS 22, 23, 24   Week 45, Day 2

Now begins a series of judicial trials. Each one reveals some further facet of Paul's ability to use his background and experience fruitfully. He can address the Jews as "brothers and fathers" (22:1), and testify to his having been educated "strictly according to our ancestral law" (22:3). But when he is about to be unjustly beaten, he appeals to his Roman citizenship (22:25-29). Before the Sanhedrin, he divides the body by pointing to his heritage as a Pharisee and by insisting that "I am on trial concerning the hope of the resurrection of the dead" (23:6).

But while taking full advantage of his rather complex background, he never wavers from his ultimate commitments. He tells his Jewish audience that God has called him to minister to the gentiles, though he knows this will influence them negatively. Before Felix, the governor, he outlines his beliefs and then his commitment: "I do my best always to have a clear conscience toward God and all people" (24:16). When Felix's wife, Drusilla, comes also to hear Paul's witness, the apostle is so impassioned about "justice, self-control, and the coming judgment" that Felix "became frightened" and postpones further conversation (24:25). Paul doesn't draw a distinction between his legal defense and his witness to Christ. For him, life is all of one piece; to live is Christ. Perhaps the best way to understand Paul's theology of being "in Christ" is simply to look at the way Paul lived his postconversion life.

PRAYER: I want, O Lord, to live in such a way that all I do honors you. Save me from lapses in this commitment; in Jesus' name. Amen.

*W*hen Saul was converted, God identified him as "an instrument whom I have chosen to bring my name before Gentiles and kings and before the people of Israel" (9:15). After years of witnessing to gentiles and the people of Israel, he now has his opportunity before kings. It's interesting to hear Festus report the case to King Agrippa; the Jews "had certain points of disagreement with him . . . about a certain Jesus, who had died, but whom Paul asserted to be alive" (25:19). That's a good summary of the unceasing issue about Christ—whether he is simply a good, dead man, or whether he is, indeed, alive.

Paul tells Agrippa, "I stand here on trial on account of my hope" (26:6). There could hardly be a nobler statement of a life purpose. Then, a question that is an issue of both logic and faith: "Why is it thought incredible by any of you that God raises the dead?" (26:8). Logic, because if God be God, there are no limits of power; faith, because it is a question of what we believe the nature of God to be.

But primarily Paul is a witness. He recounts his conversion and call, a "heavenly vision" he could not disobey (26:19). He is too brilliant a man to be accused of superstition, so Agrippa takes the opposite tack: "Too much learning is driving you insane!" (26:24). Paul, the happy warrior, wishes nothing so much for the king and his entourage than that they should find the same hope, the same joy, that he has.

PRAYER: I want a faith, O Lord, that finds joy in each challenge and that lives in the grand glory of Christ's resurrection; in him. Amen.

*P*aul's journey to Rome is full of peril—far more than there would have been if those in charge had accepted his counsel—but at last he arrives. There, true to his commitments, he presents his story first to the Jews, "testifying to the kingdom of God and trying to convince them about Jesus both from the law of Moses and from the prophets" (28:23). He gets his usual response: "Some were convinced by what he had said, while others refused to believe" (28:24). Paul is impatient with such rejection and perhaps especially so when it comes from his own people. He tells them that he will concentrate on the gentiles. "They will listen" (28:28).

As the book of Acts ends, Paul is in the rather favorable setting of house arrest, able to witness freely to those who come to see him (and also to those guarding him; tradition says many guards became converts). Here, too, he is able to correspond with his churches. Several of his New Testament letters probably come from this period. Above all, as Luke puts it, he is freely "proclaiming the kingdom of God and teaching about the Lord Jesus Christ with all boldness" (28:31).

It is generally agreed that the two years Paul spent in this fashion were A.D. 61–63. But for what follows, we rely entirely on tradition, which says that he was released, that he again traveled about, preaching and teaching, and that he was martyred in A.D. 67. And through it all, as he would say, he would "press on toward the goal" of his heavenly calling (Phil. 3:14).

PRAYER: Give me, I pray, such a commitment to your will; in Christ. Amen.

ROMANS 1, 2, 3   *Week 45, Day 5*

*M*ost of Paul's letters were written to deal with immediate problems or questions, but he had not yet preached in Rome so in this letter he is free to give a rather full synthesis of much of his theology. Paul tells us that God has revealed himself through nature, so that we human beings "are without excuse" (1:20) in claiming ignorance of God. But often our race has chosen to exchange "the glory of the immortal God for images" (1:23), choosing to worship and serve "the creature rather than the Creator" (1:25). And since this is the case, "God gave them up to a debased mind and to things that should not be done" (1:28).

248

Meanwhile the Jews have been given the Law, and they will be judged by it. But the Law and circumcision, great as they are, are not an easy guarantee of favor: "a person is a Jew who is one inwardly, and real circumcision is a matter of the heart" (2:29).

The Jews have an advantage, of course, since they were "entrusted with the oracles of God" (3:2). But Jews and gentiles alike "are under the power of sin" (3:9); "there is no distinction, since all have sinned and fall short of the glory of God" (3:22, 23). But if that seems hopeless, there is another "all" to be considered. All, also, are "now justified by his grace as a gift, through the redemption that is in Christ Jesus" (3:24). Such is the state of our human race: all of us have sinned, and with our sinning are condemned; but God has graciously offered a remedy for our sins in Jesus Christ. All of us.

PRAYER: I gladly accept your gift, O God! In Christ's name. Amen.

ROMANS 4, 5, 6   Week 45, Day 6

When Paul develops his theology of our human condition, he reasons with the intensity of a first-century rabbi, but writes with the passion of a poet. As a rabbi might, he begins with Abraham, but he contends that Abraham's greatness is not in obedience to the Law, nor in the rite of circumcision, but in faith—which, in Abraham's experience, preceded both. Then, a shout: "For while we were still weak, at the right time Christ died for the ungodly" (5:6). This happened, in fact, "while we were enemies . . . to God" (5:10). Such is the wonder of grace.

Now Paul uses another approach. Sin came into the world through "one man" (Adam), and with sin, death. "So death spread to all because all have sinned" (5:12). How can the plague be stopped? By the gift that comes through Jesus Christ. "For just as by the one man's disobedience the many were made sinners, so by the one man's obedience the many will be made righteous" (5:19).

Since God has been so generous, we ought to give all we are to God to be "instruments of righteousness" (6:13). We're done now with the sort of behavior that ends in death (6:21). Why would we even consider a way of life that has been discredited by generations of painful human experience in which the wage is death, when God freely offers eternal life in Jesus Christ (6:23)? Paul is certain that we have an easy, logical choice. How strange that we continue, perversely, to make it so difficult!

PRAYER: Thank you for offering salvation even when we are rebellious against you. I want my new life to please you; in Jesus' name. Amen.

ROMANS 7, 8; PROVERBS 4   *Week 45, Day 7*

Paul is the Christian realist in these two chapters. First, the painful facts. The Law has revealed our frailty by showing us God's standard, so that we discover that we are creatures of flesh, sold as slaves to sin (7:14). At times we're bewildered by our own behavior, when we do things we hate (7:15). Here's the rule, Paul says: "when I want to do what is good, evil lies close at hand" (7:21). No wonder he says, "Wretched man that I am!" (7:24).

But that's not the end of our story. There are other facts. Through Christ, we have been saved from condemnation. Because of his presence in our lives, we're not obligated to "live according to the flesh" (8:12). As a matter of fact, we're in an enviable position. As "heirs to God and joint heirs with Christ" (8:17), our glory is such that "the creation waits with eager longing" (8:19) to see what will happen to us.

When we are sometimes weak, not even knowing how to pray properly, the Spirit intercedes for us (8:26). In truth, everything—*everything!*—is working ultimately to our good as we love and follow God (8:28). And it will be this way to the very end, since Christ Jesus "is at the right hand of God [interceding] for us" (8:34). Nothing, therefore, in time or eternity, in heaven, earth, or hell, can separate us from the love of God. And those, too, are the facts, as real as the facts of our sin and frailty. And in the end, far more powerful.

PRAYER: When I'm up against the hard facts of my weakness

250

and failure, help me, dear Savior, to recognize the greater fact of your love. Amen.

ROMANS 9, 10, 11   *Week 46, Day 1*

*M*any first-century Jews must have seen Paul as a traitor to his people because of his conversion to Christ and his emphasis on faith more than Law. But he never lost his passion for his people; he wanted only that they come to know Christ as he had. "I could wish that I myself were accursed and cut off from Christ for the sake of my own people, my kindred according to the flesh" (9:3).

Paul argues for God's right to choose and use whom he will; it is the potter's privilege, he reasons, to use his clay for special use or for ordinary use (9:21). But Jews largely missed the opportunity, because "they have not submitted to God's righteousness" (10:3), and except for "a remnant, chosen by grace" (11:5), "the rest were hardened." (11:7).

It is at this point that the door of opportunity has opened so widely for the gentiles. Paul glories in his role as an apostle to the gentiles (11:13), but he warns them that their new prominence in the divine plan is not a sign of their superiority. The Jews are the tree of God, and gentiles are a wild shoot, grafted on. And "if God did not spare the natural branches, perhaps he will not spare you" (11:21).

In it all, Paul marvels at God's wisdom and knowledge. Some might, in unbelief, question God's plan and fairness, but Paul asks, "who has been [God's] counselor?" (11:34). And with that, Paul, in faith and adoration, cries, "To him be the glory forever" (11:36)!

PRAYER: At those times when I do not understand your purposes, give me the faith to trust and to praise you; in Jesus' name. Amen.

ROMANS 12, 13, 14   *Week 46, Day 2*

*P*aul moves now from his profound theological discussions to the routine living-out of the faith. There is an appeal for humble exercising of spiritual gifts, with the admonition, "outdo one another in showing honor" (12:10). In the same spirit, we should relate to others in such a way that we will not be overcome by evil, but rather that we will "overcome evil with good" (12:21). As for the general, civil good, realize that government performs a necessary, God-ordained role (13:1), and be obedient, not only because you fear retribution "but also because of conscience" (13:5). And that includes paying taxes! (13:6).

There's a theological basis for all of this: "the one who loves another has fulfilled the law" (13:8). It is such love that will guide us in those gray areas of conduct, where good people can hold different opinions; we would not want, for some such small matter, to "put a stumbling block or hindrance in the way of another" (14:13).

In a sense, it all comes back to the high call to discipleship with which chapter 12 begins, where we are called to present our bodies "as a living sacrifice, holy and acceptable to God" (12:1). Thus the apostle lifts a concept of the Hebrew scriptures to a grand, new level. If we are willing to live with such commitment, we will no longer "be conformed to this world"; but, transformed by the renewing of our minds, we will "discern what is the will of God—what is good and acceptable and perfect" (12:2). Great living, indeed!

PRAYER: So may I commit my life to you, O God! In Christ. Amen.

ROMANS 15, 16; PROVERBS 5   *Week 46, Day 3*

The warm, pastoral heart of Paul comes through clearly in this concluding portion of the letter. We are to consider our neighbor's good and use our strength "to put up with the failings of the weak" (15:1). We should accept one another, not caring whether one is a Jew or a Gentile (15:8). Paul appeals (as he so often does) for the people to join "in earnest prayer to God on my behalf" (15:30).

And then, the names! Phoebe, a deacon; Prisca and Aquila, "who risked their necks for my life" (16:4); Andronicus and Junia, who "were in Christ before I was" (16:7). The list goes on, and each one is a hero. What pathos, what glory in the identifying phrases: "who were in prison with me"

(16:7); "the beloved Persis, who has worked hard in the Lord" (16:12); and Rufus' mother, who has been "a mother to me also" (16:13). What a privilege, nineteen centuries later, to be part of the same body!

Paul includes a bit of counsel that seems extraordinarily appropriate to our times: "I want you to be wise in what is good and guileless in what is evil" (16:19). Many in our time pride themselves that nothing shocks them; this is the mark of their version of sophistication. Paul wants us to be very susceptible to shock—"guileless," in fact. But on the other hand, he calls for a sophistication that is almost unknown to the secular mind, being experts in goodness. This calls for a whole new mind-set, magnificently out of step with our times.

PRAYER: Thank you, dear Lord, for virtues like goodness and purity, which are so simple that they are quite beyond our understanding. Amen.

1 CORINTHIANS 1, 2, 3   Week 46, Day 4

*W*hen Paul addresses this letter "To the church of God that is in Corinth . . . called to be saints" (1:2), we see a new dimension of the expectations of the gospel. Corinth was one of the most wicked cities in the first-century world; it was not an easy place to be a saint, and the people of Corinth didn't have an easy time attaining the quality of life the gospel recommended.

For one thing, there were divisions in the church: "it has been reported to me . . . that there are quarrels among you, my brothers and sisters" (1:11). The people chose to rally around their favorite leaders—Paul, Apollos, Cephas. Paul wants the Corinthians to understand that he and the others are simply co-workers and that the glory belongs to God: "I planted, Apollos watered, but God gave the growth" (3:6). He pictures himself also as a builder, but one who remembers that the "foundation is Jesus Christ" (3:11).

Above all, Paul wishes only to exalt "Jesus Christ, and him crucified" (2:2). In his wisdom, God chose to win the world not by wisdom, but by the "message about the cross," which is "foolishness to those who are perishing, but to us who are being saved it is the power of God" (1:18); "we proclaim

Christ crucified, a stumbling block to Jews and foolishness to Gentiles" (1:23). The message is equally unattractive today to those who want their religion to be comfortable, tidy, and self-exalting. The cross is none of these.

PRAYER: Beneath the cross of Jesus, I still would take my stand. Amen.

1 CORINTHIANS 4, 5, 6, 7   Week 46, Day 5

Truly godly living is a grand achievement under even the best of circumstances, but for the people of Corinth it could have been seen as a goal quite out of reach. The apostle may seem unduly harsh when with sarcasm he says, "Already you have all you want! Already you have become rich!" (4:8). But he has reasons. The people are apparently rather pleased with themselves and "have become arrogant" (4:18), while in truth they are guilty of some kinds of conduct "that is not found even among pagans" (5:1)—and that's a strong statement to make to someone living in Corinth!

First, there is sexual immorality; specifically, a man living with his father's wife—presumably his stepmother. Paul's recommendations are severe. He fears that this "little yeast" will leaven "the whole batch of dough" (5:6), so he wants them to act immediately. God will judge persons outside the church, Paul says, but it is the business of the church to keep itself pure (5:13). Others are going to prostitutes; it was easy to do so in Corinth, with its system of religious prostitution in the temple of Aphrodite. "Your body is a temple of the Holy Spirit within you" (6:19), Paul reminds them. There were other problems of sexual conduct, too, and Paul deals with them patiently and firmly, including conjugal rights, marriage, and divorce.

Paul is embarrassed, too, that some of the believers are taking fellow believers to court: "can it be that there is no one among you wise enough to decide between one believer and another?" (6:5). He recalls what they once were, but insists that now they are a new people in Christ (6:11).

PRAYER: Help me, O God, to fulfill your best expectations of me. Amen.

*T*he issue in these chapters is our responsibility to our brothers and sisters in Christ. The immediate setting for the issue is a matter that is far removed from our day, but the principle is unchanged. In the first-century world, people offered meat sacrifices to their idols, after which the meat would be placed in the market for sale. This raised a question for many Christians. Some felt that to eat meat that had been dedicated to a pagan god was to somehow participate in the worship of that god, while others felt it made no difference.

Paul reasons through the issue carefully and gently. Idols, he points out, are not real; "there is no God but one" (8:4). But not everybody realizes this, and when such a person sees a fellow believer eating the food of idols, he or she is "defiled" (8:7). Therefore Paul vows that he would give up meat forever if he felt his eating might cause someone to fall (8:13). He underlines his conviction by pointing out certain personal liberties that he has given up in order to make the gospel more effective—particularly that he is not accompanied by a wife, and that he does not receive offerings for his support. "I have made myself a slave to all," he says, "so that I might win more" (9:19).

On fine details of conduct, Paul reasons that while all things are lawful, all things do not build up (10:23). So he concludes, "whatever you do, do everything for the glory of God," while avoiding offense to anyone (10:31, 32). The rule is as right in our day as in his.

PRAYER: May I never cause another to fall from you; in Christ. Amen.

*O*ne of the lovely serendipities of Paul's epistles is the benefit we receive through the problems and questions of the early churches. The Corinthians were abusing the Lord's Supper. In remedying the problem, Paul has left us with our best and fullest guide for the celebration of this sacrament, including the crucial words of the liturgy.

We gain similar benefit as he deals with the controversy over the use of spiritual gifts. It seems that the church at Corinth was more taken with the exercise of these gifts than any other congregation. The gifts had, unfortunately, become an issue of pride. Those with more obvious or dramatic gifts looked upon themselves as better Christians. Paul compares the church to the human body, reminding us that all the parts are needed and that, indeed, some "that seem to be weaker are indispensable" (12:22). In chapter 14, he deals particularly with the gift that was apparently the most attractive to the Corinthians, speaking in tongues. He lays down some rules for orderly use of the gifts and seeks a middle ground by reference to his own experience; on the one hand, "I speak in tongues more than all of you," but in church "I would rather speak five words with my mind . . . than ten thousand words in a tongue" (14:18, 19).

The particular favor of these chapters, of course, is Paul's hymn to love in chapter 13. We use these wonderful verses for their insight into the remarkable quality of *agape*, but Paul's original aim was to tell the Corinthians that the greatest spiritual gift is love.

PRAYER: Whatever gift you give me, Lord, please include *love*. Amen.

1 CORINTHIANS 15, 16; PROVERBS 6   *Week 47, Day 1*

*O*nce again we are the beneficiaries of a first-century church problem. Some people at Corinth were saying that "there is no resurrection of the dead" (15:12). It seems their main contention was not about Christ's resurrection but that of believers. Paul insists that the two are inseparable ("If there is no resurrection from the dead, then Christ has not been raised" [15:13]), and that if Christ has not been raised, "your faith is futile and you are still in your sins" (15:17).

In his resurrection, Christ is "the first fruits of those who have died" (15:20). Paul anticipates a question: what kind of body will we have in resurrection? He reasons out an answer with a number of analogies, and explains that the dead body which "is sown is perishable, what is raised is imperishable"

(15:42). We shouldn't expect, he says, to have the same kind of body in our resurrected state, because "flesh and blood cannot inherit the kingdom of God, nor does the perishable inherit the imperishable" (15:50).

Paul concludes with a shout. "Death has been swallowed up in victory" (15:54). But he's not really done. The resurrection is a basis for being "steadfast, immovable, always excelling in the work of the Lord" (15:58). Nor does he find it inappropriate to go from such a high moment to details about "the collection for the saints" (16:1); resurrection faith ought surely to lead to sharing. And at last, as always, the greetings for all of those long-ago believers—our kin in Christ.

PRAYER: Count me among your resurrection people, O Lord! Amen.

2 CORINTHIANS 1, 2, 3   *Week 47, Day 2*

*O*nce Paul is past the opening formalities of a letter, he usually indicates the primary burden of his writing. When he refers so early to God as "the Father of mercies and the God of all consolation, who consoles us in all consolation, who consoles us in all our affliction" (1:3, 4), we know that he has recently passed through some trying circumstances. Specifically, the people of Corinth have given him pain. They have misunderstood some things he has written, and now they feel critical of him. His writing had come "out of much distress and anguish of heart," and the intention was not to cause them pain but to let them know "the abundant love" that he has for them (2:4).

But some question Paul's apostleship, so he turns the matter directly to them. Yes, he has documents that prove his ministry, but they are not letters that he carries with him. "You yourselves are our letter, written on our hearts, to be known and read by all" (3:2). And in case any wonder about the authenticity of such credentials, Paul proceeds to glory in them. The Israelites couldn't bear to look on Moses' face when he brought back "the ministry of death, chiseled in letters on stone tablets" (3:7), and this "ministry of the Spirit" comes with far more glory; because Moses' law was eventually to be "set aside," according to Paul, but the new faith is permanent (3:11). Paul interrupts himself to note that many still read Moses with a veil, but that "when one turns to the Lord, the veil is removed" (3:16). His language is daring, but he wants his people to know how fortunate they are; they are part of God's new covenant.

PRAYER: Remove the veil of doubt that prevents my seeing your glory. Amen.

2 CORINTHIANS 4, 5, 6; PROVERBS 7   *Week 47, Day 3*

When Paul declares, "we do not lose heart" (4:1, 16), he is confessing that he has come close to doing so. At times, it is a struggle. He acknowledges that "if our gospel is veiled, it is veiled to those who are perishing" (4:3); but I'm sure he's not content that this is so. He wishes that all might come to "the light of the gospel of the glory of Christ" (4:4). If one has found that glory, he wants all to have it.

He rejoices in his role. Do some suggest that he is not much? No matter, because God puts this treasure in clay jars on purpose. Has he suffered? Yes, but never to the point of final defeat, not even when "death is at work in us" (4:12).

And there are physical problems. Paul never becomes specific, but now and again he indicates that his body suffers. His "outer nature," he says, "is wasting away," but a marvelous thing is happening: the "inner nature is being renewed day by day" (4:16). This body is a mere tent, a temporary dwelling (we groan to be done with it!), but we're heading toward "a building from God, a house not made with hands, eternal in the heavens" (5:1).

A faith of such proportions gives special credence to Paul's warning, "Do not be mismatched with unbelievers" (6:14). When one has come to see life as Paul is describing it, there is a chasm of separation from a mere temporal, secular life-style. It is, indeed, the difference "between light and darkness" (6:14), and such a union is unthinkable.

PRAYER: Give me a faith, O Lord, that keeps life in perspective. Amen.

*T*he extent of Paul's pain regarding the misunderstanding with the Corinthians is clear from the way he continues to return to the subject. Once more he talks about the letter that caused them sorrow. He's sorry, but he's not sorry. He only hopes their grief will be a "godly grief" that will produce "a repentance that leads to salvation and brings no regret" (7:10). Any teacher who has had to speak severely to a student, any minister who has preached a strong sermon, or any parent who has had to discipline a child will understand how Paul felt.

And now we see Paul taking up an offering. The need is at the church in Jerusalem, where famine threatens lives. Paul speaks first of the liberality of the churches in Macedonia, where "their abundant joy and their extreme poverty have overflowed in a wealth of generosity" (8:2). Now he prods the Corinthians that, just as they have excelled in so many other ways, they would now excel in their giving. He then reminds them of the example of their Lord, who "though he was rich, yet for your sakes he became poor, so that by his poverty you might become rich" (8:9). That must be the strongest of all arguments for Christian giving. Now Paul adds a straightforward reminder that "the one who sows sparingly will also reap sparingly," while those who sow "bountifully will also reap bountifully" (9:6). And especially this, that their gift should not be reluctant nor under compulsion, "for God loves a cheerful giver" (9:7). If we can read all that and still be sparing, we're in bad shape.

PRAYER: Give me always, O Lord, a generous heart; to your glory. Amen.

2 CORINTHIANS 10, 11; PROVERBS 8   *Week 47, Day 5*

*P*aul is so candid in this letter that we enter into his pain. He acknowledges that he may seem humble in person but bold in letters (10:1). Some say, "His bodily presence is weak, and his speech contemptible" (10:10). Paul was not an orator like Apollos, and apparently he was not physically prepossessing; we have no eyewitness details, but tradition describes him in unflattering terms.

But "we were the first to come all the way to you with the good news of Christ" (10:14). They can't take that away from Paul. And he feels "a divine jealousy" for the people at Corinth, because he had promised to present them "as a chaste virgin to Christ" (11:2). Paul's expectations for his converts—even for such erratic ones as the Corinthians!—are almost unlimited. He looks at even the dreariest soul and sees a saint struggling to come out.

At last he says that he will play the fool, and "boast a little" (11:16). He recites, first, his credentials as a Jew, to show that he is "not in the least inferior to these super-apostles" (11:5). "I am talking like a madman," he says (11:23), and somehow I like him all the more for being so human, so candid, as he lists his sacrifices and sufferings. No, he probably ought not to do so. A great saint would suffer silently, and the greatest saint might not even know he was suffering. But Paul is a struggler like you and me, and he cannot resist, this one time, telling the people at Corinth just how great a price he has paid for his faith.

PRAYER: I haven't much to boast of, Lord, which is just as well. Amen.

2 CORINTHIANS 12, 13; PROVERBS 9   *Week 47, Day 6*

*J*t is especially touching that it is out of Paul's defense of himself that we are led, first, into the hidden mystery of his most ecstatic spiritual experience, and then into the even more hidden place (and mystery!) of his "defeat." It reminds us again that we wouldn't have the riches of these New Testament letters if it were not for human frailty, and the attempts to deal with errors and questions.

He resorts to the third person to tell of the occasion when he was "caught up to the third heaven" (12:2)—that is, the highest bliss. The experience was so extraordinary that he doesn't know whether he was in or out of his body, and he doesn't tell us what he experienced because these are things "no mortal is permitted to repeat" (12:4). But he wants the people to know he has had such an experience, and it is probably true that this is an experience which, while it would impress all of us, would be especially impressive to the church at Corinth, given as they were to experience and excitement.

And then, an experience that probably meant even more. Paul had a "thorn"; he never chose to identify it, and while there have been many theories, there is no final word. Three times he prayed for its removal, only to be told that God's grace was sufficient, and that "power is made perfect in weakness" (12:9). Paul is content, therefore, not only to endure this thorn, but also the "insults, hardships, persecutions, and calamities" that come for Christ; because being weak, he is strong (12:10)!

PRAYER: Teach me, I pray, how to cope with any unremoved thorn. Amen.

GALATIANS 1, 2; PROVERBS 10   *Week 47, Day 7*

*W*e noticed earlier that as soon as a letter's formalities are past, Paul indicates its primary burden. In the case of Galatians, he doesn't even get past the formalities. In this, the most emotional of his letters, he interrupts his salutation to defend his role: he is an apostle "sent neither by human commission nor from human authorities" (1:1). This letter is often called "the Magna Charta of Christian Liberty" because of its passionate defense of the freedom that is in Christ.

Some other teachers had visited the churches of Galatia (central Asia Minor), saying that in order to be a Christian one must first of all be circumcised and come under the other requirements of the Jewish Law. Paul is livid. "Even if we or an angel from heaven should proclaim to you a gospel contrary to what we proclaimed to you, let that one be accursed!" (1:8).

He proceeds to trace his own journey of faith to establish his apostolic credentials, then recalls the series of meetings with the leaders of the church concerning the issue. He expresses his disappointment in Peter (Cephas) for hedging on his position. Paul is done with the Law as a way of pleasing God; "I have been crucified with Christ; and it is no longer I who live, but it is Christ who lives in me" (2:19, 20). To seek any other means of justification is to "nullify the grace of God" so that "Christ died for nothing" (2:21). Now let it be said that Paul's argument is not an issue limited to the first century; it reappears in each generation.

PRAYER: May I never forsake the high ground of the cross; in Christ. Amen.

GALATIANS 3, 4, 5, 6   Week 48, Day 1

*P*aul shows his rabbinical training as he makes his case through scriptures and examples from the Old Testament. First, there is Abraham; his experience is not by law, but by faith; he "believed God, and it was reckoned to him as righteousness" (3:6). The law came 430 years later (3:17). It had a purpose, of course; it was "our disciplinarian until Christ came" (3:24). But now that Christ has come, we no longer need such an aide. Nor are we any longer "minors . . . enslaved to the elemental spirits of the world"; we have been redeemed, and adopted as children of God (4:4, 5).

Paul draws an allegory from the story of Hagar. Her offspring, he says, are the children of slavery—that is, those who are held by the Law—while those who choose faith "are children of promise, like Isaac" (4:28). "For freedom Christ has set us free" (5:1).

But Paul anticipates the way some may misuse his teaching. It is all too possible that they will use their freedom "as an opportunity for self-indulgence" (5:13). So he reminds them (and us!) that they are under a new law: "You shall love your neighbor as yourself" (5:14). This means resisting the "desires of the flesh," a number of which he lists (5:19-21). He doesn't stop with the negative, however. He offers, "by contrast, the fruit of the Spirit" (5:22, 23), adding with excitement that "there is no law against such things."

Probably because of the nature of this letter, Paul offers no greetings at the end. But he reminds us again of the passion of his life: "May I never boast of anything except the cross of our Lord Jesus Christ" (6:14).

PRAYER: Me, too, Lord! Let me boast only in your cross. Amen.

262

*T*radition says this letter was written by Paul during his imprisonment in Rome, perhaps in A.D. 63. Because its style is rather formal and because there are no personal references or greetings, some feel that it was originally a "circulating letter" that was distributed to a number of churches over a relatively wide area.

If you think poorly of yourself, you'll be forced to change your mind if you take these chapters seriously. The words cascade from Paul's dictation as he describes the wonders God has in store for us. God "destined us for adoption as his children" (1:5), and he has "lavished on us" the riches of grace (1:8). We have an inheritance in Christ (1:11), and the proof of it is in our having received the Holy Spirit (1:14). Paul hopes we will come to know the "glorious inheritance" we have "among the saints," "and . . . the immeasurable greatness of [God's] power for us who believe" (1:18, 19). It is the very power that raised Christ from the dead (1:20).

And here's the marvel of it: we are people who were once "dead through the trespasses and sins" in which we lived (2:1). Besides that, we were "aliens from the commonwealth of Israel, and strangers to the covenants of promise, having no hope" (2:12). But now we are "no longer strangers and aliens"; we belong to the "household of God" (2:19). And it is all by grace, the gift of God (2:8). And this is only the beginning! There is power working in us that is "able to accomplish abundantly far more than all we can ask or imagine" (3:20). Think of that!

PRAYER: I marvel that you think so well of me! Thank you! Amen.

*T*he second half of Ephesians is just as down to earth as the first half is heavenly. If there is any key verb in these verses, it would be *walk*. Having told us how much God has in store for us, Paul now tells us how to live out the faith in our day-by-day walk. "You must no longer live as the Gentiles live, in the futility of their minds" (4:17). That's a fine phrase, reminding us that bad living begins with bad thinking.

There are specifics, with particular emphasis on the way we talk. We are urged to "speak the truth" (4:25) and to "let no evil talk come out of [our] mouths" (4:29); in place of "obscene, silly, and vulgar talk . . . let there be thanksgiving" (5:4). The person who said, "Words never hurt anyone" hasn't read these admonitions; words hurt the speaker as well as, in many cases, the hearer.

Paul then spells out the requirements of the Christian life for particular persons and relationships: wives, husbands, children, parents, slaves, masters. There is a wonderful balance in his counsel. Children, for instance, are to obey their parents, but fathers, on the other hand, are commanded, "Do not provoke your children to anger" (6:1, 4). That must have been a shocking idea in a time when parental power was unlimited.

The living that Paul recommends is possible only as we are "strong in the Lord" (6:10). The struggle in which we are engaged is not simply against "blood and flesh," but against "the cosmic powers of this present darkness" (6:12). That's why we need "the whole armor of God" (6:13-17).

PRAYER: Prepare me for battle, Lord, and keep me alert; in Christ. Amen.

PHILIPPIANS 1, 2; PROVERBS 11 *Week 48, Day 4*

*P*aul writes this letter from prison, but you'd never guess it by its tone. It is often called "The Epistle of Joy," and part of the secret is in Paul's great pleasure in the church at Philippi, his first congregation on the European continent.

Already in his greeting Paul declares that his prayers for the people are "with joy" (1:4). And when it comes to the matter of his imprisonment, he says happily that "what has happened to me has actually helped to spread the gospel" (1:12), partly through his witness to "the whole imperial guard" (1:13) and partly because both his friends and enemies are now working all the harder (1:15). He senses that death is a near possibility, and this raises a wondrous problem for him because he would love "to depart and be with Christ," but he

264

knows there is still work for him to do, especially with his dear friends at Philippi (1:24).

This letter has an especially wonderful serendipity. Paul makes an appeal for the people to relate to one another with humility, and to make his point, he refers to Christ Jesus, who "was in the form of God . . . but emptied himself, / taking the form of a slave, / being born in human likeness" (2:6, 7). It is felt that these lovely verses may have been a hymn in Paul's time, which he quoted (as preachers will); or perhaps this was the origin of the hymn, framed by Paul as he wrote. In any event, these verses are a key statement of the doctrine and nature of Jesus Christ. Our theological insight is enriched by Paul's illustration of humility.

PRAYER: May I relate to others, O Lord, with humility of heart. Amen.

PHILIPPIANS 3, 4; PROVERBS 12   *Week 48, Day 5*

*T*here are times when Paul's witness is so full of joy and glory that I wish I could put it to music. It happens this time at a surprising point, as Paul refutes those "evil workers" who insist that gentile believers must come under the law of circumcision (3:2). He decides once again to "boast," listing reasons why he might have "confidence in the flesh" (3:4). It's an impressive dossier; not many could compare with it. But I get the feeling that while Paul sets out to give his credentials, he soon finds himself on an entirely different track as he marvels at how little these things mean to him, compared to Christ. "I regard them as rubbish, in order that I may gain Christ" (3:8). And with that he recommits himself: "forgetting what lies behind and straining forward to what lies ahead, I press on toward the goal" (3:13, 14). When a person makes such a witness from a prison, it rings true and powerful.

And the mood is all joy. "Rejoice in the Lord always; again I will say, Rejoice" (4:4). The conviction is so great that the word must be spoken twice. And speaking of rejoicing, Paul wants to thank the people for their care of him. He is wonderfully independent of the matters that absorb most lives; "I have learned to be content with whatever I have" (4:11). Nevertheless, he is grateful for these special people who have sought to make his life easier. What they have done is "a fragrant offering . . . to God" and God will bless them, abundantly, in return (4:18, 19).

PRAYER: Thank you, dear Savior, for the profound joy you have brought into my life. I want to take good care of it, giving it away. Amen.

COLOSSIANS 1, 2; PROVERBS 13   *Week 48, Day 6*

*H*eretical teachings were a particular peril to the early churches. The people generally had little written material on which to draw, especially the largely gentile communities where there was little knowledge of the Hebrew scriptures. Paul's letters were often the instrument to bring a congregation back to sound doctrine. In Colossae, the problem was twofold. Some were slipping into a kind of legalism, with an emphasis on "matters of food and drink or of observing festivals, new moons, or sabbaths" (2:16). Others were caught up in a type of gnosticism that taught that "elemental spirits of the universe" (2:20) had to be worshiped because they were back of the creation and exercised power over human beings.

Paul answers with a ringing declaration about the uniqueness of Christ. "He is the image of the invisible God, the first-born of all creation" (1:15). For those who fear the "elemental spirits of the universe," Paul affirms that all things "visible and invisible," including those presumed elemental spirits, "have been created through him and for him. He himself is before all things, and in him all things hold together" (1:16, 17). Here Paul reflects the same understanding of Christ that is found in the first chapter of John. It is a high view of our Lord's deity.

Then, at a very different level, he warns the people not to become captive to laws of food, drink, and ceremonies. These things have a place, but only as "a shadow of what is to come" (2:17). Their purpose in the Hebrew scriptures was to point the way to "the substance" in Christ (2:17).

PRAYER: May nothing, dear Lord, cloud my vision of your Son; in him. Amen.

266

*T*he Bible, as we've noticed before, is a wonderfully practical book. Having confronted doctrinal errors, Paul moves now to the daily issues of the Christian life. He tells us some of the things we must be rid of: "anger, wrath, malice, slander, and abusive language" (3:8). And in their place, "clothe yourselves with compassion, kindness, humility, meekness, and patience" (3:12). Then, to complete the wardrobe, "clothe yourselves with love, which binds everything together in perfect harmony" (3:14).

Paul proceeds, then, as he did in Ephesians, with application of the faith to everyday human relationships: husbands and wives, children and parents, slaves and masters. Again, there is emphasis on the use of that troublesome instrument, the tongue: "Let your speech always be gracious, seasoned with salt, so that you may know how you ought to answer everyone" (4:6).

Several persons stand out in the farewell greetings. Notice Onesimus, "the faithful and beloved brother" (4:9); we will see more of him in Philemon. We're glad for the reference to Mark ("if he comes to you, welcome him" [4:10]), remembering that Paul was so unhappy with him earlier. When Paul tells the people to pass this letter to two other churches, and to get the letter he has written to Laodicea, we see how these letters began to be the common property and nurture of the early church. And now they are ours, too.

PRAYER: Help me to keep sound doctrine, dear Lord, and with it, good and wholesome living; and in everything, to your glory. Amen.

1 THESSALONIANS 1, 2, 3, 4, 5   *Week 49, Day 1*

*I*t is generally agreed that this was the first of Paul's letters, written in the winter of A.D. 50–51. Timothy had brought back news of how faithfully the people at Thessalonica were dealing with persecution (3:6), and Paul writes to praise them for their courage and to answer some of their questions about the return of Christ.

Paul is very proud of this congregation; he calls them his "hope or joy or crown of boasting" (2:19), and he wonders how he can thank God enough for the joy they have brought him (3:9). Nevertheless, he prods them to greater effort, especially in matters of sexual conduct (4:3-8) and honorable, industrious living (4:11, 12). Their culture was probably as sex-saturated as ours. It must have been very difficult for new converts, with no previous sense of moral restraint, to live up to the high demands of the Christian ethic.

The Thessalonians were so anticipating the return of Christ that they were worried about loved ones who had already died; would they miss the event? Paul explained that, to the contrary, they "will rise first" (4:16), and then the living believers. With such a hope, as those who "belong to the day, let us be sober" (5:8). Paul wants such hour-by-hour consistency of life, in fact, that he uses all-inclusive terms: "Rejoice always, pray without ceasing, give thanks in all circumstances" (5:16-18). That may not sound easy, but Paul reassures that this is God's will in Christ Jesus for all of us (5:18).

PRAYER: I want your best, O God. Lead me on, I pray. Amen.

2 THESSALONIANS 1, 2, 3   *Week 49, Day 2*

This letter was probably written only a few months after the first letter, and it deals with some of the same questions and problems. Again, Paul praises them for keeping the faith "during all your persecutions" (1:4). He promises them that those who now inflict hardship on them will in time suffer God's judgment (1:6). Like the Hebrew prophets, Paul believes in the justice of God.

The people are still troubled about Christ's return. Some feel "that the day of the Lord is already here" (2:2). In his first letter, Paul seemed to emphasize that Christ's return might be at any moment and that it would come "like a thief in the night" (1 Thess. 5:2). Here, however, he explains that certain things must first occur, including the appearance of "the lawless one . . . the one destined for destruction" (2:3), and that although "the mystery of lawlessness is already at work" (2:7), there is a restraining power that prevents his appearing openly.

The problem of idleness, which was mentioned briefly in the first letter, had now gotten worse. Paul reminds them of his own industrious way of life: "with toil and labor we worked night and day, so that we might not burden any of you" (3:8). His solution is severe: "Anyone unwilling to work should not eat" (3:10). In a pagan world like theirs (or ours!), the witness of the Christian life must be as above reproach as possible. Paul doesn't leave any room for casual discipleship.

PRAYER: Help me to honor your name by the industry with which I work and the integrity with which I play; in Jesus' name. Amen.

1 TIMOTHY 1, 2, 3   *Week 49, Day 3*

*H*ere we are privileged to listen in as a veteran of the faith counsels an earnest neophyte. Paul is especially proud of Timothy because he is "my loyal child in the faith" (1:2). In a way, he may envy Timothy his clean start, since Paul lives under the burden of his early persecution of the believers. But that experience has made him marvel all the more concerning God's mercy. Here's something, he says, that you can rely on: "Christ Jesus came into the world to save sinners—of whom I am the foremost" (1:15). Paul reasoned that if Christ could save him, no one was impossible. In our own way, all of us ought to have the same confidence about Christ's power to transform life.

We get some insight into the organization and the character qualifications of the early church in Paul's description of elders and deacons. We don't know much detail about their work portfolio, and perhaps that's just as well, but we know what kind of persons they were expected to be. Those of us who have positions of church leadership, whether lay or clergy, read these expectations with a solemn heart.

When Paul says, "The mystery of our religion is great" (3:16), he gives what must have been a kind of hymn of praise to Christ. Many Bibles print it in lines of poetry, to convey the idea that it was probably sung in the early church. We catch something of their spirit of adoration as we read these words, and we wish we could hear them singing.

PRAYER: In some ways I feel so far removed from those first-century believers, but I count myself one with them. Thank you, Lord! Amen.

1 Timothy 4, 5, 6   *Week 49, Day 4*

*T*his letter concludes, "Guard what has been entrusted to you" (6:20). I think the appeal includes both Timothy's personal talents and the people in his care, and that's what these chapters are about. Timothy has to protect his congregation against false teachers (it's quite astonishing how much error had crept into the church so early, yet perhaps not so surprising since it was such a young, dynamic body), and at the same time, take care of his own spiritual gift (4:14). He was in particular danger because people could easily discount him for his youthfulness (4:12).

Widows were a major concern of the early church. This is a significant insight into the quality of the church, because they lived in a culture where little concern was shown for the more helpless elements, and widows in the first century were surely in that category. There is also counsel regarding the role of elders, and the relationship of slaves and masters. Slavery was the dominant economic pattern of the times, so it was impossible to have an ethic of human relationships without facing this issue. Closely related was the issue of wealth. Paul warns that "those who want to be rich [and that includes those who are not but want to be] fall into temptation and are trapped by many senseless and harmful desires" because "the love of money is a root of all kinds of evil" (6.9, 10). If one has wealth, one needs more than ever to focus on God "who richly provides us with everything for our enjoyment" (6:17). The secret is in keeping life's material resources in their proper place.

PRAYER: Help me, I pray, to keep focused on what is eternal. Amen.

2 Timothy 1, 2, 3, 4   *Week 49, Day 5*

*P*aul is Timothy's cheerleader, wanting this young man to use to the full the gift that came to him through the laying on of hands (1:6) and following Paul's pattern of sound doctrine (1:13). He draws on several figures of speech—soldiering, athletics, and farming (2:3-7)—in graphically encouraging Timothy to effective service.

In Romans, Paul affirmed the right of God, the potter, to use human clay as he sees fit (Rom. 9:21), but he tells Timothy that we vessels have something to say about what our role will be; if we want, we can be "special utensils . . . ready for every good work" (2:20, 21).

Timothy is given a number of signs by which believers can recognize "the last days" (3:1). They have to do with human conduct and attitudes, but they are difficult to discern because they are characteristics that always exist (for example, boasters, arrogant, abusive, ungrateful, slanderers, lovers of pleasure [3:2]). It is apparently a matter of degree, and it's hard to measure matters of this kind. The secret? Always be attentive, always prepared, always sensitive to the Holy Spirit.

The letter ends warmly and gently. First there is the farewell of the happy warrior: "I have fought the good fight, I have finished the race, I have kept the faith" (4:7). Then, some needs: Paul is alone, except for Luke; he hopes Mark can come to his aid. He needs a coat he has left behind, and some scrolls. We are eavesdropping on a special moment.

PRAYER: Since I know so little about the times and seasons, help me, dear Lord, to be ready for your purposes at all times; in Christ. Amen.

TITUS 1, 2, 3; PROVERBS 15   Week 49, Day 6

*T*itus, like Timothy, is Paul's "loyal child in the faith we share" (1:4). Paul has left Titus behind in Crete to get the churches in order. We notice again that elders are a key figure in leadership. It's interesting to see the similarities and the differences with which Paul describes their qualifications in these three pastoral epistles to Timothy and Titus.

When Paul tells the young leader to "teach what is consistent with sound doctrine" (2:1), he becomes specific in a rather surprising way by applying doctrine to ages and categories: older men, older women, younger women, younger men, and slaves. This indicates again the pragmatic style of the scriptures. All of us have to live out our faith in the peculiar settings of our personal lives, so the Apostle spells out his directions in that fashion. Very practical!

He has high expectations for believers. They may be only a little distance removed from a pagan world, but he expects them to "live lives that are self-controlled, upright, and godly" (2:12), especially since "we wait for the blessed hope and the manifestation of the glory of our great God and Savior, Jesus Christ" (2:13). Whatever one's understanding about the nearness or not of Christ's return, we should live with the impetus that such an expectation brings. And that includes being "careful to devote [ourselves] to good works" and avoiding "stupid controversies," which are "unprofitable and worthless" (3:8, 9). The Lord is always coming, and we ought always to be ready.

PRAYER: I want to live my life on tiptoes of holy expectation. Amen.

PHILEMON; PROVERBS 16, 17   *Week 49, Day 7*

*T*his little letter is a model of Christian gentility and persuasiveness. A runaway slave, Onesimus, has been converted by Paul's witness. As it happens, Onesimus' master is one of Paul's earlier converts in Colossae. Paul convinces Onesimus to return to his master, Philemon, and sends this letter with him.

After a warm, gracious opening, Paul gets to the heart of the matter. He wants Philemon to give Onesimus his freedom so he can be an aide to Paul. He calls the slave "my child . . . whose father I have become during my imprisonment" (10). He employs a playful pun: "Onesimus" means *useful* or *beneficial*, so Paul says, to cast it in our words, "Formerly he was un-Onesimus to you, but now he is indeed Onesimus both to you and to me" (11). In sending him back, Paul says he is sending his very heart (12).

Paul says, somewhat daringly, "welcome him as you would welcome me" (17), and if he owes anything, "charge that to my account" (18). Then, a gentle but direct touch: Paul reminds his convert Philemon, "I say nothing about your owing me even your own self" (19).

Paul sees the providence of God in all that has happened.

272

Philemon lost a slave but now is getting back "a beloved brother" (15, 16), since Onesimus was converted in the interim. "Perhaps this is the reason," Paul suggests, "he was separated from you for a while" (15). The story may be even greater. Some scholars feel that this is the Onesimus who later became a bishop, and who was responsible for collecting Paul's letters.

PRAYER: Help me to believe for reasons I can't see; in Christ. Amen.

HEBREWS 1, 2, 3   *Week 50, Day 1*

*T*his book, even more than the Gospel of Matthew, relates the new faith in Jesus Christ to the teachings of the Hebrew scriptures. It was written to some new converts who had apparently become discouraged and were tempted to return to their former beliefs. The author, who is never specifically identified, makes a powerful statement about the uniqueness and superiority of Jesus Christ.

He begins his case by demonstrating that Jesus is superior to the angels; nothing, he observes, that was ever said of an angel can be compared with the statements that have been made about the Son. And the marvel is this, that this One "had to become like his brothers and sisters in every respect, so that he might be a merciful and faithful high priest . . . to make a sacrifice of atonement for the sins of the people" (2:17).

Next, the writer explains, Jesus is greater than Moses, who "was faithful . . . as a servant, to testify to the things that would be spoken later" (3:5). But whereas Moses was a servant in God's house, Christ is a son in the house (3:5, 6).

At this point he interrupts the flow of logic to warn the people that they are in danger of "an evil, unbelieving heart that turns away from the living God" (3:12). The people of Moses' day missed their chance to enter God's rest because of their unbelief. He fears his group of believers are in real danger of committing the same tragic sin.

PRAYER: In a time and a culture where so many ask for my allegiance, help me, dear Lord, to hold Christ high above all; in his name. Amen.

*T*he Christian life is described in quite different ways, often by the same writers, because it has so many facets. The language of battle and warfare is often used, but here the writer speaks of it as entering God's rest. "A sabbath rest still remains for the people of God; for those who enter God's rest also cease from their labors as God did from his" (4:9, 10). This is an emphasis on that quality in the Christian life in which we rely more surely on the grace and mercy of God and less on our own striving.

The author now returns to the excellence of Christ. He is our "great high priest who has passed through the heavens" (4:14); he is one who can "sympathize with our weaknesses" because he was tested as we are, "yet without sin" (4:15). Although he was the Son of God, "he learned obedience through what he suffered" (5:8). Our Lord's greatness is shown through his readiness to submit himself to all human indignity in order not only to be our Savior, but also to be sympathetic with our human state.

But the issue and burden of this book is the danger that its readers will leave the faith. The writer wants his people to "go on toward perfection," because if they do not—if, instead, they keep struggling at the lowlands of their faith—they will lose out completely. He speaks a hard word to those who might consider denying their faith. If they do, "they are crucifying again the Son of God" and they cannot be restored to repentance (6:4-6). If it seems that he leaves little room for mercy, keep in mind the circumstances and severity of his times.

PRAYER: Keep me at the center of your will, dear Lord, always. Amen.

*R*emember Melchizedek, king of Salem, whom we met long ago in Genesis? Everything about him is special. His name means *righteousness* and the name of his realm (Salem) means *peace*. He receives tithes from Abraham, the father of the chosen people and one who was called the friend of God. He is without genealogy. The writer doesn't try to tell us who Melchizedek is; he wants simply to note that he is not only different from the Levitical priesthood, but also superior to it, and then to identify that Christ is a priest, not after the Levitical order but after "the order of Melchizedek" (7:11). Christ has his role, "not through a legal requirement concerning physical descent, but through the power of an indestructible life" (7:16).

Jesus is therefore "the mediator of a better covenant, which has been enacted through better promises" (8:6). The purpose of a priest is to provide access to God. Under the old covenant that process was limited, because the priests themselves were human and imperfect. In Christ we have a better covenant, and since that is the case, the old covenant has been made "obsolete" (8:13).

The writer now touches upon some of the elements and sacrifices of worship according to "the first covenant" (9:1). In each he finds symbols of the greater reality, which is now accomplished in Christ. Above all, Christ fulfills the "shedding of blood," without which "there is no forgiveness of sins" (9:22), so that by his one offering he is able "to bear the sins of many" (9:28).

PRAYER: I gladly accept your sacrifice for me, dear Savior. Amen.

HEBREWS 10, 11; PROVERBS 18 *Week 50, Day 4*

*T*he writer has almost finished making his case. He rejoices still further in the excellence that is now ours in Jesus Christ. We come now "by the new and living way that he opened," and we can come "with a true heart in full assurance of faith" (10:20, 22). But because this is a more excellent way, to reject it is unthinkable.

But if they are to hold fast, they will need faith. Fortunately, they have a heritage upon which to draw. The writer leads us into a gallery of faith that is wondrous in every way. This chapter is to faith what 1 Corinthians 13 is to love; perhaps there is more that could be said on the respective subjects, but in all our days on earth we will never finally plumb the depths of these two chapters. They will always challenge us.

The story begins with God and the creation, which was a faith event. Then to Abel, who pleased God, "and without faith it is impossible to please God" (11:6). And Noah, Abraham, Moses, Rahab (did you expect to find her here?), and several of the judges. But the writer realizes he is running out of time, so he goes into a grand symphony of phrases, trying to describe persons "of whom the world was not worthy" (11:38). And the marvel of it all is this, that as extraordinary as these persons were, they didn't receive what was promised! They were looking, waiting, and living for what is now ours, through Jesus Christ. That lets us know how blessed we are. It also reinforces that it would be out of the question to let it go.

PRAYER: Thank you for my heritage in faith! In Christ my Lord. Amen.

HEBREWS 12, 13; PROVERBS 19, 20   *Week 50, Day 5*

The writer isn't done with our faith ancestors. He sees them now as "so great a cloud of witnesses" surrounding us, perhaps even cheering us on, as we "run with perseverance the race that is set before us" (12:1). They have a stake in us since we are privileged to complete the journey in which they have preceded us through the centuries.

And with that, we are once again dealing with the day-by-day business of the Christian life. There is a glory in all of this journey, but it is usually found in routine places. Discipline, for instance. It "always seems painful rather than pleasant at the time," but we need it (12:11). And "pursue peace with everyone" (12:14)—there's a big assignment! Beware lest we become like Esau, "who sold his birthright for a single meal" because he was "an immoral and godless person" (12:16). Watch out for "all kinds of strange teachings" (13:9); there is a continuity in Jesus Christ, for he "is the same yesterday and today and forever" (13:8).

The readers were told, through Abraham's experiences, that faith-people are "strangers and foreigners on the earth . . . seeking a homeland" (11:13, 14). Now they are reminded that "we have no lasting city, but we are looking for the city that is to come" (13:14). I expect it is easier for people to believe such a word when they are suffering persecution, or even in hard economic times; I think I heard more singing about heaven during the Depression of my boyhood. But it's difficult for us to remember, when all is reasonably well, that this earth is not our permanent address.

PRAYER: Help me to know, dear Lord, that I am part of eternity. Amen.

JAMES 1, 2, 3   *Week 50, Day 6*

*A*s you read this book you may feel at times that you're reading Proverbs, or perhaps one of the Hebrew prophets. It resembles these books in style, content, and emphasis; yet it is unmistakably Christian. The author, James, is traditionally thought to be either the brother of Jesus or the apostle James the Less. His style of writing has a sense of authority; there are 54 commands in the 108 verses of the book. It is an extremely practical book, committed to "religion that is pure and undefiled before God"—the kind of religion that proves itself by seeking to "care for orphans and widows in their distress" and in keeping its followers "unstained by the world" (1:27).

The church was still in its first or second generation when this book was written, yet already people are catering to those "with gold rings and in fine clothes" (2:2). James reminds them that "God has chosen the poor in the world to be rich in faith" (2:5)—a matter their Lord had surely made clear again and again—but it is somehow hard for us really to believe this. In his emphasis on the pragmatic, Jesus calls for *works*, and he proves his case by using the same example— Abraham—other New Testament writers use to prove the importance of faith (2:14-26). And speaking of practical works, James deals emphatically with how we use our tongues. "No one can tame the tongue," he says, because it is "a restless evil, full of deadly poison" (3:8). He's warning us to be careful.

PRAYER: Help me, I pray, to live out my discipleship in all the practical matters of daily conduct; and always to your glory. Amen.

*W*e are surrounded by temptations, but James has some down-to-earth advice for meeting them: "Resist the devil, and he will flee from you. Draw near to God, and he will draw near to you" (4:7, 8). That's basic and it makes sense, and we wonder why we don't more readily follow its counsel. So, too, with James' advice concerning our planning. We are "a mist that appears for a little while and then vanishes," so we should couch all our thoughts of tomorrow in a spirit that reasons, "If the Lord wishes" (4:15).

As James nears the end of his letter, he comes back to the subject of the rich. He sounds like the prophet Amos when he warns of wealth that has been gotten at the pain and expense of others. When he urges his readers to have patience, it sounds as if he is thinking especially of the retribution he is sure the evildoers will eventually receive. "The Judge," he promises, "is standing at the doors!" (5:9).

James provides a method for Christians to pray for the sick. The Catholic Church sees this passage (5:14, 15) as a basis for its sacrament of extreme unction; and groups that emphasize divine healing, such as most Pentecostal bodies, use it as their method of prayer for the sick. I like it that James, after telling us that "the prayer of the righteous is powerful and effective," uses as his example Elijah, noting that he was "a human being like us" (5:16, 17). If a person as human as Elijah qualifies as one of the effectively righteous, there's hope for you and me.

PRAYER: I'm thankful you are patient with our failings, O Lord! Amen.

1 PETER 1, 2; PROVERBS 22   *Week 51, Day 1*

*T*his letter is written to Christians who were suffering persecution. This was a common experience in the early church; the Christians had many enemies, so any period of relative calm was likely to be interrupted by a new outbreak of persecution.

What does one write to persons living in such circumstances? Remind them, first, that they have "a living hope" and "an inheritance that is imperishable, undefiled, and unfading, kept in heaven for you" (1:3, 4). Thus this "little while" of "various trials" is only going to make the "genuineness of [their] faith" all the better (1:6, 7). And with that comes an appeal to the kind of living that is appropriate to people who have been purchased by "the precious blood of Christ" (1:19).

Peter makes any number of direct and indirect references to the Hebrew scriptures in his appeal for godly living, including the Psalms, Isaiah, Deuteronomy, Exodus, and Hosea. When terms like "a chosen race, a royal priesthood, a holy nation" (2:9) are applied to the believers, you realize how deep are our Christian roots in Judaism, and how convinced the early church was that their new faith was the fulfillment of the expectations of the Hebrew scriptures.

But they have to live out this faith as "aliens and exiles" in this world, and they have to know that there is a war to be waged (2:11). The gentile world may be inclined to despise them for their faith, but that's all the more reason to make an honorable witness.

PRAYER: Help me, O Lord, to honor your name by my life; in Christ. Amen.

1 PETER 3, 4, 5   Week 51, Day 2

*L*ike Paul, Peter spells out his theology in the practical terms of our stations in life. But where Paul usually balances a message to the slave with one to the master, Peter urges the slaves to pattern their lives after Christ, who "when he was abused, he did not return abuse" (2:23). His counsel to wives includes a warning against expensive adornment, which may indicate that believers were by now coming into a higher level of economics. Husbands are warned that thoughtlessness toward their wives may hinder their prayers (3:7), which is a further reminder of the connection between the spiritual and the everyday.

Mainly, however, Peter is dealing with the issue of persecution. He pleads with them not to be intimidated by their enemies, and to remember that Christ suffered as "the righteous for the unrighteous" (3:18). Nor should they be "surprised at the fiery ordeal" they are enduring (4:12); instead, "be glad and shout for joy" (4:13). I've been privileged to know some people who, in our time, have suffered real persecution, and I've been impressed that joy seems to be their dominant quality. Peter knew what he was talking about.

Yet isn't it strange, in a time when people were living with such heroic faith, that Peter needed also to warn Christian leaders against serving "for sordid gain" (5:2), and that it was necessary to urge them not to "lord it over those in [their] charge" (5:3)? We human beings seem always susceptible to petty, selfish sins.

PRAYER: Help me, I pray, to keep up my guard against evil; in Christ. Amen.

2 PETER 1, 2, 3; PROVERBS 23   *Week 51, Day 3*

This letter deals primarily with two issues, false teachers and the return of Christ. Peter lays out a rule that can keep us from error when he says that "no prophecy of scripture is a matter of one's own interpretation" (1:20). Believers are part of a body; we need one another to correct and to confirm us. And this body is made up not only of fellow believers in our own time, but also those of centuries past; that is, tradition helps us in understanding the faith.

Peter speaks sharply about false prophets. If God didn't spare angels that sinned or the people of Noah's and Lot's generations, then surely the unrighteous of this time will suffer. He describes them in language that is bitter enough to let us know how seriously they are sinning in their false teachings. Perhaps the most descriptive phrase is this, that they are "waterless springs" (2:17); seeming to offer benefit, they bring only disappointment.

But what of the coming of Christ? Some will scoff, saying "all things continue as they were from the beginning of creation!" (3:4). Remember, Peter pleads, that "with the Lord one day is like a thousand years, and a thousand years are like one day" (3:8, 9). God is patient, "not wanting any to perish, but all to come to repentance" (3:9). When it seems to some that all signs point to the return of Christ, never forget this, that God is bound more by his mercy than by the signs.

PRAYER: Help me, I pray, to be sensitive to your love for our human race, and to work with you for the fulfilling of your purposes. Amen.

1 JOHN 1, 2; PROVERBS 24   *Week 51, Day 4*

*A*t the very heart of Christian doctrine is the belief that Jesus Christ is both human and divine. In our day this doctrine is more likely to be in danger from those who deny or minimize his divinity, but in the early church the issue was made by those who denied his humanity. They were part of a movement known as gnosticism, a philosophy that taught that salvation was possible only through *gnosis*, or knowledge. Those who applied this philosophy to Christianity taught that Jesus inhabited a human body only temporarily, and therefore they denied both his death and resurrection. The first sentence in this letter rejects this heresy, as the apostle declares "what was from the beginning, what we have heard, what we have seen with our eyes, what we have looked at and touched with our hands" (1:1). All of his verbs are firsthand encounters with a real, physical person.

But this isn't by any means the whole burden of the letter. The writer is concerned about the quality of the believers' walk with God, and his argument with the doctrine is not only for its error but also for its effect on the lives of his people. He hopes that we will not sin, but if we do, he reassures us that "we have an advocate with the Father, Jesus Christ the right-eous" (2:1). The quality of life John recommends is fulfilled in the "new commandment" that we love one another. To live in the light is to live in love; and conversely, if we hate a brother or sister, we are walking in the darkness (2:9-11).

PRAYER: Fill me with your love, O Lord, so I will walk in love. Amen.

1 JOHN 3, 4, 5; PROVERBS 25   *Week 51, Day 5*

*T*his letter, like the Gospel of John, emphasizes love. It constantly urges us to love one another, but it recognizes the divine source of real love. "We love because he first loved us," John says (4:19); it is through God's love that we have come to know what love is.

Love is sometimes referred to as the new commandment, but it has also been around forever: "this is the message you have heard from the beginning, that we should love one another" (3:11). But it is far more than the fuzzy commodity so often offered by the secular culture. You can't claim to have God's love, John says, and refuse a brother or sister in need (3:17). Our love must be, "not in word or speech, but in truth and action" (3:18). Love is an action verb!

We can hardly imagine the difficulties in living the Christian life in the first century. Christians were a minuscule minority, yet well known for their impact on society, and therefore feared by many and often subject to persecution. Yet they had a commanding radiance. This book helps us understand why. See the sense of victory when John marvels that "we should be called children of God," and the almost breathless hope when he says, "What we will be has not yet been revealed," but "we will be like him, for we will see him as he is" (3:1-3). Do our hearts sometimes condemn us? If so, "God is greater than our hearts" (3:20). Does the world seem overpowering? No matter; "the one who is in you is greater than the one who is in the world" (4:4). They couldn't lose. Nor can we.

PRAYER: I take glad new hope this day! Thank you! Amen.

2 JOHN; 3 JOHN; PROVERBS 26   Week 51, Day 6

These two short letters deal with the needs of some early congregations. Some feel that the "elect lady" (2 John 1) was a specific person, but it seems far more likely that John is referring to a church, with "children" being the individual members. Thus the letter concludes with greetings from "the children of your elect sister" (13), another church—perhaps the church at Ephesus.

In both letters the Apostle rejoices that many are "walking in the truth" (2 John 4; 3 John 3). In this case, "the truth" refers specifically to two matters, one relational and one doctrinal. The doctrinal matter is the continuing problem of

282

gnosticism: "Many deceivers have gone out into the world, those who do not confess that Jesus Christ has come in the flesh" (2 John 7). John minces no words; anyone who so teaches is a deceiver and the antichrist. (This reminds us that the antichrist is not simply a particular individual, but the spirit that is opposed to Christ.)

The other issue of truth has to do with the call to love, the commandment "we have had from the beginning," "love one another" (2 John 5). But again, love is more than just a feeling; it is to "walk according to his commandments" (2 John 6).

Do church fights bother you? Me, too! But it seems they've been with us from the beginning. John warns against a man named Diotrephes, "who likes to put himself first, does not acknowledge our authority" (3 John 9). As long as the church is made up of human beings, it is likely at times to act human!

PRAYER: Help me, dear Savior, to rise above pettiness; in Christ. Amen.

JUDE; PROVERBS 27, 28   *Week 51, Day 7*

*A*s we've noticed before, we wouldn't have the priceless New Testament epistles if there hadn't been questions and troubles in the early church. Jude is another example. It is an impassioned appeal to the people to "contend for the faith that was once for all entrusted to the saints" (3).

The problem with which Jude deals is immorality. Some have chosen to "pervert the grace of our God into licentiousness" (4). Jude compares them with Sodom and Gomorrah, where they "indulged in sexual immorality and pursued unnatural lust" (7) and to the sins into which Israel was led by Balaam (11). Like Peter (2 Pet. 2:4), Jude refers to the fallen angels (6). The scriptures give us no specific doctrine in this matter, but there are enough references to let us know that such a doctrine existed in the early church.

Jude reminds the people that the apostles had warned of such apostasy (18), and he pleads, "Build yourselves up on your most holy faith" (20). When all around you things are falling, the secret is to reinforce your own foundations. And remember, of course, that we are not in this battle alone.

Jude's closing words, which have become favorite benedictory sentences throughout the Christian world, are so fitting for a people who might easily lose heart in the midst of persecution and heresy: "Now to him who is able to keep you from falling, and to make you stand without blemish in the presence of his glory with rejoicing . . ." (24). These great words sound good for our times, too. Take firm hold of them.

PRAYER: Keep me from sin, O God, and show me your glory; in Christ. Amen.

REVELATION 1, 2, 3   *Week 52, Day 1*

*T*his is a book for all seasons, but especially for dark times. John was in exile "on the island called Patmos" because of his witness, but he was also "in the spirit on the Lord's day" (1:9, 10). Such is the quality of this book; one may be imprisoned by circumstances, but one can still be "in the Spirit," so that the glory of the Lord is revealed.

Above all, this book is "the revelation of Jesus Christ" (1:1). John sees his Lord in a dramatic vision, in which he identifies himself as "the first and the last," "alive forever and ever," and holding the "keys of Death and of Hades" (1:17-19). Above all, he is the Lord of the church, and he has a message for the seven churches.

The churches are identified by the names of seven first-century cities. Some feel that these brief letters are simply that—messages to the cities that are named. Others feel that the number seven, as is often the case, is symbolic, representing all of Christendom, since seven is the number of completeness. Still others have tried to make the seven identifications fit seven consecutive periods of church history, from the first century to the present time.

In any event, each letter has basically the same structure: a phrase identifying the speaker, an evaluation of the congregation, words of commendation and chastisement, the formula sentence ("Let anyone who has an ear listen"), and a promise to the faithful. The churches are imperfect, but challenged and loved.

PRAYER: Let all my reading draw me nearer to my Savior; in his name. Amen.

284

*R*eaders of Revelation are likely to be looking for predictive factors and thus miss one of the truly dominant
qualities in the book, *worship*. At this point we are ushered to
the heavenly throne, where "day and night without ceasing
they sing,

> 'Holy, holy, holy,
> the Lord God the Almighty,
>   who was and is and is to come.'" (4:8)

Then, twenty-four elders who sing, "You are worthy, our Lord
and God" (4:11). When the Lamb of God is presented,
another song is begun:

> "You are worthy to take the scroll
>   and to open its seals." (5:9)

Soon there is a choir numbering "thousands of thousands,
singing with full voice, 'Worthy is the Lamb that was slaughtered'" (5:11, 12), and then a chorus made up of "every creature in heaven and on earth and under the earth and in the
sea," praising the Lamb (5:13).

Worship characterizes this book because it reports the final
victory of God and goodness. There is reason to sing! And
see the focus of the worship. When John weeps because no
one is worthy to open the scroll, he is told that "the Lion of
the tribe of Judah" has conquered and is able to open it.
While he waits to see this conquering Lion, he finds instead
"a Lamb standing as if it had been slaughtered" (5:5, 6).
God's victory has come through gentleness sacrificed. Love is
winning.

PRAYER: Let me never forget that your Lamb will triumph.
Amen.

REVELATION 6, 7; PROVERBS 30   *Week 52, Day 3*

*V*irtually everything in Revelation has symbolic value—
every person, object, number, color, garment. Numbers
are given significance all through the Hebrew scriptures, and
especially so here. Seven is the number of completeness, as

we have noticed before, so the series of judgments are presented in sevens: seven seals, seven trumpets, and so on. Another symbolic figure—144,000—builds on the figure twelve. Twelve is, of course, the number of the people of God, as in the twelve tribes and the twelve apostles; and 144,000 is twelve multiplied by 12,000, conveying the idea of greatness. Incidentally, when you see the listing of the tribes you will notice that Levi, Joseph, and Manasseh are included, while Ephraim and Dan are not.

The first order of business is judgment. In this respect, Revelation seems to reflect one of the moods of the Hebrew prophets. It is the time of "the wrath of the Lamb; for the great day of their wrath has come, and who is able to stand?" (6:16, 17). But the people of God (represented by the 144,000) are protected from these disasters. Others, however, have already died for their faith. Having "washed their robes and made them white in the blood of the Lamb" and having come out of "the great ordeal,"

"They will hunger no more, and thirst no more . . .
for the Lamb at the center of the throne will be their shepherd . . .
and God will wipe away every tear from their eyes." (7:14-17)

PRAYER: Grant, me, I pray, the faith and the insight to read your Word in such a way that I will become a better disciple; for Christ's sake. Amen.

REVELATION 8, 9, 10   Week 52, Day 4

We noticed earlier that Revelation is full of symbolism. I don't believe anyone in our century can interpret all these symbols; I doubt that anyone should try. I'm not even sure that the first-century readers were meant to interpret every detail. When one watches ballet, he or she can see meaning in particular segments, but not in each step, turn, or movement. But all the individual parts combine to convey a certain mood and a certain understanding. We can't hope to catch every symbol in Revelation, but we can be enlightened and blessed by the total sweep of the book, with each symbol playing its part.

We sense the awe as the seventh seal is about to be

opened, and the value of "the prayers of all the saints on the golden altar" (8:3). The seventh seal becomes the entry point for a new series, the seven trumpets; again we are in symbolism—perhaps referring to Israel's victory at Jericho. And although the plagues and woes are fearful beyond description, those who are not destroyed "did not repent of their murders or their sorceries or their fornication or their thefts" (9:21). We can harden our hearts against judgment as surely as we can against miracles. John learns the severity of the prophetic task when he takes the "little scroll" and eats it; it is sweet as honey in the mouth, but bitter in the stomach (10:10). Some of life's tasks are like that. And he, like the prophets before him, ministers to "many peoples and nations and languages and kings" (10:11). They are all in God's domain.

PRAYER: Let the light of your Spirit rest on my reading, I pray. Amen.

REVELATION 11, 12, 13   *Week 52, Day 5*

Someone has said that Revelation could be called "the Book of Sevens." That number arises again, this time in half-form, in the 42 months and the 1,260 days, each of which represents 3½ years. Who are the two witnesses? Theories include Enoch, Moses, Elijah, and Zerubbabel, among others. They might also be the two peoples of God, Israel and the Church. The woman in chapter 12 is often thought to be Israel, and the son, the Christ; but I wouldn't build a doctrine around such an uncertain matter.

The descriptions of the two beasts (13) remind one of the prophet Daniel; the two books are related in many ways. The war between Michael and the hosts of Satan also reminds us of Daniel (10, 11). There may be a specific event in mind, or this may symbolize the age-long warfare between good and evil, with the added factor that it is now drawing to a close and that the forces of goodness will win. At What cost? +

And then there is the mark of the beast. Scores of interpretations have been placed on this number over the centuries; I've seen several in my own lifetime. In a broad sense, the beast is evil personified, and the mark is proof of his absolute

Isaiah 45:7?

Amos 9:4?

287

control of those who cooperate with him. I wouldn't be too quick to accept any contemporary identification of this mark. Whatever it means, it is no ultimate threat to those who choose to keep their lives committed to God's purposes. And while reading all these somber portions, rejoice that they are so frequently interrupted by songs from heaven. For those who believe, Revelation is a book of glad singing.

PRAYER: When the scene is dark, dear Lord, give me a song. Amen.

REVELATION 14, 15, 16, 17   *Week 52, Day 6*

*R*evelation is marked by the conflict between good and evil. Notice how good has its counterpart in these chapters of conflict. God the Father has such in Satan, the dragon; Jesus Christ, the Lamb, is opposed by Antichrist, the beast; the Holy Spirit by the False Prophet (the second beast); the woman clothed with the sun is countered by the great whore; and Jerusalem by Babylon.

Revelation has more quotations from and allusions to the Old Testament than any other New Testament book. It is as if the author were making special effort to show that the people of God—Israel and the Church—are all one. That quality comes through in special fashion in "the song of Moses, the servant of God, and the song of the Lamb" (15:3). To link Moses and Christ is, of course, to link the Old and New, Law and Grace. They have a common witness, a song of praise to "Lord God the Almighty" (15:3).

The bowls of wrath are poured out, but although the pain is so intense that they gnaw their tongues in agony, still "they did not repent of their deeds" (16:11). Now it is time for judgment on the city "with whom the kings of the earth have committed fornication" (17:2). She is identified as Babylon, which was the Hebrew symbol of ungodly power, but it is commonly agreed that Babylon is the code name for Rome, which held that role in the first century, as for several centuries both before and after. She "rules over the kings of the earth" (17:18) but the end is near.

PRAYER: In the midst of symbolism, help me, I pray, to see you. Amen.

*O*ne of Shakespeare's characters says, "O God, seest Thou this, and bearest so long?" We are at the place in Revelation when God's bearing with injustice, entrenched evil, and human brutality is at an end. The victory begins with the fall of Babylon. Babylon seems to me to symbolize not only Rome, but the very principle of arrogant and unprincipled government. The scriptures have had an argument with such power since Babel. It is linked with immorality, exploitation, and crude luxury (18:3-17), and as such is an offense to God. Power is to be used to bless the earth and its inhabitants, rather than in selfish excess.

By contrast, we have the scene at the "marriage of the Lamb" (19:7). The bride—the people of God—is "clothed with fine linen, bright and pure—for the fine linen is the righteous deeds of the saints" (19:8). Purity of life is the finest of all garments.

But one more battle remains to be fought. Satan, "that ancient serpent" (20:2), is bound for a thousand years so he can "deceive the nations no more" (20:3). There is a millennial reign of perfection; one assumes the nations will want nothing else. But when Satan is released, he is successful again at deceiving the nations, and brings them together for a final battle, Gog and Magog (Ezek. 38, 39). But this battle is settled by fire from heaven (20:9), and Satan, too, is finally removed (20:10); and then, what other generations called "the Great Assize," the final judgment when the books of our deeds are opened.

PRAYER: Help me this day, I pray, to make good entries in your book. Amen.

REVELATION 21, 22   *Week 53, Day 1*

*P*eople often talk about "the end of the world," but Madeleine L'Engle reminds us that as far as the Scriptures are concerned, it is not so much an ending as a beginning. Revelation tells us now of "a new heaven and a new earth" (21:1). Some things, yes, are at an end: tears, death, pain (21:4). They must go so that all can be new (21:5).

The new Jerusalem is described in highly symbolic terms, with twelve gates named for the tribes of Israel and twelve foundations named for the apostles; it is, that is, the city of God's people. There's something almost playful about the ornateness that is described, as the most cherished gems and wealth of the earth become masonry and pavement! "The river of the water of life" flows through this city, beginning at the throne of God (22:1), with the tree of life on either side. We last saw the tree of life in Genesis; now it will not be taken from us, because "nothing accursed will be found" in this place (22:3).

We have been a long time in getting here, and our journey has been uneven and often faltering. We seem at times to have lost as many battles as we have won. But now the war is at an end, and God is Winner, beyond dispute, and we with him.

The closing verses are in the nature of warning and prayer and benediction, but the end of the book proper, it seems to me, is verse 17. It is an invitation, and in triplicate at that: *Come, come, come!* "Let everyone who wishes take the war of life as a gift." God's last word to us is *come*.

PRAYER: World and life without end! Hallelujah! Amen!